BREXITERNITY

I.B. TAURIS
Bloomsbury Publishing Plc
50 Bedford Square, London, WC1B 3DP, UK
1385 Broadway, New York, NY 10018, USA

BLOOMSBURY, I.B. TAURIS and the I.B. Tauris logo are
trademarks of Bloomsbury Publishing Plc

First published in Great Britain 2019

Cover design by Liron Gilenberg
Cover image © Bakai/iStock

A catalogue record for this book is available from the British Library.

ISBN: PB: 978-1-8386-0132-4
       epDF: 978-1-8386-0783-8
       eBook: 978-1-8386-0784-5

Typeset by RefineCatch Limited, Bungay, Suffolk

Printed and bound in Great Britain

To find out more about our authors and books visit www.bloomsbury.com
and sign up for our newsletters.

BREXITERNITY

The Uncertain Fate of Britain

DENIS MACSHANE

I.B.TAURIS
LONDON • NEW YORK • OXFORD • NEW DELHI • SYDNEY

CONTENTS

CONTENTS

INTRODUCTION

Brexit England is a changed country. Far from ending in 2019, Brexit is only just getting under way. The vote of mainly Englishmen and women in June 2016 was not Brexit. Nor was the proposed mini-treaty known as the withdrawal agreement and political declaration of November 2018, which was repeatedly rejected by MPs and public opinion in 2019.

This is the beginning of Brexeternity. The corrupted 2016 campaign of lies and disinformation – the culmination of a 20 year long anti-European ideological project – is just the prologue. Brexit will unfold over the coming years, if not decades. The Brexit revolution has already devoured two prime ministers. Boris Johnson, the new prime minister, faces exactly the same problems that David Cameron and Theresa May faced. His temporary suspension of Parliament's right to scrutinise the government was a sign of political fear not confidence. Johnson like his predecessors is unwilling to tell the truth to Britain about Europe. They went along with the populist hostility to European partnership that year by year in the 21st century rose from the deep bowels of the Tory Party where it had long been present but not determinant in the party's identity and ideology..

Now the government, other political forces, economic actors, journalists, opinion and policy shapers and all of Britain's allies, partners, rivals, friends and foes have to face up to Brexiternity. The era of Brexit that began in January 2013 when David Cameron announced his referendum and ended with the election of Boris Johnson as prime minister is closed. A new era of Brexiternity opens. It encompasses all the decisions that Britain will now take on how to interpret the June 2016 plebiscite decisions, on how and if a fresh democratic decision can be taken, on what will be the outcome of either a total amputation from commercial and citizens' exchanges with other European nations or years and years of negotiations to establish a new legal relationship between the UK and the EU.

In 2015, Labour chose as its leader an MP who has never liked the European Union. Jeremy Corbyn voted against all its treaties since entering the Commons in 1983 on a Labour general election manifesto committed to pulling the UK out of Europe. The Labour opposition has been unable to define a convincing position on Brexit since 2016 and thus has not profited from a Tory prime minister and the Conservative government and party making themselves a national and global laughing stock. Labour says it will support staying in the EU and oppose any deal proposed by the Conservatives. But were Labour to win an election and form a government, Jeremy Corbyn would not necessarily call for a Yes vote to staying an EU member in any new referendum. Few could make sense of this ever-changing chameleon approach by Corbyn to Brexit. Voters certainly were unimpressed as Labour fell below the Liberal Democrats in the European Parliament election of May 2019. Some opinion polls showed the Liberal Democrats and Nigel Farage's newly formed one-man Brexit Party coming ahead of Labour if a general election was held. Labour just scraped home in a by-election in Peterborough in June 2019, with the Brexit Party losing by a few hundred votes. But the Labour majority in Peterborough fell well below the same constituency's Labour vote in the general election two years previously.

Nine years into an unpopular Conservative government, this was a lamentable performance. Jeremy Corbyn had seen off two Tory prime ministers, but only 16 per cent of voters thought he would make a suitable prime minister. Brexit has thus reduced the leadership of the main political parties to a new low in British history.

In Brussels, a new European Union leadership team emerged, with strongly pro-European leaders taking over. The new president of the European Commission, Ursula von der Leyen, is an Anglophile German centre-right minister who went to the LSE and who has friends in London. But for her, Brexit is a 'burst bubble of hollow promises . . . inflated by populists' who 'had promised that Britain would benefit from Brexit. The fact is today that Brexit is a loss for everyone.'

So we enter a Brexiternity of conflict, rows with our European neighbours, political divisions within as much as between parties. Friends and families are divided, as people close to each other voted differently in the referendum. Someone who was counting on retiring to Spain faced a brother or a daughter who had voted to abolish the EU citizenship rights that made this option free and easy. Colleagues at work in the private sector or in public service regarded each other suspiciously, as someone you thought you knew was revealed to have a deep dislike of a European Union you thought added value to the nation – or vice versa.

Workers at Ford in Wales, Honda in Swindon, British Steel in Scunthorpe, Nissan in Sunderland faced losing their jobs as uncertainty over Brexit continued. Firms in the financial services sector in the City of London and elsewhere quietly relocated jobs to EU capitals in order to keep access to the EU single market. Two major internationally respected supervisory agencies based in London, the European Medicines Agency and the European Banking Authority, had to relocate to the continent. On the eve of one of the most anti-European politicians, Boris Johnson, entering Downing Street a report by the Governing Office of Budget Responsibility warned that UK public finances would take a £30 billion hit with state borrowing doubling under even a 'relatively benign' no deal Brexit as favoured by Mr Johnson. The OBR said the UK's budget deficit would more than double putting pressure on financing core public services. Mr Johnson also insisted as part of his bid to persuade Conservative Party members to vote him into Downing Street that he supported the Nigel Farage call for a full No Deal amputation from the EU. The OBR said such a no-deal Brexit would bring about a 'full-blown recession' shrinking the economy by 2 per cent, sending unemployment soaring and house prices down by 10 per cent.

There is now an open conflict between centuries of parliamentary representative democracy as the supreme mechanism of democratic rule in Britain and the different democracy of plebiscites. In truth, the two are not compatible. But neither will cede supremacy to the other – hence the biggest-ever defeat for a serving prime minister and government early in 2019, when a majority of 230 MPs voted against Theresa May's proposed deal to withdraw from the EU. This was followed by another defeat the following month on St Valentine's Day, when the Commons refused to support her deal or her negotiating strategy by a 303–258 vote.

The prime minister put in place after the 2016 plebiscite refused all compromise. It was the May Way or No Way and soon Mrs May was on the way out, with few mourning one of the worst-ever premierships in British political history.

Mrs May, her supporters and many journalists and voters castigated MPs for refusing to take clear decisions. This misunderstands the democratic process. Houses of Parliament, congresses, national assemblies, senates are not executive bodies. Their job is precisely to reflect, pause, consider, or demand changes in what the executive – the government – seeks to do. Far from Parliament being unable to decide, MPs did what they always should: they held the government to account and found it wanting. This will go on – one way or another – for some time, as Brexiternity sinks roots in Westminster.

Britain has no written constitution and no precedents for this stand-off between the democracy of the plebiscite and the democracy of an elected parliament. A new general election is almost certain to return another divided parliament and, in any event, clarifies nothing, as Brexiternity means there can be no closure on Britain's relationship with Europe under today's genera-tion of politicians and others who influence public opinion in England. The Scottish Nationalists will continue to insist on their secessionist agenda. And why shouldn't they, as English MPs have shown themselves incapable of handling the outcome of the Brexit plebiscite?

Margaret Thatcher, quoting Clement Attlee, described referendums as 'a device of dictators and demagogues'. The Brexit referendum was not about dictatorship, but it was the culmination of more than two decades of anti-European demagogy. As the French political aphorist, Charles Péguy, noted: 'The triumph of the demagogues fades but the ruins go on forever.'

The Irish question has been reopened. After 300 years, a Tory prime minister had to concede that Spain could look to get back some control over Gibraltar. Brexiternity will dominate the next general election, whenever that may be. It will alter the economy. It will plague businesses. It will change the lives of up to two million Brits who have invested money and hope to make a home or a living on the continent.

Never in the lifetime of most adults in Britain has there been such a sense of uncertainty about the political and governing institutions of the London-run state, the future of the British economy, or England's relationship with its longest-lived formerly occupied colony, Ireland, or with Scotland. Wales voted for Brexit in 2016, but three years later, in the European Parliament elections, the anti-Brexit votes in Wales outweighed those voting to leave the EU. The Brexit generation of politicians seems out of touch with the nation's future needs.

There are divisions between the young and the old, between London and university cities and the deindustrialized regions of the north, within parties more than between parties, and everywhere a deep apprehension about the nation's future. There is disappointment in the role of the BBC, which celebrates its centenary in 2022. In treating the demonstrable untruths about Europe, both during the 2016 referendum and ever since, as of equal weight and validity as established facts, it could be argued that the BBC has done immense damage to Britain's global reputation as home to truthful, impartial broadcast journalism.

The Irish writer, Fintan O'Toole, sees England obsessed by 'pain and self-pity'. He locates Brexit in a long list of failures, such as the Charge of the Light Brigade, Captain Scott dying after reaching the South Pole, or the defeat of the British Army in France in May 1940 and evacuation from Dunkirk, which are somehow turned into glorious celebrations of Englishness. It is hard to see Brexit entering that category. It is closer to the Suez crisis or the failure of appeasement politicians in the 1930s to read Europe correctly.

O'Toole, like almost every writer from outside Britain, just observes with bewilderment the spectacle of the comprehensive mess Britain has been in since June 2016. 'The Island of Losers' was the influential German political weekly *Die Zeit*'s front-page headline early in 2019.

Ian Buruma wrote a short book called *Occidentalism* – a play on a more famous text, *Orientalism* by Edward Said, which argued that Euro-Atlantic intellectual accounts of the Arab world were biased by colonial-era stereotypes. Buruma's argument was that Occidentalists, that is, those writing outside the western tradition, were equally prejudiced in depicting everything in the Euro-Atlantic world as negative and worthy of disrespect. In present-day England there has been a similar prejudice from much of the opinion-forming class – at times an almost religious hostility to any positive understanding of modern Europe. If Europe cannot be made to fit into the English order of things – an English idea of an economy dominated by financial, not industrial engineering and a currency whose value changes by the day, English traditions of state administration and how the law should be devised and upheld – then Europe must be at fault. Brexit is the expression of an English sense of superiority. God, after all, is a protestant Englishman, not a continental Catholic!

The divisive vote by 37 per cent of the UK electorate to leave Europe in June 2016 came to be called Brexit – a term I first used in 2012, little realizing it would become reality. Politics and government in Britain since that vote are as if one of Adam Smith's 'invisible hands' has squeezed a giant tube of superglue into the interstices of Westminster and Whitehall machinery, blocking all the normal movement of democratic politics and sensible governance of the great democracy of the United Kingdom.

Four Conservative prime ministers – David Cameron in 2016, John Major in 1997, Margaret Thatcher in 1990 and Edward Heath in 1974 – were driven out of office because they got European politics wrong. Now the question of Europe has obtained the head of a fifth British Conservative prime minister, Theresa May. Boris Johnson will find the crushing weight of Brexiternity making normal politics and governance all but impossible.

In July 2016, the first Brexit-era prime minister, Theresa May, could have reached out to a divided nation where just 37 per cent of the registered electorate voted to leave the EU without anyone defining what 'Leave' meant. At that time there were 52 million people in Britain aged 18 or older. Around a third – 17.4 million – decided on behalf of the other 36 million that Britain should tear up decades of laws and treaties that allow open trade with Europe and permit British citizens to live, work, travel or retire without let or hindrance anywhere on the continent. Given that two out of three people of voting age did not vote for Brexit, Mrs May might have worked on a non-partisan basis with opposition parties, the UK's nations and great cities, set up Royal Commissions or joint CBI–TUC working parties, asked universities to produce reports, or tasked Chatham House and other international policy think tanks on what different forms of Brexit might mean for the UK's geopolitical role. There were many possible forms of Brexit. Instead she spoke for just the hard Europhobe end of those who voted to cut Britain apart from Europe. Brexit meant Brexit, No Deal was better than a Bad Deal, declared our prime minister. EU citizens who had lived in Britain for years and added value to the British economy through their contribution to the professions and universities or as health workers and carers were castigated as 'queue-jumpers'.

Mrs May tried to capitalize on what she thought was the anti-EU mood of the country when she called a general election in June 2017 – three years ahead of its due date in 2020. However, she lost the majority she inherited from David Cameron. The result was to give the whip hand to Ulster's Democratic Unionist Party (DUP), a religious cultural identity party which has only 25–30 per cent support among British citizens living in Northern Ireland. The DUP rejects Kipling's concept of 'One Law, One Land, One Throne', written to defend English supremacy over the people of Ireland at the beginning of the last century, and repudiates UK law in areas such as gay and women's rights.

Mrs May tasked committed politicians such as Boris Johnson, David Davis, Liam Fox and Dominic Raab, whose dislike for European Union partnership goes back decades, to deliver the vision they promised in 2016 of a born-again Britain of growth, trade and prosperity outside of Europe.

It has not been the fault of any civil servant that the politics of Brexit, including the non-opposition of the Labour Party, has been what it is. Like the men who walk behind elephants in Disneyworld sweeping up the pachyderm droppings, UK civil servants have done all that was asked of them; but they cannot make water flow uphill, or get twenty-seven sovereign states to bow before the atavisms of English nationalism.

The Labour Party is bothered and bewildered by Brexit. One day the Labour leader, Jeremy Corbyn tells the German news weekly *Der Spiegel* that Brexit 'cannot be stopped' and the next day Labour's shadow foreign secretary, Emily Thornberry says 'Oh yes it can', because the Labour Party might support a new referendum. Then another Labour shadow minister pops up to say 'Oh no – holding a People's Vote is not a Labour priority'. Tom Watson, Labour's deputy leader, and Emily Thornberry, seen by many as the most likely successor to Jeremy Corbyn, openly defied their leader and his inner clique of advisers for their refusal to challenge the damage Brexit was doing to British jobs and public revenue. Corbyn himself is a veteran of five decades of demonstrating in London marches and rallies against right-wing xenophobia. Yet when one million marched in London in the spring of 2019 in favour of Europe and against the ideology linked with the hard right UK

Independence Party (UKIP) or British National Party (BNP), the Labour-hating Murdoch or Rothermere press, and admirers of Donald Trump and Steve Bannon, Corbyn was nowhere to be seen. The Labour shadow cabinet was ordered to boycott the demonstration. Truly Brexit has rotted the brains of Labour as well as Tory elite politicians.

The Brexit plebiscite was about many things, but the most important was immigration. Theresa May as home secretary (2010–16) fought a cultural identity war, proclaiming that European Union citizens coming to work in Britain were unwelcome and the numbers coming were 'unacceptable', as she told the Conservative Party conference in October 2015. She won a standing ovation for her attack on EU citizens.

Most Conservative politicians this century have been unable to hide a provincial Home Counties disdain for the foreigner in our midst. The same was true for many Labour MPs who fell in behind the slogan of 'British jobs for British workers' uttered by Gordon Brown as prime minister in 2009. Mr Brown appeared not to know that the slogan had been coined by the racist, antisemitic BNP. If the xenophobic populist politics on immigration in Italy, east Europe, France, Germany, Austria, the Netherlands or Denmark were aimed at Middle Eastern and North African – mainly Muslim – migrants, in Britain it was EU citizens arriving since 2004 who were instrumentalized by anti-immigrant populists and which led to Brexit.

EUROPHOBIA EMBRACED TWENTY YEARS AGO

The embrace of anti-European nationalism by Conservative Party leaders, starting with William Hague, as a means of regaining power after 1997 failed. Not even the disaster of the Iraq war could stop Blair's re-election in 2005. Unlike his immediate predecessors or successor as prime minister, Blair left office not as a result of defeat, or party turmoil leading to his overthrow, but at a time and in a manner of his own choosing.

But instead of asking if anti-European demagogy infused with anti-immigrant rhetoric was really the best way for the Conservatives to emerge as an effective twenty-first-century party of government, the Tories doubled down on anti-European populism. David Cameron after 2005 and when in Downing Street after 2010 never missed an opportunity to sneer at or mock

Europe and EU officials such as the Commission president, Jean-Claude Juncker. Mrs May after July 2016 sounded as hostile to the EU as ever she did before she became prime minister.

Thus Brexit Britain. A nation that no longer knows how to live in the modern world. Mrs May was living on borrowed time. Like an elderly maid-servant who lights the fire in the grate and is then dismissed, the Conservative male elites did not like, respect, admire or fear their leader, our prime minister. The language was ugly, hateful, misogynistic, full of accusations that she was a 'traitor' who would destroy the Conservative Party. Political knock-about in Britain is rough, wounding, aggressive. But the sheer vile, extravagant, hate-filled, crude insults hurled in public at Mrs May from Tory MPs, the DUP, Nigel Farage and other right-wingers in Britain is without precedent. Brexit has badly coarsened political discourse.

President Trump came to Britain and insulted Mrs May, saying she had negotiated Brexit badly and adding that Boris Johnson would make a good prime minister. On the eve of his state visit in June 2019, Trump opined that Nigel Farage should be put in charge of negotiating Brexit and that Britain should simply crash out of Europe without any agreement, even at the cost of total disruption to all commercial relations. In return, the Labour mayor of London, Sadiq Khan called Trump a 1930s-type 'fascist'. Brexit was reducing all normal international relations to screeching insults at partners and allies across the Channel and the Atlantic. Arnold Toynbee, the founder of the Royal Institute of International Affairs, the first great international policy think tank, Chatham House, asserted that 'civilizations die by suicide, not murder'. Britain, in drinking the Brexit hemlock, may prove the Toynbee thesis correct.

Brexit is part of a wider western political phenomenon – the turn away from the Enlightenment values of reason, separation of powers, a respect for law, and value on intellectual labour and professional expertise as well as the value of compromise over confrontation and of international cooperation and partnership over the assertion of national identity and ethnicity. This new ideological project for the twenty-first century is defined by the American writer Michael Tomasky as 'the annihilation of liberalism [and] the restoration of a white ethno-nationalist hegemony'. It is central in Europe to the belief system of politicians such as Nigel Farage, who helped bring about Brexit. Leaders such as Vladimir Putin in Russia, Matteo Salvini in Italy,

Marine Le Pen in France, Jarosław Kaczynski in Poland, Viktor Orban in Hungary, Geert Wilders and Thierry Baudet in the Netherlands, along with a range of parties including the Swedish Democrats, Germany's *Alternative für Deutschland* (AfD) and Austria's Freedom Party, founded in the 1950s by ex-SS officers and Nazi functionaries, unite in their dislike of the European Union and its core values and enforceable law and its operational organization based on supranational compromise, not assertion of national identity and national demands *über Alles*.

Brexit and Trump were plebiscited by voters in 2016. But before we go further, a word of warning. It is fashionable in some pro-European circles to decry all those who supported or voted for Britain leaving the European Union as reactionary, xenophobic, or nostalgic for a country that can never return to its imagined past. This is unfair. Over twenty-five years I took part in more debates at public meetings, on TV and radio and in the House of Commons on the question of Britain and Europe than on any other issue in my life. Of course, I disliked the obvious untruths that more rancid anti-Europeans used. But always tugging at me was the fact that what I was defending had so many flaws.

Also, as a Labour MP from a trade union background, there was no doubt in my mind that the governing elites of Britain in Westminster and Whitehall had done nothing to help working-class Britons since the 1992 EU Treaty of Maastricht. Working-class voters needed and deserved to be trained, to have access to state employment and social housing, to see their workplace rights defended, or even to feel that their state, the United Kingdom, knew who was in the country or coming to work here from Europe.

So I accepted that many of those who fought over years to get Britain to leave the European Union were sincere and motivated by genuine passions for the country, as much as I argued the opposite case. If there was a simple up-and-down case against which no one can argue, then there would be little point in politics. Europe is bigger than its proponents or opponents realize. I believe that for all its flaws, the European Union with Britain as a leading partner and participant is a force for good for my country, for my fellow Europeans and for the part of the world I live in.

I accept, however, that others equally sincerely have different views. In a sense it is the age-old political debate between what in the early years of Germany's Green Party were known as the *Fundis* and the *Realos* – the fundamentalists and the realists. Professor Stephen Walt of Harvard University, writing on different schools of thought in international relations theory, defines the difference between 'realism' and 'liberal idealism' thus: 'Realism tries to explain world politics as they *really* are, rather than describe how they *ought to be*' (emphasis in original).

The plight of those who argue for Europe is that we have to be the boring realists as well as remaining European idealists who see strengthening the nations of Europe by strengthening the European Union as a romance, not drudgery. Brexit is a massive win for the nationalist, intolerant politics of a Donald Trump or a Vladimir Putin. Both men want to see the European Union broken apart into small rival nations that will never be able to stand up to Russia or America or the new world powers such as China.

American right-wingers poured money into the anti-European softening up of British public opinion in the years before Brexit. Brexit was hailed by France's Marine Le Pen. After the referendum, she put the British Union flag into her Twitter and Facebook handles, sent congratulations to Boris Johnson and announced: 'The UK has begun a movement that cannot be stopped.' Europe's most violent neo-fascist party, Greece's Golden Dawn, hailed 'the brave decision of the British people. Golden Dawn welcomes the victory of the nationalist and patriotic forces in Great Britain against the European Union.'

IF BREXIT WINS, EUROPE FAILS

Jeremy Hunt, the then foreign secretary, told the Conservative Party conference in October 2018 that the EU was like the 'Soviet Union'. His crass comparison produced a backlash from east Europeans, who see the EU as their safeguard against any return to European Sovietism. I was briefly imprisoned in 1982 in communist Poland when detained by the security police while running money to the underground resistance operation of the Polish Union Solidarity. The dream of Poland becoming a member of the European Union seemed impossible in the dark days after the suppression of Polish Solidarity in December 1981. But it happened, as the giant magnetic pull of a Europe that could live together in peace with its nations open to commerce, ideas and freedom of movement overcame the dead weight of nationalism and communism.

The Latvian ambassador to Britain broke all the rules of diplomatic protocol as she reacted to the British foreign secretary's comparison of the EU to the Soviet gulag. 'Just for your information – Soviets killed, deported, exiled and imprisoned hundreds of thousands of Latvia's inhabitants after the illegal occupation in 1940, and ruined lives of three generations, while the EU has brought prosperity, equality, growth, respect', Ambassador Baiba Braže told Hunt.

In private, many European ambassadors and politicians across the Channel agreed that Brexit was a fork in the road for the future of Europe. It would be a mistake to view it as just another political-diplomatic hiccup that a few clever words could smooth over. If Brexit is seen to succeed, Europe is heading for failure. The stakes are very high indeed.

One of the most regularly repeated myths is that in 1973 we only joined a common market, a simple free trade area, without any political purpose. The government in 1975 sent a brochure to every household urging support for the Treaty of Rome and the European Economic Community in order:

- To bring together the peoples of Europe.
- To raise living standards and improve working conditions.
- To promote growth and world trade.
- To help the poorer regions of Europe and the rest of the world.
- To help maintain peace and freedom.

'Peace and freedom'; 'helping poorer regions of Europe'; 'bringing together the peoples of Europe'; 'improving working conditions' – if this is not about politics, then words have lost all meaning. Peace we take for granted. Instead we focus on EU laws and rules. The texts are mind-numbingly technical. Some ideas are simple. You can trade with, invest in, buy from, sell to or live, work, retire in other European countries thanks to a common EU rulebook. The British passport after Brexit, whatever the colour of its cover, will be worth far less unless the UK comes to a compromise on so-called freedom of movement. European laws insist that our personal data remains private unless we agree it can be exchanged.

BRUSSELS IS ABOUT PLUMBING, BREXIT ABOUT PASSION

The Brexit *passionaras* stand in contrast to the plumbers of the EU, the realists who tried to make the thing work through messy, complicated, half-satisfactory compromises between different national systems, traditions and priorities. Mrs May's chancellor, Philip Hammond – 'Spreadsheet Phil', as this bean-counting businessman is known among Tory MPs – said in 2015 that Brexit 'would light a fire under Europe'. The arsonist metaphor was typical of the hyperbole ambitious Conservative MPs felt compelled to use as they outbid each other in denunciations of Europe in the first years of this century.

The journalist David Goodhart, in a much-cited argument, divided the British population into 'anywhere' and 'somewhere' people. Theresa May picked up this theme in her most notorious post-Brexit speech when she told the 2016 Conservative Party conference: 'Today, too many people in positions of power behave as though they have more in common with international elites than with the people down the road, the people they employ, the people they pass on the street . . . but if you believe you are a citizen of the world, you are a citizen of nowhere.' The Goodhartian sneer is very old; it was Socrates who said: 'I am neither Athenian, nor Greek, but a citizen of the world.' The leader of Germany's AfD extreme right-wing party, described by the *Financial Times* commentator Wolfgang Munchau, a German, as a Nazi party, said in 2018: 'The globalised class live in big cities, speak fluent English, and then they move from Berlin to London to Singapore for jobs, they find similar flats, houses, restaurants, shops and private schools.' In 1933, Hitler mocked 'people who are at home both nowhere and everywhere . . . who live in Berlin today, Brussels tomorrow, Paris the day after that, and then again in Prague, or Vienna or London, and who feel at home everywhere.' Kaiser Wilhelm II described pre-1914 social democrats and their commitment to internationalism as *'Vaterlandslose Gesellen'* – men without roots in their nation.

On the other hand, Winston Churchill, in a passage no longer much read by Europe-hostile Conservatives, said in 1948: 'We hope to see a Europe where men of every country will think as much of being a European as belonging to their native land, and that without losing any of their love or loyalty of their birthplace. We hope wherever they go in this wide domain . . . they will truly feel "Here I am, I am citizen of this country too".' That generosity of spirit and vision had long left English political discourse well before the Brexit plebiscite in 2016.

Let me be clear. There is no comparison between the Kaiser, Hitler and anyone in Britain opining on Brexit today. It is very old conservative politics to divide in two those not afraid to move to different regions – even across frontiers – to live, work, or love and those who stay rooted close to where they were born. Such a binary divide makes a cute comment column, but has little bearing in real life, where we are usually both 'anywhere' and 'somewhere' people at one and the same time. The 'somewhere' people, it is argued, were those who voted for Brexit, while the 'anywhere' people liked Europe, and were happy to sacrifice some national sovereignty or even identity to a post-national existence.

Yet many 'somewhere' Brits seeking what Keats called 'a beaker full of the warm south' have flocked in their hundreds of thousands to take advantage of EU citizenship to buy apartments and small houses in southern Spain, Portugal, France, Italy and Greece. They sold their council homes, took early retirement and opened British-themed pubs and cafés on the Costa del Sol. Many voted for Brexit as they were told that their 'somewhere' identity was under threat from EU membership. But it was the hard work of the 'anywhere' officials in London and Brussels and the signing off by British ministers twenty or thirty years ago that allowed their relocation to a warm climate to come true.

Was Margaret Thatcher a 'somewhere' or an 'anywhere' prime minister? Working with Jacques Delors, the most capable of his generation of Brussels bureaucrats, Mrs Thatcher destroyed the national sovereignty in economic terms of European states. She outlined at the time the potential benefits of a market of some 320 million people in 1985:

> Just think for a moment what a prospect that is. A single market without barriers – visible or invisible – giving you direct and unhindered access to the purchasing power of over 300 million of the world's wealthiest and most prosperous people.
>
> Bigger than Japan. Bigger than the United States. On your doorstep. And with the Channel Tunnel to give you direct access to it.
>
> It's not a dream. It's not a vision. It's not some bureaucrat's plan. It's for real. And it's only five years away.

For three decades, political leaders and officials from different European countries have had to put up with the passionate insistence of the British for Margaret Thatcher's European project, which, in the eyes of many other European nations, ran roughshod over their national sensibilities, especially in terms of economic management. Each EU member state had its priorities. France, for example, insisted on taking Greece into the European Community without any of the reforms needed to modernize that country's administration and economy or eradicate its endemic corruption. For Germany, having EU member states on all its borders after the end of communism was a priority. Tony Blair also wanted to see ex-communist countries upgrade their economies by being obliged to follow EU norms and rules. Other politicians were happy to leave East, Central and Baltic states in Europe out in the cold. 'Why are you so obsessed with letting all these east European countries into the EU?' they complained to me during the eight years I worked for Tony Blair in the Foreign Office. The point is that there was a made-in-Britain European project, as London pushed its centuries-old policy of seeing all of Europe open to trade without a single dominant political power.

The anti-European *Fundis* rejected all this and won the vote in 2016. Now the *Realos* are raising their heads. But the process will be long and full of difficulties. A Brexiternity of negotiations and internal political wrangling in Britain lies ahead.

In 1948 Winston Churchill debated Europe in the House of Commons with Ernest Bevin, the Labour foreign secretary. Bevin adopted the Brexit argument that Britain should avoid 'any reference to the surrender of sovereign rights' and Europe should be built on intergovernmental negotiations. Churchill replied with his alternative of 'countries acquiring an enlarged or enriched sovereignty through membership of a European Union'. In the years since the Brexit plebiscite, both Tory and Labour political leaders have been closer to Bevin's belief that national government should guard jealously their prerogatives behind national frontiers, in contrast to Churchill's concept that the European Union actually enlarges and enriches the sovereignty of its member states.

The government Boris Johnson formed in July 2019 was light-years away from the One Nation Tory government that Churchill shaped in 1951. Most of Johnson's ministers came from the hard anti-European right of the

Conservative Party. Churchill set up the European Convention on Human Rights and its court but Johnson's Foreign Secretary, Dominic Raab, had called for Britain to leave the ECHR.

The new prime minister, Boris Johnson, refused to meet fellow heads of government in Europe unless they first agreed to his demands on re-writing the mini-Treaty called the Withdrawal Agreement to appease fundamentalist Ulster protestant politicians.

Johnson before June 2016 had said the UK would stay in the Single Market. Now any such pro-business compromise with the EU including calls in 2016 by his chief advisor, Dominic Cummings, for a confirmatory referendum on any final deal appeared to be ruled out.

The nation was confused. Johnson lost a long-held Conservative seat in a by-election. There was much talk of an early general election. Businesses did not know which way to turn.

However, one thing was clear. The next chapter of British history will continue to be dominated by the question of Europe. Brexiternity is now the uncertain future of the United Kingdom.

1

WHY BREXIT?

Before we proceed, we must try and analyse why the UK voted for Brexit in 2016. In January 2015 I wrote a book, *Brexit: How Britain Will Leave Europe*, written in the course of 2014. Over 250 pages I laid out my reasons why, if David Cameron did indeed impose a plebiscite on Europe on his country, there would be only one answer. I assumed I was stating the obvious. My confidence that an EU plebiscite would turn into a vote on immigration seemed clear enough to me, even if all my friends in politics, the civil service, journalism and the think-tank world pooh-poohed my fears – with one or two exceptions – and said David Cameron would easily win his referendum.

On the day of the plebiscite, 23 June 2016, I bumped into an old and admired friend, Professor Anand Menon, who heads a major European policy studies institute at King's College London. I asked him for his prediction. 'I know the English, Denis. They will bottle it and vote to stay in.' He was in good company, as David Cameron's pollster, Lord Andrew Cooper, assured the then prime minister on the day of the vote that Remain would easily win.

But, for me, twenty-first-century British politics had once again become obsessed with the question of immigration. It all sounded so familiar.

My political and journalist life began in the West Midlands after leaving Oxford in 1969. It was utterly dominated by Enoch Powell and the surge of xenophobic anti-immigrant populism he unleashed.

That such anti-immigrant or anti-foreigner passions run like a deep coal seam in British life was hardly a secret. The *Daily Mail* in the 1930s ranted against the arrival of Jews from Nazi Germany. A headline in that newspaper in 1938 stated: 'German Jews Pouring Into This Country', and the article went on to write of 'aliens' entering the UK through the 'back door'. Lord Rothermere's journalists argued that these immigrants were taking jobs that might have gone to true-born British citizens. Britain, with half the population of today, was for the *Daily Mail* of the 1930s already an overcrowded island with no room for any foreign incomers from Europe. Under the newspaper's editors up to September 2018, the same language was used against incomers from Europe in the twenty-first century. In 2008, the Federation of Poles in Great Britain produced a dossier of fifty hate headlines from one single paper – the *Daily Mail*.

In the 1970s, I did vox-pop interviews for the BBC in the West Midlands. Time and again I recorded remarks against immigrants working in our midst that could not be broadcast as they were so offensive.

From 1965 to 1975 the BBC broadcast a comedy series called *Till Death Us Do Part*, which featured a loudmouth London know-all character called Alf Garnett who kept denouncing 'wogs' – a repulsive, ugly, racist epithet. The BBC and its middle-class viewing public laughed at his stupidity and crude racism, but it was taken for granted that racism was part of the British working man's psyche. Other popular BBC programmes such as *Steptoe and Son* or *Fawlty Towers* had characters using derogatory terms like 'wogs', 'sambos' or 'Pakis.' It is extraordinary today to watch these mass audience shows on YouTube and wonder how the BBC – and the viewing public – was so deaf and blind to such foul racism.

Sadly, I have to report that during more than four decades as a political activist knocking on doors to ask people to vote for my candidate, or indeed myself, I have heard many unpleasant remarks about colonial immigrants and non-white British citizens. (No one in the Midlands or the north of England would be in the least bit shocked at this statement, but unless you explain to readers just how much casual racism there is out there, the argument that it is one of the roots of Brexit will not convince.) After the end of communism and the arrival of hundreds of thousands of Poles and other east Europeans from the 1990s onwards, the insults switched to Europeans. This was openly whipped up by UKIP and the BNP as they sought and won election to the European Parliament in 1999, 2004, 2009 and 2014. William Hague as Conservative Party leader said Britain would become a 'foreign land' if the pro-European Tony Blair was re-elected as prime minister in 2001.

TORY LEADERS AFTER 1997 UNLEASH ANTI-EU FERVOUR

Hague's successors as Tory leader, Iain Duncan Smith and Michael Howard, also made anti-immigration themes central to their political leadership between 2001 and 2005. Theresa May, as home secretary from 2010 to 2016, never missed a moment to brand Europeans coming to live in the UK as a problem that needed to be solved rather than a source of hard work, income tax and more consumers of British economic output.

Let me again underline that many of those who opposed membership of the European Community and then the European Union did so for perfectly honourable motives. I think they are wrong, but much of the critique of the Brussels institutions was on target. There is a democratic deficit in Europe just as there is in Britain. A total of 45,000 bureaucrats work for EU institutions, mainly in Brussels. Ten times that number of bureaucrats are employed as British civil servants and often get things as badly wrong as their equivalents in Brussels. We can all think of ways the EU could spend its money better, just as we can all think of ways the British government could spend our money more wisely. Britain should certainly have controlled the volume and velocity of new hires coming from Europe to work for British firms.

So I don't demean or criticize the millions of my fellow citizens who voted for Brexit. But equally it is wrong to assert that anti-immigrant, often xenophobic hostility played no part. The generation that made sure they stayed in to watch *Till Death Us Do Part* were finally given a chance to vent their feelings about immigration in 2016. These feelings had never been allowed a ballot box outlet, as no party that hoped to win seats in the House of Commons countenanced such openly xenophobic anti-immigration policies in its manifestos or programme.

A cliché about Brexit is that working-class voters in former industrial areas in the north of England carried the day as they rose to vote against better-off elites in the south. In fact, it was the south that won it. Fifty-two per cent of middle-class, property-owning, decently pensioned people living in the south of England voted for Brexit. As Mary Creagh MP likes to point out: 'There are more Remain voters in Wakefield than in Oxford.'

In his 1935 book, *It Can't Happen Here*, the American writer, Sinclair Lewis sketched the victory of a populist candidate who led 'The League of

Forgotten Men'. Crude anti-immigrant propaganda was whipped up and poor, left-behind voters were promised a wonderful new world if only they voted for the populist appeal. Citizens who feel ignored by elites and left behind as capitalism endlessly mutates come from all classes and social categories. The wins for Donald Trump and for Brexit were like bricks thrown through the windows of the liberal elites. In 1979 in South Yorkshire or Cornwall the average GDP per capita was 94 per cent of the EU average. By 1997 this had fallen to 75 per cent. Millions lost their jobs and inequality grew dramatically after 2010. Britain's League of Forgotten Men and Women were itching to take their revenge.

In rural England and in smaller urban communities in Kent and Lincolnshire, as well as Sunderland and Stoke, they had been told for years by their newspapers that too many immigrants were coming into Britain and now was their chance to protest. Wondrous promises of £350 million a week for the NHS or that prescription charges would be abolished were dangled in front of people. These were lies. An official poster produced by Tory MPs campaigning for Brexit said Turkey with its 79 million people was about to join the EU, with the implication that all those Turks might come to Britain. It was untrue. Brexiters argued that, despite lying only fifteenth in the EU league table of exports per capita, Britain would be transformed into a trading giant conquering new markets, as in the days of the East India Company, if only we left the European Union. This was fantasy.

Twentieth-century politics in Europe – at least after 1945 – was fashioned by three interlinked political groups that shared power: the centre-right Christian Democrats or Conservatives in Britain, the centre-left Social Democrats (Socialists in France, Spain and Italy), and Britain's Labour Party and the classic Liberals. There were other populist parties – notably the French and Italian communist parties – which could win up to 30 per cent of votes even if their Marxist and often pro-Soviet orientation prevented them from finding political allies to enter government.

The French Communist Party was anti-immigration, anti-European, anti-Brussels bureaucracy. Nationalist populist anti-European politics can be as loud on the left as on the right. As communist parties faded after the end of Soviet communism, the need for populist politics was filled by rightist parties such as the *Front national,* now the *Rassemblement national* in France, PiS (Law and Order) in Poland, Lega in Italy or Fidesz in Hungary. In the 2014 elections to the European Parliament, such anti-immigrant, EU-critical parties won 31 per cent of the vote in Sweden (Swedish Democrats), 26.6 per cent of the vote in Denmark (Danish People's Party), 23 per cent in France (*Front national*), 20 per cent in Hungary (Jobbik), 20 per cent in Austria (Freedom Party), 18 per cent in Finland (True Finns), and 17 per cent in the Netherlands (Party for Freedom). In Britain, UKIP was the biggest party, with 26.5 per cent of the vote. A British academic, Professor Matthew Goodwin, wrote in the press that UKIP had four or five parliamentary seats 'in the bag' before the 2015 general election. Yet there are currently no UKIP MPs, and in the 2017 general election the party could only achieve 1.8 per cent of all the votes cast. British voters used the European Parliament elections in both 2014 and 2019 to cast angry anti-immigrant, or anti-Brussels, votes, but when it came to choosing a government to run national affairs – to decide on tax, pensions, healthcare, education, social, environmental and cultural policies, or geopolitical issues – voters on the whole turned away from the extremist parties that did well in the European Parliament elections.

From time to time, another branch of populist politics – nationalist identitarian – took off. The Scottish Nationalists, the Catalan Separatists, or the Northern League in Italy are examples of this strand of populist politics. They would win regional power, but could not, even after resorting to violence like the Basque or Irish nationalists, break up the settled state order of existing democracies. Italy's Northern League had to drop its demand for the break-up of Italy, rename itself, focus on Islamophobia and anti-refugee populism and then depend on the more left-wing, green Five Star Movement to form a coalition government in 2018. But the new Italian populist government made clear it was not proposing to return to the lira as the national currency, still less copy Britain and quit the EU. Viktor Orban in Hungary enjoyed berating Brussels. His acolytes claimed they were in favour of a white Christian Europe but, unlike British anti-Europeans, they never for a moment suggested leaving the EU or rejecting the four core principles of the EU single market – notably freedom of movement.

There were populists of the left as well – Podemos in Spain, Jean-Luc Mélenchon in France or Yanis Varoufakis in Greece – who denounced Europe and Brussels as being the source of all their nations' problems, often using identical language and metaphors of condemnation to those of Nigel Farage or Boris Johnson, but none of them were inspired by Brexit to call for their own nations to quit the EU.

Systems of proportional representation and constitutional separations of power between regional and central power obliged a permanent compromise in ruling a state. Another key compromise was between capital and labour, enshrined in the idea of a social market economy. Workers on the continent who did not possess the educational capital to advance into the professions or higher-paid jobs in state administration, or become managers in private firms and banks, at least had strong trade unions to promote and defend their interests. This historic compromise between capital and labour put in place after 1945 in most western democracies was terminated in Britain during the Thatcher years. It left many citizens open to arguments that the problems they and their families faced in daily life were the fault of immigrants and Britain having to share sovereign power in economic and trade policy with other partners in the EU.

In the media and opinion-forming classes in the universities and research institutions, representatives of liberal politics and belief systems had the upper hand and occupied the majority of posts as professors and columnists. They tried to maintain an equidistance between the main right and main left political and social forces and groups in European economies and social systems, but – as often happens when one tries to do the splits – their posture became ungainly.

The year 1990 was the *annus mirabilis* for the liberal idea of world order when communism and apartheid in South Africa ended, authoritarian or military rule in southern Europe as well as in Latin America and South Korea had been buried, and an American political scientist, Francis Fukuyama, announced 'the end of history' and the triumph of liberalism as a world – and especially Euro-Atlantic – model of governance.

In Europe, this triumph was commemorated in the 1992 Treaty of Maastricht, which renamed the European Economic Community, later the European Community, as a new entity called the European Union. The European Union took forward liberal, conservative free market and social market ideas and announced the concept of European citizenship.

Four remarkable leaders had brought this about. In Britain, Margaret Thatcher seized the moment to bring about a long-held British mercantilist dream – namely, a Europe without trade barriers to anything Britain could produce and sell at a profit across the Channel. These were not just goods; Britain's wealth now came from its financial, professional and creative industries and educational services. The latter were a star new industry, as several British universities were among the top twenty in the world. There are now 130 universities in Britain and a total of 165 higher education institutions receiving public funds. In 1973, when the Open University was launched, there were 130,000 university students. In 2019 there are 2,320,000, of which 450,660 are foreign students paying handsomely for degree courses in Britain, including 138,000 young EU citizens. The high tuition fees received from these students from Europe, China, Russia and Africa are used to hire more professors and lecturers. British universities seek endowments from the world's super-rich and research partnerships with global business. UK universities, helped by able British diplomats and officials in Brussels, won the lion's share of EU grants for research across many fields. These in turn attracted partnership financing from richer European universities. Thanks to the EU, British universities have enjoyed a golden age, which ends with Brexit.

Mrs Thatcher offered world capitalism a grand bargain. If Japanese car firms and American or Swiss banks came and invested in Britain, she would guarantee not just a supportive welcome from planning and other authorities, but a guaranteed free access to the world's biggest and growing market – hundreds of millions of consumers – for whatever Britain could produce.

Japanese car firms such as Toyota, Nissan and Honda reinvented the made-in-Britain automobile. In the 1930s, Britain had imported Ford and General Motors (called Vauxhall in Britain) in order to make motor cars. In the 1970s, a combination of bad management and intransigent trade unions combined to destroy British-owned car firms. Mrs Thatcher persuaded Japanese firms to bring modern car manufacturing to the English regions in exchange for the guarantee they could export freely to customers in Europe.

The same was true for foreign banks, insurance firms, investment funds, specialist but profitable financial services firms such as clearing houses and foreign exchange traders. Thousands of American, Swiss, French, German and in due course Arab, Russian, African and Latin American firms set up in London because of Mrs Thatcher's creation of the European single market.

In France and Germany, two remarkable leaders, François Mitterrand and Helmut Kohl, who between them governed for fourteen and sixteen years respectively over their countries' destinies, supported Mrs Thatcher's vision of a single internal market for Europe. They were both young men in the Second World War and were determined to sink the differences that had

caused such damage and disaster to their great nations in a jointly construc-
ted European Union.

Mitterrand had sat at Winston Churchill's feet at the European Movement's
founding congress in The Hague in 1948, which launched the idea of
European cooperation, including sharing some sovereign powers in a new
concept of partnership. In 1942, Churchill had minuted the cabinet thus: 'I
look forward to a United States of Europe in which the barriers between the
nations will be greatly minimised and unrestricted travel will be possible.'

The first moves led to the creation in 1950 of the supranational European
Coal and Steel Community (ECSC). A tired, insular Labour government, in
office since 1945 but by 1950 exhausted and poorly led, missed the opportunity to be a founding member of the ECSC. Churchill criticized Labour
for refusing to take part in the first steps of European partnership, telling the
House of Commons 'national sovereignty is not inviolable' and may be 'resol-
utely diminished'. Writing in 1930, Churchill had been far more cautious as
he looked out on a Europe heading towards the nationalism and xenophobia
of fascism, Nazism and Francoism that culminated in the Second World War
and the Holocaust: 'We are with Europe, but not of it . . . We are interested
but not associated.' The Churchill of 1930 could look at a map of the world
with one-sixth coloured red as part of the British Empire, while the post-
1945 Churchill filled the Albert Hall with giant rallies in favour of Europe.
By the 1950s, imperial Britain was over; though to judge by some of today's
anti-Europeans and the idea of 'Global Britain' – or 'Empire 2.0', as it had
been dubbed by Whitehall wags – the dream lives on.

The prime minister at that time, Labour's Clement Attlee, had commen-
ted back in 1939: 'Europe must federate, or perish.' But once in Downing
Street, Attlee reverted to being a sovereignist nationalist and the Labour
government tried to block Churchill's European Union enthusiasms. To be
sure, Churchill saw the union of continental European countries as a first
step. Britain was one of the so-called 'Big Three', with the United States and
the Soviet Union. Had London sought to lead a European Union after 1945,
the UK would have been so dominant and the British presence so heavy that
the project would have capsized. But Churchill was angry that Labour would
not even join the less ambitious ECSC in 1950. That summer Churchill
proposed 'the immediate creation of a unified European army subject to
proper European democratic control'. Such calls nearly seventy years later

sent anti-EU British politicians and columnists wild with fury, because they were made by European leaders such as Angela Merkel. But the original idea belonged to a British statesman, Winston Churchill.

After refusing to be a founder member of the ECSC in 1950, Britain had to wait twenty-three years before joining the European Economic Community. But at least Churchill, when back in office after 1951, powered ahead with creating the European Court of Human Rights (ECHR) – a court that, although not formally part of the EU, has had far more influence through its rulings, which have overridden British judges and law, than the Court of Justice of the European Union (usually called in English the European Court of Justice – ECJ).

In 1990 Helmut Kohl presided over the unification of his country. Germany expanded from roughly the same population and economic weight of France into a much bigger country, as Weot and East Germany came together and the capital moved from the quiet Rhine city of Bonn to the monumental Prussian city, Berlin. François Mauriac, the most influential public intellectual – and a liberal – in France after 1945, famously wrote that he admired Germany so much, he was glad there were two of them in the 1950s and 1960s.

After 1990, Mitterrand had to work out how to maintain French partnership with a country that had overnight increased its population by one-third and now was by far the most dominant country in Europe, particularly the new Europe with a centre of gravity at its midpoint rather than its Atlantic coastline.

His answer was to bind France and Germany together in a European Union with a common currency as its most stand-out symbol alongside the single market. Europe already had its symbols. The first European Coal and Steel Community Treaty of 1951 had enshrined non-discrimination on grounds of nationality in hiring workers. Digging up coal and working at the arduous, dirty, foundry end of steel making had always required immigrant labour. Many coal miners in northern France and Belgium before 1939 had been Polish. Britain's Labour government after 1945 allowed 200,000 Polish soldiers to stay in Scotland and northern England, where they were sent down mines to dig coal – an essential British export after 1945 to earn precious foreign currency. English miners refused to work on the same shift as their Polish comrades and the Polish miners had to set up their own working men's clubs, as the English miners refused to share an after-shift pint with the European foreigners.

NO DISCRIMINATION IN HIRING ON GROUNDS OF NATIONALITY

So, at the first moment of European economic integration, the concept of non-discrimination in hiring workers from other European countries was built into the treaties. This idea was later ennobled by being called the principle of freedom of movement, which has also been a target for populist nationalists. The French communist leader, George Marchais, in the 1980s was calling on the French government to impose controls on European citizens to stop them working in France. The Stalinist French politician used the same language as Nigel Farage, or indeed Theresa May when she told the Conservative Party conference in October 2015 that 'the number of European immigrants coming to Britain is unsustainable'. Marchais was applauded by French communists in 1980 and Mrs May was given an ovation by English Conservatives thirty-five years later as she appealed to the prejudices latent in all of us about incomers who arrive with their own language, customs and faith and seem to disturb a settled order.

Well before 1992 and the Maastricht Treaty, Europe had given itself a flag: the twelve gold stars on a blue background. This was originally designed for the Council of Europe in 1954 by an official in its accounts department. It had no special significance; it was just a pretty geometric design that graced Council of Europe letterheads and documents, until copied by Brussels and given greater prominence by being designated as the European Community logo. Beethoven's Ninth Symphony, which incorporates Schiller's poem about all men becoming brothers, became a sort of theme tune or anthem for European partnership and cooperation.

In the 1957 Treaty of Rome, the preamble stated that the peoples (not the states) of Europe were desirous of 'creating an ever closer union among the peoples of Europe'. There was no reference to a closer union of states, still less of a federal European superstate. These warm words of people coming closer together had no legal weight at all, as they were in the preamble, not the main legally enforceable text, of all EU treaties to this day. They were removed from the draft text of the European constitutional treaty of 2004 when I was Europe minister. After the constitutional treaty was shot down in referendums in France and the Netherlands, the drafters in Brussels simply cut and pasted the old 1957 language onto the replacement Treaty of Lisbon.

The 1992 Maastricht Treaty was the child of a remarkable French politician, Jacques Delors, who had been president of the Commission since 1984. He was never elected to any public post and had worked in the Banque de France and as an adviser to the centre-right French prime minister, Jacques Chaban-Delmas. In economics Delors was a social-liberal. In politics he was a technocrat linked to the moderate trade union, *Confédération française démocratique du travail* (CFDT). He was made France's finance minister by François Mitterrand in 1981 and persuaded the French socialist president to steer away from his protectionist 1970s ideas of socialism in one country and instead embrace a more open border market economy. An important strand in Delors's make-up was his commitment to Catholic social justice theory and practice.

Delors never won election to Parliament and was selected for appointment to all the important posts he held, including the decade 1985–95 as president of the European Commission. Perhaps because he had never faced voters, Delors was given to grandiose statements about Europe. He told the European Parliament that soon MEPs would be making 80 per cent of the laws in Europe. It was nonsense, but the suggestion that the EU was about to replace national parliaments was seized upon by nationalist politicians.

Delors made a pro-trade union speech to Britain's Trades Union Congress in 1988 that accelerated the move by the British unions and the Labour Party away from their primitive anti-Europeanism, which reached its nadir in 1983 when the Labour Party manifesto for the general election included a pledge to withdraw from the European Community. The Delors TUC speech provoked fury in Mrs Thatcher's every fibre. She had made her name and had won three elections on a promise to tame trade union power and bring to heel what she and all Tory MPs (and not a few modernizing non-Tory MPs) saw as the usurpation of democratic control of the economy and public services by trade union general secretaries and militant syndicalist local union activists.

By the time she was ousted from office in 1990, provoked in large part by a mishandling of Britain's links with the rest of Europe over the question of the pound's relationship to other currencies, Mrs Thatcher had begun her turn against Europe. Patrick (Lord) Wright, the permanent under-secretary at the Foreign Office, the UK's top professional diplomat, records in his diaries how Mrs Thatcher became embittered and obsessively anti-German as the Berlin Wall crumbled and a new post-communist Europe emerged.

29 September 1989

Margaret Thatcher has also been showing signs of her Germanophobia over the past few weeks, and has very unwisely discussed the Germans both with Mitterrand and Gorbachev. This phobia also colours her attitude to community enlargement, since she regards the Austrians as another sort of German and seems obsessed by a feeling that German speakers are going to dominate the community. She is also, of course, deeply suspicious of [Hans-Dietrich] Genscher [German foreign minister]; any talk of German unification is anathema to her.

1 November 1989

Christopher Mallaby [UK ambassador in Bonn] looked in, having seen the PM today. At one point she blurted out: 'I hate Europe.'

This hatred of Europe took over Margaret Thatcher's being in the 1990s and she became the patron saint of anti-Europeanism. There has been no satisfactory explanation of her trajectory from a passionate pro-European to a bitter opponent of European partnership and integration. Biographies of her are either hagiographic or polemical denunciations. But as with the three Conservative prime ministers who followed her, John Major, David Cameron and Theresa May, the European question ended her career. Her predecessor, Edward Heath, entered British history as the prime minister who took Britain into Europe in 1973. But the following year Heath lost two general elections when both the Labour Party and the most prominent Conservative politician of the day, Enoch Powell, urged a vote against Heath by criticizing his embrace of Europe and offering a referendum on his decision to enter the European Economic Community.

Yet in 1998, Geoffrey Howe, whom Thatcher humiliated and destroyed as foreign secretary because of his opposition to her by then obsessive anti-Europeanism, told me at a diplomatic reception she had to be seen as one of the architects of modern Europe. I recorded the encounter in my diary:

5 March 1998

I circulate a bit and have an odd conversation with Geoffrey Howe. He says the two biggest shapers and makers of Europe have been Helmut Kohl and Margaret Thatcher. I find the thesis challenging. He explained that she was the initiator of the single market and the revolutionary who showed that Europe could be made to work by her economic reforms while Kohl was the creator of the single currency and held it all together to fruition.

The Delors–Kohl–Mitterrand–Thatcher quartet became a troika, as John Major, who became prime minister after Mrs Thatcher was ousted in 1990, was a pleasant, accommodating man but not remotely in the big league of prime ministers.

In 1992, the European Union was born, with its commitment to greater integration. Britain was sidelined as Major was bullied by what became known as Eurosceptics – Michael Howard in the cabinet and a new generation of right-wing anti-Europeans including Iain Duncan Smith and Bernard Jenkin. They had their queen over the water in Margaret Thatcher, new think tanks like Open Europe financed by City financiers who hated the idea of the EU imposing any control or accountability on the way they made money, and above all, the weight of the offshore-owned press – the Rupert Murdoch papers, the *Daily Mail, Daily Telegraph* and others – who decided to adopt populist anti-Europeanism as their cause. Twenty-four years later they won with their Brexit campaign. In my diary in 1998 I recorded my presence at one of their gatherings:

14 May 1998

In the evening I went to a dinner organised by Carla Powell, the woman whose salon, thanks to her marriage to Charles Powell, Margaret Thatcher's great assistant, has been the most famous in Conservative circles for years. The event is to launch a book by a man called Rodney Leach on Europe who works at the same bank as Charles Powell. We turn up at a posh hotel in Knightsbridge and bit by bit a coven of Europhobes assembles. There is Paul Johnson with his watery eyes and his once flame-red hair now turning white. Then there is William Rees-Mogg looking more gaunt and white-haired than ever but still passionate in his hatred of all things European. Michael Howard appears with his model wife and then Bill Cash. There was one of the Saatchi brothers who was close to the Conservative Party. Then the divine apparition came in. It was Margaret Thatcher coming through a side entrance in a fluorescent light blue dress walking very slowly and sedately like an ageing goddess amongst her fawning servileurs.

Then an introductory speech from Charles Powell and up stands Rodney Leach who is introduced as some kind of polymath because he is a great bridge player as well as being a banker and has written his book. He makes a rather tedious speech attacking Europe for its social policies, its federal inclinations and all the usual rant of the Europhobes. I mutter under my breath getting noisier all the time and I see blacker and blacker looks at me. The publisher of the book says I am behaving disgracefully and Mrs Leach is very angry.

Leach helped set up and financed the leading anti-European think tank Open Europe. He was ennobled by David Cameron in 2006 as a sop to the hard anti-European MPs Michael Howard and William Rees-Mogg's son, Jacob, who won their campaign to cut links with Europe two decades later after rich men like Rodney Leach decided to put their money into anti-EU campaigning. By the mid-1990s the pro-Europeans in Britain were faint of heart and weak in belief. Already in 2000 I noted in my diary:

27 January 2000

On BBC I am all over the place with Bill Cash [leader of the Eurosceptic Tories]. He is actually becoming a moderate within the Conservative Party, which has been taken over by hard-faced men who know only one thing – that they really hate Europe.

Far from 1990 announcing a triumph of liberalism, the next quarter-century saw its roll-back. The Irish political writer Paul Gillespie offers the view that the 1992 creation of the European Union and the push for more and more Europe 'have privileged freedom over equality, neoliberal economics over deliberative politics, a technocratic over a more political EU and a private, atomised individualism over public and social values'.

The EU has indeed been much more about classic liberalism: upholding private property rights, creating individual rights for citizens to live, work or retire anywhere in Europe or, for example, to use their mobile phones without extra charges for crossing the frontier. This has not involved a transfer of power to Brussels, but an increase in individual citizen rights and protection of the private and economic space of the individual.

In the past, political practitioners and commentators, at least in European democracies, debated from a classic conservative and Christian democrat perspective the relationship and the power of the *Gemeinschaft* (community) with and over the individual, while for social democracy or Labour and trade unions it was the power of the *Gesellschaft* (society) over individual rights, especially property rights than needed to be privileged. The creation of the European Union was a big win for classic liberalism. The individual firm and individual citizen were privileged. Community, social and national identity were relegated. Workers saw the protection of effective trade unions lessened as the European Court of Justice favoured the rights of capital and multinational firms. Local communities could not defend themselves against big money coming in to buy up property but not live in the community. National governments could not take some national measures to protect their people.

This change did not lead to the creation of a European superstate. In fact, the very opposite happened. Europe became weaker and weaker as classic liberalism won its battle on behalf of the individual at the expense of community or social cohesion. The response of national politicians was to blame Europe for things they were not allowed to do. At times this transference of blaming big bossy Brussels became silly. Policies and directives that national leaders had voted for in European Council meetings were criticized by the same national leaders once back home and having to respond to local criticism. It was easy to transfer blame to Brussels for a decision taken with the agreement of national leaders. All national heads of government played this game.

In his book *Counter-Revolution: Liberal Europe in Retreat*, a critique of the EU as it evolved after 1992, Professor Jan Zielonka of Oxford University argues: 'The post-1989 liberal elite assumed that governance is a kind of enlightened administration on behalf of an ignorant public.' On the contrary, elected politicians in the quarter-century since the end of communism and the creation of the European Union became ever more sensitive to national voters. In many regards, since the Lisbon Treaty was signed in 2007, the EU stopped functioning, as national political leaders refused to share burdens or enforce commonly agreed policies and were happy to boast about blocking or diluting EU policies. This was already the case in Britain, where all four prime ministers between 1992 and 2016 took public pride in being seen to thwart, opt out of, or simply refuse to implement European Union policy and decisions of the Commission for as long as they could.

PRIME MINISTERS REFUSED TO MAKE CASE FOR EUROPE

No British prime minister felt confident about being European, as Gordon Brown, then the chancellor of the exchequer, explained in a talk I had with him in the Treasury when I was minister for Europe.

23 February 2003

'I am pro-European, Denis,' Brown said. 'The political case for Europe has been met. I think the economic tests have been passed. But is the country ready for Europe yet? Does the country feel that European values are our values? Do they not see Europe still as being too corporatist and capitalist and not really embracing British values?'

I did a little bit of gratuitous arse-licking saying that I had always regarded him as the strategic Bismarck of the Labour Party and he snorted at the reference to Bismarck but, of course, everyone loves to be flattered. He urged instead that I should seek to make the case for Britain to see its values as being in tune with those of Europe. 'It's not the economic case we have to make really, it's the political case. People will vote yes in a referendum on economic grounds but then they will vote no on political grounds because they don't trust Europe and they don't see Europe as being in line with British values. That's what we have to change.'

Those are powerful arguments and I said to him that they needed to be advanced. Of course I didn't want to say that you can't persuade Britain to like Europe if people like the Chancellor, especially a good and popular one like Brown, never makes the case for Europe. I am not allowed to be impertinent. 'Well, I am thinking about making a speech on Europe. I am not sure yet but maybe I need to say something,' he grunted.

He never made the speech. In the end Brown did produce a pro-EU book on the eve of the Brexit plebiscite. Entitled *Britain: Leading, Not Leaving: The Patriotic Case for Remaining in Europe*, it was well argued and, like all his writing on politics, a serious, intellectually cogent, heavyweight product. But it was published too late to have any impact. Brown never made the case for Europe when he was at No. 11 or No. 10 Downing Street. When national leaders are not willing to explain, defend and promote a key part of what the country is – in the manner, for example, that all prime ministers and ministers will always speak positively about the North Atlantic Treaty Organization

(NATO) or Britain's place as a permanent member of the United Nations Security Council or the usefulness of the Commonwealth – then others will fill the void.

Thus the conventional cliché that the Brexit vote was a protest against liberal elites is easy journalism and instant political science when, in truth, a large number of factors played their part. The most important was the long-organized campaign by powerful, wealthy individuals, firms and above all the offshore-owned press against Europe. They played the anti-immigrant card day after day. Many Conservative MPs entered into a bidding war with their UKIP opponents to see who could most excoriate Brussels, the EU and the number of Europeans working in Britain. In that contest it was hard to be outflanked on the right. Nick Griffin, the leader of the xenophobic BNP, was asked by the BBC on the night of the 2014 European Parliament elections if he had lost his seat because voters had turned away from a racist party. 'Oh no,' he cheerfully replied, 'they've found another one to vote for.'

The BNP leader's jibe at Nigel Farage's one-man UKIP 'party' was perfectly accurate. The anti-immigrant ideology used to attack the EU had long since become normal politics. David Cameron in 2006 correctly called UKIP 'closet racists'. He was swiftly reminded by anti-immigrant Tory MPs as well as a procession of commentators in the anti-European, anti-immigrant press that these were potential Tory voters and the Conservatives, if they were to win power, had to win back the voters who had fallen for UKIP's anti-immigrant rhetoric. Cameron collapsed into appeasing UKIP. The Tory MP and cerebral former minister, Nick Boles, said in 2019 that if Mrs May conceded to the demands of the hard anti-European Conservative MPs, the Tory Party would become 'NUKIP'. It was too late. Cameron and his friends who took control of the Conservative Party after 2005 did so by making concessions to the 'NUKIP' tendency of militant anti-Europeans within the Conservative Party. Brexit was the inevitable end result.

TOO EASY TO BLAME NIGEL FARAGE

The BBC massively promoted UKIP, even though the party could never get its leader, Nigel Farage, chosen by voters, to represent them in Parliament. However, it is too facile to place the blame for whipping up anti-European populism solely on the Conservatives and political right, as I noted in my diary:

14 January 2012

I went to the session on Europe at the Fabian New Year conference and it was absolutely dreadful. Helen Goodman, a North East Labour MP was ranting about all the foreign immigrants who have come in in the last period of the Labour Government. I couldn't believe my ears. There was a very good study this week by something called the Migration Advisory Group or Committee which actually showed that the rise in unemployment especially amongst young people was due to the economic slowdown and cannot be blamed on foreigners. As I said to the session, in the 1970s we heard complaints from Labour supporters and from the poorer elements of the working class that too many Pakistanis were being allowed in and were taking their jobs and their homes and their benefits. Now once again the same right-wing rubbish is being said about East European immigrants, Polish Catholics and others who actually pay taxes and social security and that are far less of a drag on the economy than many British citizens. But now it's being endorsed by a shadow minister.

Chris Leslie was even worse, explaining why Britain would show no solidarity to anybody in trouble in the Eurozone via the IMF and complaining about democratic accountability. He sounded just like a UKIP guy. Linda McAvan, the MEP, called me and I had the last little burst at them. But when I spoke to her afterwards she said she was shocked and dismayed at the Euroscepticism on offer from the two Labour MPs there.

Europeans working in Britain thus became the whipping boy for populists around the political compass. The deputy head of Immigrant Watch, another anti-European organization funded by wealthy supporters of anti-EU politics, insists that immigration was the main driver in winning the Brexit result.

2

THE POLITICS OF REFERENDUMS AND WHY THE BREXIT MAJORITY HAS VANISHED

In June 2016 there were 44.56 million voters entitled to vote in Britain. It did not include roughly two million younger citizens aged 18–24 who were not on the electoral register, as the government changed the electoral registration rules, which had the effect of making it more difficult for younger people to vote. Opposition politicians said Tory ministers thought younger voters would not vote Conservative in the 2015 and 2012 parliamentary and London mayoral elections. Whatever the motives, the Brexit referendum did not include many potential voters. According to the Office of National Statistics, there were 52 million people aged over 18 in 2016 but only 44.56 million were on the UK electoral register.

There were a further almost two million British citizens living in Europe. Only 246,000 of them voted in the referendum. Unlike an American or French citizen who carries his or her right to vote to the grave, no matter where they live, Britain is snooty about those of Her Majesty's subjects who live abroad and discourages them from voting.

Unlike the Scottish independence referendum of 2014 when 16 and 17-year-olds could vote, the 1.4 million young members of the generation that would be most affected by the outcome of David Cameron's Brexit plebiscite were not allowed a say.

Of the 44.56 million British voters, 27.1 million did not vote for Brexit
– they either voted Remain or did not vote at all; 17.4 million voted for
Brexit and 16.1 million voted against. Since then that majority has evaporated. Partly demography has played its part. About 1.5 million people, mainly
older citizens, who voted strongly for Brexit in 2016, have passed on in the
normal order of things. At the same time, roughly the same number of
younger citizens have reached the voting age of 18 and they tend to support
keeping their European rights by staying in the EU by 4–1. Of course, until
votes are tested no one can be sure, but all polls carried out in 2019 showed
a majority for not leaving the EU.

Of course, an opinion poll is not the same as placing a ballot paper in the
box in the voting booth, but the direction of travel is clear. Thirty-seven per
cent of those on the electoral register – the same number as those who voted
for Brexit – voted in the nationwide European Parliament election three years
after the Brexit plebiscite. A clear majority of them voted for candidates
hostile to Brexit and in favour of a new consultations. Polls in December
2018 and January 2019 showed leads for staying in Europe of up to 9 points.
As with the majority in support of a second referendum, and the remarkable
poll showing more than 80 per cent of Labour Party members opposing the
party leadership line on Brexit and supporting staying in the EU, it was clear
on the third anniversary of the Brexit plebiscite that the nation had moved on
from its vote of June 2016.

I accept that in 2016 there was a majority for Brexit of those who voted
and having stood for election to Parliament and local councils as well as in
trade union ballots and voted countless times on laws in the House of
Commons, I accept that a majority of one is enough in a democracy.

The 2016 referendum was not binding on MPs. It was consultative. But
MPs agreed to accept the result. The opposition Labour Party, under the leadership of a man whose ideas on Europe were formed five decades previously,
did not want to make the case for Europe. Worse, as Mrs May floundered and
her Brexit ministers contradicted each other, the Labour leadership was
unable to exploit the government's Brexit disarray.

Some Labour MPs spoke out with verve and vigour, but Jeremy Corbyn
and others followed Mrs May in saying the UK had to leave the single market,
had to impose an immigration bureaucracy on those Europeans willing to
work in Britain, and although a small move was made in favour of staying in

the customs union, it was hedged in with condition and caveats so that Labour's position was hardly different from that of the Conservatives. And when the chance came in a Commons vote to at least keep the UK in a customs union with the EU, four Europhobe Labour MPs ignored their leader, refused to vote with their comrades, and instead voted with Conservative anti-Europeans. Little wonder that British citizens and foreign observers found Labour's position hard to understand. On any definition, Brexit would cause unemployment and relocation of industrial firms that provided secure, working-class jobs. But for ageing Labour anti-Europeans, none of this seemed to matter.

By any standard, Brexit has produced the biggest constitutional-political-economic-geopolitical crisis in British history. Britain has faced previous crises on different fronts that governments have had to deal with. These included:

- Economic dislocation in the 1920s and 1930s, as it seemed no government could rise to the challenge of unemployment, despite the urgings of John Maynard Keynes.
- Political challenges in the 1970s when Britain seemed ungovernable, as weak prime ministers had no idea how to deal with trade union militancy or respond to external economic shocks such as the hike in oil prices or the subjugation of government to orders from the International Monetary Fund. It was an era when the cabinet secretary, Sir William Armstrong was found naked under the coffin-shaped cabinet room table, kicking his bare feet against the underneath of the table surface. He was taken away quietly and, in the best manner of the British establishment, put in the House of Lords and made chairman of Midland Bank.
- There were foreign policy challenges as in the 1930s when governments refused to face down fascism and both the Conservatives and – to begin with – Labour supported a policy of non-intervention, which encouraged the brutalities of Mussolini, Franco and Hitler as they established fascist order in their own and other countries.
- Britain was humiliated in the Suez debacle of 1956. The Labour government 1964–1970 refused to take action to stop the white settler regime in Rhodesia seizing power and opening a conflict with the majority African population, which continued with racist violence until 1981 and which has held back Zimbabwe's development for fifty years.

- The interventions and regime change policies supported by Tony Blair and David Cameron in Iraq, Libya and Syria led to chaos in all three countries as they became centres for Islamist terrorism and transit centres for unending flows of refugees and economic migrants. A total of 626 British soldiers lost their lives and studies estimate a quarter of the 220,000 British military personnel – some 75,000 men and women – who were sent to Afghanistan and Iraq have suffered physical and mental scarring that will last to their graves.

- The Irish conflict, when the British military executed after a summary trial the teachers, a trade union leader, and intellectuals who called for Irish independence in 1916. This was followed by a brutal war involving British military death squads – the 'Black and Tans' – after the Irish people voted massively in peaceful elections for independence in 1918. The behaviour of supremacist protestant politicians in the six counties of north-east Ireland which remained under London's rule provoked sporadic resistances, culminating in a thirty-year-long civil war which resulted in 3,600 killed and many thousands wounded between 1968 and the Good Friday peace agreement of 1998.

But all these varying crises were solved by British democracy. A poor prime minister could be replaced, as Churchill took over from Chamberlain in 1940 or Macmillan displaced Eden after the Suez disaster. Elections could remove weak, incompetent prime ministers and ministers and replace them with more dynamic leadership for the country.

At different moments, different forces shaped and reshaped public opinion. Sometimes political leaders shaped policy, sometimes the press took a lead, as the *Sun* did in opposing employee rights in the 1970s or 1980s, or *The Times* and the *Daily Mail* did in supporting appeasement of fascist dictators in the 1930s.

BREXIT PLEBISCITE HAS REWRITTEN BRITAIN'S UNWRITTEN CONSTITUTION

However, the Brexit plebiscite takes us into entirely new territory. In countries with a written constitution, there are very clear rules on the validity of a referendum. The Swiss held one in February 2014 on freedom of movement and voted to end immigration into Switzerland of EU citizens.

As they contemplated the full impact of such a move on the Swiss economy or health and old age care services, there was a gradual awakening among Swiss MPs, who still work as employees or professionals and are not paid salaries by the Swiss federal parliament. They decided to modify slightly the internal rules of the Swiss labour market – something a sensible British government could and should have done at any time this century – and quietly filed away the referendum result. In Britain, the 2016 plebiscite has been treated with almost religious reverence. Almost every day since 23 June 2016 has produced new facts or evidence not available to voters when they made their decision.

The ballot paper was vague in the extreme. It did not mention the EU customs union or single market, freedom of movement, the border in Northern Ireland, the reintroduction of mobile phone roaming charges, or the loss of access for British firms to essential agencies such as the European Aviation Safety Agency or the European Chemical Agency.

The referendum was consultative, not mandatory. It has taken a sequence of political decisions to turn a vote of little more than a third of the nation into a mandate for the most dramatic change in British history in living memory, or indeed in the three centuries since representative parliamentary democracy became rooted down as our way of governance.

It is not often that a great, historic nation decides the game is over and risks relegating itself out of the top rank of economic and geopolitical players. But future historians may decide that is exactly what Britain has done in its convulsions over Brexit.

A personal confession. I first used the term Brexit in 2012. My diary noted:

21 October 2012

In the FT Philip Stephens uses the word I coined some months ago, 'Brexit'. It's a neologism that is gaining currency.

Why Brexit? In 2012, the buzzword for those interested in European politics at the time was Grexit – the idea that Greece might exit the euro single currency or even the EU itself. I was much occupied by the fate of Greece. The cradle nation of democracy, of philosophy, of logic, of debate, of beauty in all the arts had been suffering at the hands of some of the most small-minded politicians that have ever crawled upon the face of the earth.

It would be difficult to make a list of the errors of the Greek ruling elites – right, left, or technocratic – ever since democracy was restored after the ugly rule of a military junta from 1967 to 1974. Taxes were not required to be paid by the rich, who provided the money for political parties. The nation's richest landowner, the Orthodox Church, which was more nationalist and populist than any nationalist populist party anywhere else in Europe, paid not a drachma or a cent on its fabulous wealth and investments. Northern European banks, corporations and weapons manufacturers bribed their way into contracts.

The Greeks had hoped to buy their way into modernization by folding their drachma into Europe's new currency, the euro, at the end of the twentieth century. But as with joining the European Community in 1981, Greece refused to adopt the reforms necessary to sustain EC and then EU membership. Greece made no effort to change economic and fiscal or labour market or planning policy after 2000. Instead a tsunami of cheap euros flooded into the country and when the US-induced financial crash of 2008/9 hit Greece, the country's political class proved utterly unable to rise to the challenge, as I noted at the time:

22 March 2011

The Greeks are in a dreadful state. Having lived for years without reforming the way they spend public money or even having reasonably open and accurate accounts, the international markets have now caught up with them and want huge savage deficit reduction cuts in place as quickly as possible. I read a very stupid article in the Guardian *by a Greek professor at London University saying it is all a plot by the northern European capitalist powers against the periphery of Greece, Spain and Portugal. What utter drivel. The Greeks have lied to and cheated themselves as much as to Europe over who gets the money the state raises. Each ministry has its own pay and pension scheme. There are not just 13 months in December but 14 months are paid instead of 12 and in the Ministry of Foreign Affairs it is 16 and a half months. Different ministries have got different arrangements for free travel or cheap mortgages.*

The new PASOK government under George Papandreou doesn't know what to do. It is appealing for European solidarity because Greece is a member of the Eurozone but Greece doesn't play the foreign policy game on Kosovo, or Cyprus, or Macedonia and there is not much sympathy for Greece in northern Europe. Mrs Merkel has become very hard line as she faces a German public opinion that simply isn't prepared to keep on being the banker of Europe especially when the Germans themselves are having to tighten their belts and accept long working life and lower social expenditure to try and keep the German economy strong.

The one exception was the donnish American-educated, Swedish-speaking prime minister, George Papandreou, who wanted to put a reform package to the people of Greece to decide in a referendum. As Professor Georges Prévélakis, who teaches at the Sorbonne and is one of Europe's best analysts of recent Greek history, argues, there was a possibility of what he calls a 'rupture' with the prevailing Greek economic model that had not been reformed since Greece entered the European Community in 1981. It was not taken because Nicolas Sarkozy and Angela Merkel and the Brussels chieftains were nervous of a Greek referendum that would have rejected their model of how the Greek debt crisis should be handled after the crash.

GREXIT, THEN BREXIT

So, while writing about Grexit, I found myself looking at the ever-increasing language against Europe I could see in my own country from many politicians, most of the press by readership and on the BBC, where the words 'European Union' produced an almost curled lip of disdain from the monolingual presenters of key BBC radio and television current affairs programmes.

Might Brexit happen before Grexit, I wondered back in 2012? When I first stood for Parliament in 1974, Britain had never taken a decision by means of a referendum or plebiscite. By the time I stood down as an MP in 2012, demands for referendums had become normalized. William Hague, as leader of the Conservative Party, began the regular call of all Tory leaders in opposition after 1997 for referendums on any and all EU treaties.

The biggest cheerleaders for a referendum on being in or out of Europe were the Liberal Democrats. In their frustration that the British first-past-the-post electoral system denied them the number of Commons seats that a more proportional electoral system would have provided, the Lib Dems found a substitute in insisting that a referendum was a purer form of taking decisions than the debate and deliberations in two Houses of Parliament, followed by a vote of elected representatives. The Tory leader of the opposition, David Cameron, repeatedly called for a referendum on the 2007 Lisbon Treaty of the European Union, but the Lib Dem leader, Nick Clegg, said what was needed was a referendum on EU membership itself.

Tony Blair was opportunistic over referendums, holding them when he was certain of winning, such as those to endorse the 1998 Good Friday Agreement for Northern Ireland, to create an elected mayor of London, or to set up a parliament in Scotland. He accepted a referendum on regional government in the north-east on which he was agnostic, though confident it would fail, as indeed it did.

Blair's most important referendum decision was in 1997. Before the general election that year, the Conservatives under John Major had made an election pledge that entering the single European currency required a referendum. Blair did not want to leave the Tories as the only party offering a plebiscite, so he matched John Major's offer. It turned into a plebiscite prison for Blair. He dared not risk a referendum on eurozone entry. He knew that nearly all the press would campaign for a No result. Even the *Guardian* newspaper, broadly supportive of Europe from a liberal-left position, was hostile to the euro. When pressed about holding a referendum on the euro early on in his premiership, when his popularity and authority were at their highest, Blair would respond bitterly: 'I am not going down in fucking history as the prime minister who took Britain out of Europe.'

The five economic tests cooked up by Gordon Brown on eurozone entry were a complete red herring. I was in the ministerial team in the Foreign Office after 1997 specializing in EU politics, and I never found anyone there or in Downing Street who thought for a second that Blair would risk a referendum on the euro. He was a much better judge than David Cameron of how the British people would vote in a plebiscite on an EU question.

In 2004, looking at the Commons arithmetic, Blair conceded to holding a referendum on the 2004 EU constitutional treaty. Had it been held, voters in Britain would have rejected it. It would have been a good signal ahead of Cameron's Brexit referendum in 2016. Blair's face was saved by the French and Dutch voting down the EU constitutional treaty in 2005. There was no hiding the relief in Downing Street as the news of the French and Dutch 'No to Europe' arrived, thus avoiding the need for a UK referendum.

As soon as he became prime minister in 2010, David Cameron dropped his promise to hold a referendum on the Lisbon Treaty. But now he was in coalition with the most pro-referendum party in British politics, the Lib Dems. As I noted in the daily diary I kept as an MP and minister, the Lib Dems were obsessed with holding an In–Out referendum on Europe. In March 2008, there was a Commons debate on holding a referendum on the Lisbon Treaty. Gordon Brown was clear Parliament should decide international treaties, not populist plebiscites.

5 March 2008

The big story has become the fact that Nick Clegg has ordered his MPs to abstain rather than vote for or against the referendum. This has provoked the most extraordinary derision from almost everybody else. Nick's argument is that there should not be a referendum on the Lisbon Treaty, which is perfectly acceptable, but instead a much bigger referendum on the question of whether Britain should stay in or out of the EU. But everyone knows that a referendum like that would simply have all three parties agreeing to stay in though arguing about the terms. It wouldn't settle the divisions in the country on the question of Europe one little bit any more than the 1975 referendum settled the matter. Moreover, the Lib Dems had an opposition day debate putting up this very idea in the autumn and were defeated by 500 votes to 60. So this is rather odd posturing and three Lib Dem front bench spokesmen have said they will resign from the front bench in order to vote for a referendum.

In January 2013, David Cameron proposed an In–Out referendum on Europe. Soon after, Sir John Major endorsed Cameron's plebiscite proposal, saying it 'could heal many old sores and have a cleansing effect on politics'. Five years later, Sir John declared that the reappearance in Ireland of internal border checks, as a result of the six counties ruled by London that would be outside the EU facing the rest of Ireland inside the EU, could see the return of violence.

So far from healing old sores, David Cameron's referendum, so warmly endorsed by Sir John Major, has made politics far worse. The referendum

Major supported now threatens the Irish peace process which he helped bring about, and he has recently called for a second referendum to undo the damage caused by the one he enthused about in 2013. Such weathervane politics leaves most citizens even more disenchanted with the quality of national leadership.

So, with hindsight, the political leaders such as Major and Clegg, who supported referendums in place of representative parliamentary democracy, or Blair, who offered referendums to avoid having to make difficult political decisions, bear considerable responsibility for creating a political culture of referendums, thereby allowing the proposal in 2013 by David Cameron to hold a Brexit plebiscite to turn into today's political reality.

No one talks of Grexit any more – but Brexit is the biggest thing to hit Europe since the collapse of Soviet communism. In the Queen's tenth decade, she does not know if her successor will reign over a truly united kingdom, as Scotland and Northern Ireland are coldly bitter at the triumph of an English nationalism that won the Brexit vote.

Britain does not do revolutions – or at least not since the 1640s, when a king's head was chopped off at the end of a civil war that helped create the supremacy of the Westminster Parliament over the state and the nation. Yet it is hard to see Brexit as anything other than a revolutionary moment. It has already destroyed two prime ministers and will almost certainly destroy the new one. It has transferred power from representative elected institutions to a populist plebiscite.

Together with Trump, the Brexit neo-isolationism implies that the long nineteenth- and twentieth-century hegemony of English-speaking power – the United Kingdom and then the United States – could be over. To be sure, new powers – China, India – are on the rise. But North America combined with a Europe in which Britain plays a leading role could still help shape the world. Brexit and Trump make that unlikely.

Because of Brexit, paradoxically, Britain has had a massive impact on continental European politics – although not the one that the 'Leave' voters wanted – as the rest of Europe has recoiled in horror at copying the Brits. European leaders are now more united on the need to stay together and not let Britain have a special status by which it has all the economic benefits of EU membership but none of the political burdens, such as the sharing of sovereignty or paying a share of the EU's running costs.

The twenty-seven other EU member states have found new virtues in the much-criticized European Union, and a new unity on Brexit. Rightist populist nationalist leaderships in Hungary, Poland or Italy are full of condemnation for policies emanating from Brussels they don't like. But they have all dropped calls about leaving the EU or even ditching the euro, as they see how badly the Brexit plebiscite has damaged Britain.

That's good for the EU, bad for Britain. To be sure, there are tensions and contrasting visions for the direction of travel in the EU27 in the third decade of this century. But there were tensions and conflicting visions of where Europe should go in 2009 at the height of the economic crisis, in 1999 as the euro came into being, in 1989 as communist Europe crumbled, in 1979 at the end of the inflation shock high unemployment decade, and so on back to 1949 when the first proposals for a supranational European authority over the coal and steel industries were being made. The cliché that Europe is in dreadful trouble and the EU is about to implode have been staples of newspaper columns and books, especially in Britain, for more than half a century. But the EU is still with us and will outlive the monolingual English commentators who have been announcing the end of Europe since 1950.

Government ministers and pro-Brexit commentators like to look at the rate of job creation in Britain. With the massive taxpayers' subsidy to low-paid employees – 34 per cent of working age people in Britain in 2018 were so poorly paid they were eligible for state benefits, according to the UK's Department for Work and Pensions – it is little wonder there were such high employment figures. A different measure might be the 1.3 million food parcels issued to low-income families and individuals in the year up to March 2018. According to the Office of National Statistics, nearly 600 homeless people had died on the streets of Brexit Britain in 2018 as the slow decline of the economy and the shrinking revenues for public services took their toll.

Economists at the International Monetary Fund (IMF) have identified the United Kingdom as having the largest trade deficit of twenty-eight of the world's biggest economies, running at 4.4 per cent of GDP, in contrast to a surplus for eurozone countries. UK government debt is currently 87 per cent of GDP, more than double the level in 2007, at the end of a decade of Labour government and before the financial crisis. British workers have had no significant wage rises in over a decade. The middle classes have only been able to maintain consumption by going massively into debt.

For the UK, the economics of Brexit are almost entirely negative. Today, any firm based in Britain – British or foreign owned, from modern media or creative firms to banks, to car manufacturers such as Nissan, Honda and Toyota, to universities or management consultants – can produce in Britain and sell into every corner of the world's biggest market, the European Union. Britain runs an enduring trade deficit in goods but a surplus in services – notably the giant network of financial-sector services based in the City of London, the Wall Street of Europe. But EU leaders have made it clear that automatic access to selling bonds, or investment and pension funds, or trading euros is conditional on being in the European Union, or at least agreeing to abide by EU laws and regulations, much as a foreign bank or firm in the United States has to abide by American laws as well as federal and state ordinances.

British car production by mid-2019 had been reduced by nearly half because of Brexit uncertainty. British Steel was threatened with closure as a result of Brexit. Every day seemed to bring reports of financial sector firms relocating some of their business to EU capitals such as Frankfurt, Paris or Amsterdam. British citizens are not fools. Their gut feelings remain in dislike mode on the EU. But their wallets and their heads were telling them Brexit was no longer a good idea. But where could they find the politicians able to represent the desire of a majority for a compromise solution to the Brexit conundrum?

3

HAS BREXIT KILLED BRITISH PARTY POLITICS?

The London political class likes to look down its nose at the erratic and financially dubious political behaviour elsewhere in Europe. Yet it has been Britain which has been plunged into six major national votes in just five years (the 2014 and 2019 European Parliament elections, the 2014 Scottish independence referendum, the 2015 general election, the 2016 EU referendum and the 2017 general election). It had a ruling party without a majority, a prime minister so cordially disliked by many of her own MPs that she had to step down, and a cabinet openly at war with itself, making the Trump White House look like an oasis of Eisenhower calm by comparison. Labour has little purchase on public opinion and the Labour leader's tergiversations on the question of Brexit have provoked open contempt and derision from Labour MPs and younger members of the party, leading finally to a number of MPs walking out to form a short-lived pro-European independent group.

At times of major crisis about the identity and the future of a nation, the existing politics – ideas, parties, leaders – mutate. It barely matters in England if you are Conservative or Labour, a reader of the *Guardian* or the *Sun*. The period since the Brexit vote has put British political parties and the broad political class, including the political media, to the test as never before since the 1930s. Few trust politicians and still less the media. A survey published in 2018 of 27,000 voters across Europe carried out by the Paris-based Foundation for Political Innovation found that in Britain 40 per cent thought 'democracy works poorly in my country'. More than half the British respondents said they had no trust in Parliament, which is still full of many MPs who made lots of money fiddling expenses – a practice seen as corrupt and illegal in most democracies. A few were sanctioned, but most were not. Their constituents know who they are, even if the story as a media event has died away.

Only 26 per cent of Brits polled said they trusted the British media – the fourth lowest of all EU member states. In the US, 39 per cent of the population say they trust the media, while in the Netherlands and Norway 58 and 59 per cent of respondents trusted their journalists – more than twice the UK figures. Prior to the 2016 referendum, many newspapers became propaganda sheets against the European Union, full of bilious comment and indifferent to facts. The public enjoy robust comment, but a press that gives up on factual reporting, as has been the case this century on the European question, gradually loses the respect of the people.

Thus, the period since Brexit shows traditional politics melting. So far, no new politics has emerged. The breakaway of ten Labour and three Conservative MPs in February 2019 to form an independent group lasted only a few months, until the new Change UK party broke apart. Their departure was immediately followed by the Labour leadership softening its Brexit position to give the impression of meeting some of the concerns of the departing MPs, notably on allowing the people a new referendum. A poll published just after the Labour MPs walked out on Jeremy Corbyn showed that 84 per cent of those who had reached voting age since 2016 would now vote to stay in the EU and 87 per cent would vote against Theresa May's proposed deal in a referendum.

Labour was badly out of touch with the new voters the party needed if it was to win enough seats to form a government. Of twenty-six members of Labour's shadow cabinet, twenty-two will be aged 60 or over at the time of a 2022 general election. Some, including the party leader, will be in their 70s, with one aged 80.

To be sure, Britain's first-past-the-post electoral system puts a premium on joining one of the two big political formations to secure election at all levels from local council to Downing Street. Across Europe, twentieth-century party political formations are being shaken. The arrival of a new politics in France, which propelled Emmanuel Macron to the Elysée Palace and gave his new party *En Marche* a big majority in the French National Assembly elections, is one example. Another is the arrival of two populist parties in power in Italy. In other countries, new coalitions have emerged based on parties that did not exist fifteen or twenty-five years ago.

It would be wrong to assume that Britain is inoculated against similar political tectonic plate shifts. Had UKIP not been led by a xenophobic loud-mouth rent-a-quote buffoon, might it have become a serious English nationalist party in the manner of Scotland's nationalists? If Europe was the only or main question on the ballot paper, Nigel Farage did well. But no one took him seriously to vote him in as MP or thought anything he had to say on the wider governance of Britain was of importance. When his one-man Brexit Party tried to win a Parliamentary seat in Peterborough or Brecon in the summer of 2019, it failed.

It takes courage and a great deal of money to do new politics in Britain. Sadly, the Liberal Democrats did much damage to faith in radical political change by being poodles for David Cameron and George Osborne in the 2010–15 coalition. The efforts since the Brexit plebiscite by ex-Lib Dem ministers from the Cameron government to offer themselves as a vector for new politics do not have credibility. The same is true of Tony Blair, whom many in the nation will never forgive both for the invasion of Iraq and then for the way he made so much money after he stood down as prime minister.

It is too facile to make pro- or anti-Europeanism the dividing line. Brexit is dissolving the already weakened bonds that bound together disparate and contradictory forces into a single big UK-wide Conservative or Labour Party. Indeed, the only MPs animated on the subject of Europe this century have been obsessives for whom British partnership in the EEC 1973–92 or the EU since has been seen as an enslavement. But where were the rational, moderate MPs able to put the case for European partnership and British participation and leadership in the affairs of the continent? They were thin on the ground, as I noted a year before David Cameron announced his referendum:

26 January 2012

Into a little debate on Europe. This should have been the normal pre-Council European debate of a full eight hours but under the insane new arrangements it is truncated to just 90 minutes. There weren't many speakers though and the time limit was just five minutes so I was able to have my blast. Where on earth are

Labour MPs? They are not interested at all in the EU. There are huge areas of policy debate on which now we have just about nothing to say. It's very very worrying.

Over the question of EU membership, neither Theresa May up to her departure nor Jeremy Corbyn have shown leadership, articulated a convincing vision or enthused their MPs, party members or the public. As Brexiternity bites, we can expect different politics to surface, but even at this stage it is too early to define or describe what form they will take. The collapse of the Change UK project illustrates the difficulties for any new politics, but the traditional parties remain shaken and confused by Brexit.

The opposition Labour Party has a leader who is a big fan of Fidel Castro and Nicolas Maduro, the latter of whom has reduced Venezuela to degrading poverty despite sitting on the world's biggest oil reserves, who has supported Slobodan Milosevic, and is accused by his own MPs of being unwilling to purge his party of rank antisemitism. Ignored or marginalized for most of his time in the Commons since 1983, Corbyn found that there was finally an audience for his denunciations of the shameful inequality and cruelty of austerity cuts on public services and indirect tax rises for the poor, while the better-off get richer by the second. The architect of making the poor poorer and his rich friends richer was the prime minister between 2010 and 2016, David Cameron. He thought he was sailing to an easy win in his referendum on the European Union. By the end of the count, Cameron was finished. If Lord North in British history books is the prime minister who lost America in the 1780s, David Cameron is the prime minister who lost Europe 230 years later.

THE FIRST POLITICAL BREXIT AS CAMERON QUITS EPP FEDERATION OF EUROPEAN CENTRE RIGHT PARTIES

In 2009, in his first essay at a political Brexit, Cameron took the Conservative Party out of the Europe-wide federation of centre-right parties such as those led by Germany's Angela Merkel, the then president of France, Nicolas Sarkozy, Poland's Donald Tusk, or Spain's Mariano Rajoy. The federation, known as the European People's Party (EPP), allows all the mainstream conservative parties to connect, debate and network. It has moderate centre-right parties from

Nordic countries sitting with national identity parties like Fidesz from Hungary, which wins votes by constantly attacking Brussels and European Union values.

David Davis told me how in 2005, when he ran against Cameron for leadership of the Conservative Party, he won the support of more MPs in the first ballot – sixty-two – than David Cameron's forty-two MPs. The key swing vote MPs were the forty-two Tory MPs who voted for Liam Fox, who campaigned for the leadership on a hard-line anti-European ticket.

'Liam came to see me and David Cameron,' Davis told me. 'He offered his support to whichever of us agreed to leave the EPP. I was much more Eurosceptic than Cameron, and had been critical of the EU since the 1990s. But it made no sense to me for the Conservative Party, a big international party, to leave an important international federation, even if we strongly disagreed with some of their more pro-European federalist members. Liam went to see Cameron who immediately signed up to the demand to quit the EPP and with that Cameron won the leadership.'

Walking out of the EPP into 2009 had no impact on the 2010 election, when Cameron won enough seats to form a coalition government with the Liberal Democrats. Was it then that he decided that he could make an offer about allowing voters to leave Europe in a referendum, thinking that it would never happen? That, like quitting the EPP, a referendum would be just an anti-European gesture of little consequence? Until Cameron writes his own honest account of what led him to propose his Brexit plebiscite, we shall not know.

The xenophobic and antisemitic BNP won two seats in the European Parliament in 2009, and UKIP under its populist demagogue anti-immigrant leader, Nigel Farage, was also winning votes. The BNP was never able to win a seat in the House of Commons, and although two Tory MPs who defected to UKIP remained in their seats for a short period, no UKIP candidate standing for the first time under the UKIP banner was ever elected to the Commons – including Nigel Farage himself, who was rejected by voters in five general elections and two by-elections. Yet the BBC and the press treated Farage as a major mainstream political figure. In the manner of Senator Joe McCarthy, claiming communists were taking over America in the 1950s, or Donald Trump insisting the United States was swamped by Mexican and Muslim immigrants, Farage won a major profile with his claims that the European

Union was taking over Britain and a tsunami of European 'immigrants' – Polish, Italian, Spanish – was overwhelming English towns and public services. He claimed it was possible to travel through London without hearing English spoken and said: 'This country, in a short space of time, has frankly become unrecognizable.'

Trump invited Farage to visit him in Trump Tower soon after winning the US Presidency in November 2016 and tweeted: 'Many people would like to see @Nigel_Farage represent Great Britain as their Ambassador to the United States. He would do a great job!' Trump in 2019 urged the UK to leave the EU, if necessary without paying the money owed or any kind of agreement. This ultimate fusion of Brexit and Trump has not come to pass, but in their appeal to xenophobic, anti-immigrant, anti-Muslim nationalism, both Farage and Trump have much in common.

Arguments merging into open hostility to Europe, especially on the impact of EU membership since 1973 upon traditional beliefs and misbeliefs about national and parliamentary sovereignty, have been like a political virus eating into the innards of traditional British politics and making parties lose coherence and shape.

In his book *Beyond Brexit: Towards a British Constitution*, Professor Vernon Bogdanor, one of Britain's leading constitutional political scientists, argues that the nearly five decades of British membership of first the European Community, then the European Union has fundamentally changed the UK's previous constitutional arrangements. As on the continent (or in most democracies, including the United States), British judges slowly obtained the power over the years of interpreting European law (emanating from both the EU and the Council of Europe's European Court of Human Rights) as it has been incorporated into UK law to overrule what ministers want to do if the rights of British citizens as guaranteed by European law are judged to be threatened or reduced. As Bogdanor notes, following Brexit, 'Britain will become once again a country which provides no legal remedy for breaches of human rights'. The stand-off between Mrs May and MPs which led to her resignation reflected a constitutional clash between the authority of Parliament and the authority of direct democracy, as expressed in the June 2016 plebiscite. Since Britain has no written constitution, we have no rules on whether the direct democracy of the plebiscite or the indirect parliamentary representative democracy of the House of Commons was supreme.

In many countries, for example, a referendum that could affect constitutional norms to the extent that the Brexit plebiscite has done – altering laws, rights of citizens to live in Europe, changing the UK's geopolitical status – would need the consent of at least 40 or even 50 or 60 per cent of all the electorate. The Brexit upheaval was based on just 37 per cent of the registered electorate with, as has been noted, millions of younger British voters or British citizens living in Europe not getting to vote. For Bogdanor, all this points to the need for a written or codified constitution. The paradox of such a move is that 'if Britain is to have a constitution, Parliament must explicitly abdicate its sovereignty'. So, in or out of the EU, the supremacy of parliamentary sovereignty is drawing to a close. Bogdanor notes:

> It is just possible that we are now approaching a peaceful constitutional moment, one marked not by revolution or a struggle for independence, but by the concatenation of inter-connected constitutional problems, all pressing insistently for resolution.

By the third anniversary of the Brexit plebiscite, the level of anger, fury and hate language of 'treason', 'betrayal' and 'selling out' used against Theresa May by the proponents of the full rupture with Europe, advanced by Boris Johnson, Nigel Farage and the UKIP fellow traveller MPs in the Conservative Party, had reached such intensity that the hopes of Bogdanor and others that there could now be a calm, rational discussion of a new constitutional settlement were perhaps premature. But no one could doubt that Brexit had melted down existing political structures and out of the Brexit process some kind of new politics had to emerge.

It is doubtful if any of these considerations were foremost or even present in David Cameron's mind when he surrendered to UKIP and conceded the only demand the party had made since first winning a seat in the European Parliament in 1999 – namely, that a plebiscite should be held on British membership of the EU. Cameron calculated that the pro-EU vote would easily win, UKIP would be finished, and anti-European Tory MPs would be marginalized. Rarely has a British prime minister gotten the internal politics of his own country and his own party so hopelessly wrong.

In forming her cabinet, Theresa May promoted rabid anti-Europeans, including Boris Johnson into the prestigious post of foreign secretary. Johnson had a long record of falsifying news stories and indeed was fired from his first job at *The Times* for making up quotes. His reporting in the 1990s for the *Daily Telegraph* about Brussels was often sheer invention. For twenty-five years Johnson had been making Tory audiences laugh and jeer with his inventions about the EU. In his biography of Winston Churchill, Johnson wrote that a 'Gestapo-controlled Nazi European Union' was proposed in 1942 with 'a single currency, a central bank, a common agricultural policy and other familiar ideas'.

LABOUR TRIES BUT FAILS TO GET ANYONE TO LISTEN TO ITS BREXIT POLICY

The failure of Labour to carry out what constitutionally is seen as the first duty of Her Majesty's Opposition – namely to oppose – is a symptom of how Brexit has overturned all political norms and rules. Corbyn's predecessor as Labour leader was Ed Miliband, a kindly, thoughtful, well-meaning man, but more a second-rank cabinet minister than a politician with the ability to destroy a party in power and win an election. He became Labour leader in 2010, defeating his brother, David. I was an MP at the time and told David Miliband, whom I nominated to be leader, that in my judgement there was very little chance of Labour winning the next election:

It's not whether Labour is good or Cameron is bad, but just that voters, after they have switched votes from a party that has been in power for more than a decade, enjoyed a few terms in office, will tend to stay with the new party they now support. There are hardly any examples in European or Australian or Canadian history of a party of the left doing more than a decade in office, losing and then bouncing back at the next election. It's not excluded, but the pattern of history says Labour is going to be in opposition for at least two terms.

David Miliband looked crestfallen as I gave him my honest assessment based on three decades of observing the fortunes of centre-left parties in other countries. I added that I thought the Conservative–Lib Dem government had the potential to be an attractive coalition after the drab last years of Labour under

Gordon Brown, who was a brilliant chancellor of the exchequer but did not inspire as prime minister. 'Cameron and Clegg are young, and fresh faces, in tune with metropolitan, socially liberal Britain and unless they make a big mistake they should be OK for five years', I told the elder Miliband.

His younger brother won and straight away made mistakes that led indirectly but inevitably to Labour's inability to handle Brexit after June 2016. Ed's first mistake was to abolish the rough-and-ready system of shadow cabinet elections by Labour MPs. This system allowed Labour MPs who had the shrewdest idea of which of their number could make an impact in the Commons, on television, or with the public to elect twelve of their number – known as the Parliamentary Committee – to form a shadow cabinet. The leader could add one or two other members. To be sure, there were regional and political groups that swapped votes, but it allowed the MPs who impressed their peers to emerge.

Ed Miliband moved to make personalized appointments. He quickly put into the shadow cabinet two brand new, very young MPs, Rachel Reeves and Chuka Umunna. Both were highly able but had little political experience. Their instant promotion was resented by other MPs with equal or better claim to the roles. After Miliband's defeat and resignation in 2015, Reeves moved to select committee work. After an initial flirtation with seeking to control European workers entering into the UK labour market, which sounded at the time close to Brexit ideas, Umunna threw himself with considerable energy into campaigning against Brexit and finally left Labour to join the breakaway Independent Group of MPs, saying he had never really felt at home in Labour. In the end he joined the Liberal Democratic Party. This was quite a journey, as ten years previously Umunna was selected at a young age to be the Labour candidate for his safe Labour seat in south London because he appealed to local Labour activists as the most left-wing of the those who sought the nomination, recalls the journalist Polly Toynbee, a Labour Party member then living in the constituency.

Umunna was stylish and eloquent and showed dash and courage as he spoke out against the folly of Brexit while most Labour MPs kept their head down and went with the line of accepting the vote of 37 per cent of the electorate as unchallengeable. However, older Labour MPs representing seats far away from the fashionable centres of modish metropolitan Labour circles in London, who had watched Umunna's startling rise to front bench status and instant promotion by Ed Miliband, did not rally to support him. His break-way party quickly split apart and Umunna, once seen as the Barack Obama of British left-liberal politics, now appears to be a young man with a political past but no clear future.

Ed Miliband's next mistake was to allow anyone to register as a 'supporter' of the Labour Party on payment of just £3. It did not help him win the 2015 election when his election campaign coffee mug bore the slogan 'Controls on Immigration'. After his inevitable resignation, Labour Party membership soared, as Miliband's departure was seen as the final end of the New Labour era that began twenty years previously under Tony Blair and Gordon Brown when the two Miliband brothers, David and Ed, worked for Blair and Brown respectively and after 2010 were seen as the continuation of the Blair–Brown years by younger protégés.

The Labour Party was swollen by many young millennial activists who had been radicalized by the massive increases in student fees accepted by Nick Clegg and the Liberal Democrats in clear breach of a solemn 2010 Lib Dem election promise not to make going to university more costly for young people. Others from a pre-New Labour left background in Trotskyist or communist party and trade union activism joined or rejoined the Labour Party for the nominal membership fee Ed Miliband had initiated. Labour membership was either very young or quite old.

When the election to replace Ed Miliband took place, it was a walkover for Jeremy Corbyn. He had been in the hard left Campaign Group of MPs for twenty years. Every time there was a Labour Party leadership election, members of the Campaign Group took it in turns to be the flag-bearer for the anti-New Labour hard left. Before 2015 they stood no chance. After Ed Miliband's reforms, the Labour Party was handed over to committed left-wing socialists who took all the leadership positions bar that of deputy leader. Tom Watson, who had manoeuvred against Tony Blair on behalf of Gordon Brown after 2005 and had a deserved reputation as a political schemer, became Corbyn's deputy.

The Ed Miliband and Blair–Brown generation of MPs then made matters far worse by refusing to serve under Corbyn who, to begin with, sought a balanced shadow cabinet other than one or two trusted veteran leftist friends such as John McDonnell and Diane Abbott. The Labour MPs who considered a Corbyn-led Labour Party unelectable resigned as front bench spokespersons and insisted on a second leadership election in 2016. Corbyn turned back to the membership, now in the hundreds of thousands – young, angry, passionate, with a stratum of experienced far left organizers who had worked with anti-European leftists such as Tony Benn after 1979 and who had pushed Labour to endorse an early form of Brexit in the party's 1983 general election manifesto. They had been marginalized by Labour leaders including Neil Kinnock, John Smith and the Blair–Brown team, for whom winning power was a priority rather than maintaining leftist anti-European political purity.

The young neophytes and old reawakened left re-elected Corbyn, who was reinstalled as leader of the Labour Party without any serious challenge until the next general election currently scheduled for 2022. The new prime minister, Boris Johnson may take a risk and call an early election, as Theresa May did in 2017. But as in 1974 or 1951, when the British people are invited to have an election ahead of the normal schedule just in order to confirm a prime minister in post, any Brexit election based on Boris Johnson's character might produce a result uncomfortable for the denizen of Downing Street.

In June 2016, Jeremy Corbyn, reconfirmed as Labour leader, had to take a position on Brexit. During the referendum campaign he kept as low a profile as possible. His natural lifelong dislike of European economic integration, with its focus on open trade and competitive market economics, prevailed over his natural international and almost libertarian support for open borders, social justice, worker rights and environmental progressivity, which also formed part of the overall European Union political project, so his campaign was half-hearted. After the referendum he also had to take into account the shock many Labour MPs felt, especially in traditional working-class constituencies in the industrial north of England, Wales and the Midlands, as they saw a majority of voters in their own constituencies voting to leave Europe. In the immediate aftermath of Brexit, there was a panic in pro-EU Labour ranks in these seats which had been badly hit by the deindustrialization policies of the 1980s and 1990s.

The reaction was curious. In most solid Labour seats in the north and Midlands, up to half the voters were in normal circumstances Tory or UKIP voters. In the 2010 general election the BNP polled 3,000 votes or more in constituencies in Stoke-on-Trent, West Bromwich, Leeds, Rotherham and Pendle, with 6,620 BNP votes registered in a single Essex constituency. Two Labour MPs for Stoke-on-Trent seats, Gareth Snell and Ruth Smeeth, argued in June 2019 that Labour had to appeal to pro-Brexit voters. Yet in both their seats Labour won 39 per cent of the votes in the 2015 general election, while the combined Tory–UKIP vote was 52 per cent in Snell's constituency and 48 per cent in Smeeth's. Was there much point in Labour trying to devise a policy for Europe that would convert Tory and UKIP voters plus the BNP voters of 2010 into supporters of Labour and Corbyn?

Other Labour MPs in solid working-class seats such as Sunderland, Sheffield, Wolverhampton and Redcar that voted Leave in 2016 stood up for their commitment to protect jobs and investment and retain the right of their constituents to live, work or retire in Europe.

Immediately after the Brexit plebiscite, some Labour MPs started calling for stringent controls on European workers with proposals for quotas, or seasonal limits, or special permits for London or South Wales. The language sounded similar to ideas promoted by Nigel Farage in his campaign against European workers in Britain. Labour wits dubbed them 'Red UKIP', which upset some Labour MPs promoting these ideas, but showed the disarray that the party found itself in as a result of the Brexit vote.

Opinion polls have turned steadily against Brexit since the referendum, with most showing a desire to stay in the European Union free-trade single market and customs union. By the end of 2018 there was not a single serious opinion poll that showed a majority for leaving the EU. A YouGov poll held on the eve of the Labour annual conference in September 2018 showed 91 per cent of Labour Party members saying Brexit would be bad for Britain and 86 per cent urging a new referendum. But at the conference itself Corbyn could not find words to oppose Brexit and instead focused on criticizing Mrs May's handling of the negotiations. Later he confessed that if a new referendum were to be held, he did not know how he would vote.

Corbyn himself is thus no enthusiast for the European Union and he has refused to lead Labour against the prime minister's pro-Brexit stance. However, I have examined all of Corbyn's interventions on Europe in the Commons since 2005, and while he urged the European Commission to take more action in support of his favoured causes, he has never actually called for Britain's withdrawal.

A year before the referendum Owen Jones, the newspaper columnist who has significant influence on the left in Britain, urged his *Guardian* readers to support what he called Lexit – a left-wing exit from the EU. Jones condemned the EU in language that was common to members of the Campaign Group, the hard left block of Labour MPs who carried the torch for Tony Benn's 1970s and early 1980s hostility to Europe that inspired Jeremy Corbyn and his No. 2, the Labour shadow chancellor, John McDonnell. Jones proclaimed that EU treaties and directives enforce free market policies based on privatiz ation and marketization of our public services and utilities:

> If indeed much of the left decides on Lexit – it must run its own campaign [which] would focus on building a new Britain, one of workers' rights, a genuine living wage, public ownership, industrial activism and tax justice. Lexit may be seen as a betrayal of solidarity with the left in the EU: Syriza [the Greek leftist party] and Podemos [Spain's populist hard left party, whose leaders have taken money from the Venezuela regime] are trying to change the institution, after all, not leave it . . . the threat of Brexit would help them . . . The case for Lexit grows ever stronger, and – at the very least – more of us need to start dipping our toes in the water.

Owen Jones has elected to make himself the main promoter and defender of Jeremy Corbyn in the press. To be fair to the *Guardian* writer, he soon dropped his support for Lexit and campaigned to stay in the EU. The arguments he advanced in the summer before the Brexit plebiscite were identical to those advanced by many on the anti-European left since the 1970s. The parties he hailed as models to emulate – Podemos in Spain or Syriza in Greece – faded.

It is too simplistic to paint Corbyn as a socialist anti-European. He supports the right of Europeans to live in the United Kingdom and, like any 1970s internationalist, he believes in open borders. He does not like the European Union of free markets, rules-enforced competition, and bans on state subsidies to prop up money-losing industries. At times, he can use UKIP-sounding language about European workers in Britain driving down wages.

LABOUR FAILS TO EXPLOIT MAY'S BREXIT VULNERABILITY

At the general election of June 2017, Labour won many seats in pro-European cities and university towns and gained votes among the young. This gave the opposition a golden opportunity to tear into Prime Minister May and pour salt on the open wounds of senior Tory politicians who disagreed on how to handle Brexit. Instead, Labour turned in on itself. Corbyn fired three shadow ministers who voted to support the United Kingdom staying in the single market, even though leaving the single market was UKIP and hard-line Tory Brexit policy. Labour spokespersons contradicted each other. In March 2018 he dismissed the highly effective Owen Smith as shadow secretary of state for Northern Ireland because Smith had argued for a soft Brexit and for the right of voters to be consulted before a final amputation with Europe takes place.

Usually Corbyn focused more on his demand for a new general election. But when eight well-known and popular Labour MPs left the party in February 2019 in protest at Corbyn's laid-back approach to Brexit (and the party's sad, bad record on antisemitism), Corbyn came straight back to tell the weekly meeting of Labour MPs in Parliament that he now stood four-square behind a new referendum – dressed up as a confirmatory referendum on any final deal to leave Europe. The Labour MPs who had walked out of the party in protest at Corbyn's relegation to minor importance the idea of consulting the people had achieved their goal of forcing the Labour leader to be a little warmer about a new referendum, but at the expense of their future as Labour MPs.

But again and again, Labour in the spring of 2019 slalomed around the issue of a new referendum, suggesting it might be needed on a Tory-negotiated deal to give effect to Brexit but not a Labour one. However, the shadow foreign secretary, Emily Thornberry came out strongly for a new referendum without ifs or buts. As one of the main possible successors to Jeremy Corbyn if – as some reports suggested – the Labour leader might stand down after entering his eighth decade in May 2019, Ms Thornberry was appealing to the hundreds of thousands of young Labour Party members who had joined for £3 after 2015 and been enthused by Corbyn's appeal to mobilize against austerity, poverty, and for social justice in the election campaign of 2017. The Labour signalling was confused, contradictory and at times indecipherable as different members of the shadow cabinet opined on the issue of allowing the people a new vote.

Already rank-and-file party members at the 2016 Labour Party conference, shortly after the referendum, agreed a resolution stating Conference 'recognises that many of those who voted to leave the EU were expressing dissatisfaction with the EU or national policy and were voting for change, but believe that unless the final settlement proves to be acceptable, then the option of retaining EU membership should be retained'.

A core element of 'retaining EU membership' is, of course, staying in the customs union and single market. The Labour conference resolution goes on to state as formal party policy that 'The final settlement therefore should be *subject to approval through Parliament and potentially through a general election or a referendum*' (my emphasis). This policy was confirmed at the 2018 Labour Party conference, but with most emphasis on holding a new general election. Both trade union leaders and shadow cabinet members dismissed the idea of a new referendum even though there was a clear reference to it in a conference resolution.

In the past it was often Jeremy Corbyn himself who insisted, in his disagreement with the then party leadership, that decisions taken at the party conference were sacrosanct and should be treated with respect, indeed reverence. He voted 500 times against Labour leaders in Commons votes before 2015 and so can neither demand nor expect unquestioned loyalty from current Labour MPs. In fact, it has been fellow Eurosceptic Labour MPs such Kate Hoey and Frank Field, also of the Corbyn generation of 1970s Labour politicians who were hostile to Europe, who have shown their disloyalty to him by voting to support Theresa May in key Commons votes when Corbyn whipped Labour to oppose the government.

The broad mass of Labour MPs are bemused and uncertain and without leadership will do what politicians do at any time, anywhere in the world: keep their heads down. There is certainly a sense that Brexit is completely and utterly a Conservative Party mess, with the strains inside the Tory Party and among Tory ministers and MPs at breaking point. Corbyn shares this assessment. Labour in this analysis should simply lie back and enjoy Conservative Party convulsions in the expectation that voters will not again entrust government to a party that is so badly led and full of swivel-eyed factionalism about Europe.

In addition, Labour MPs are far from certain where their own voters want to be. Four Labour MPs lost their very safe seats in working-class constituencies in the Midlands and north England in the 2017 general election. Strongly pro-European Labour MPs in seats far away from the more liberal, metropolitan Remain cities and university towns of England were very cautious in profiling themselves as ardent pro-EU Remainers in the 2017 election. I canvassed for Labour MP friends who were strongly Europhile but in their local literature they talked of respecting the referendum result and the need to control immigration from Europe. One long-standing pro-European Labour MP representing a Lancashire seat explained that every time he went back to his constituency after the referendum, he met many people who were proud to have voted Leave and expected him to support them in votes in the House of Commons.

This is real-time, real-experience politics that was not well understood by the many enthusiasts who have never stood for election and who assumed that all but diehard pro-Brexit MPs would support moves in the Commons or campaigns in public to reverse the referendum by any means possible.

Corbyn promoted as his main Brexit *consigliere* Keir Starmer, a former QC with a flair for self-publicity who had been elected to a safe London (and Remain) seat in 2015. Like any good lawyer, he could produce words that seemed to cover over as far as possible Labour's internal contradictions on Brexit. They made sense at north London liberal Labour dinner parties and on national radio or TV interviews, but were irrelevant in Bootle, Bradford or Barnsley.

Labour shadow cabinet members contradicted each other on the Sunday morning political TV shows or said something different from what Corbyn had said in a preceding interview. This made good copy for mocking columns by the commentariat in the press, but among Labour members, activists and voters no one really noticed or cared. Brexit was a Tory product and a Tory problem. What Labour had to say was irrelevant and that suited many Labour MPs nervous of repudiating the choice made by many of their voters in June 2016.

Being lectured on Brexit or told what they should do, think or vote in the first two years after the referendum by Tony Blair or by Blair-generation peers in the House of Lords was, if anything, counterproductive. Labour MPs elected in 2010 or 2017 and the new, more left-wing membership of the Labour Party did not listen to declarations from unelected or retired pro-European Labour politicians. Labour taken as a whole simply felt no responsibility for Brexit. They were under little pressure from local businesses or trade unions or local Labour councillors. This changed somewhat when, in the autumn of 2018, major foreign-owned manufacturers said they would have to relocate out of the UK if access to the EU single market was lost. Nevertheless, the biggest trade union, Unite, did not come out and urge a rethink on Brexit and the majority of Labour MPs continued to keep their heads down.

The weekly and regional evening papers barely discussed Brexit. The local radio phone-in programmes were full of loudmouth know-alls who got their views from the *Sun* and other anti-EU tabloids like the *Daily Mail*. It was easy to parrot slogans about how badly Mrs May and her ministers were handling Brexit. But there was no real pressure on Labour to come up with a distinct line of policy and seek to win support for it from the public.

Labour talked grandiloquently about forcing a general election and replacing the Conservatives. There is nothing wrong with an opposition party proclaiming that all the nation's problems would be solved if it were to replace the government. But Labour could offer no convincing narrative, policy, or different negotiation priorities on Brexit. This non-policy on Brexit neither impressed nor enthused, but it kept most Labour MPs, elected councillors and the bulk of trade unions who are an integral part of Labour in an uneasy coalition of leaving Brexit as a Tory problem for Mrs May to solve.

The nadir was reached at the Labour Party conference in Liverpool in September 2018. Jeremy Corbyn had proclaimed his desire to return control of the Labour Party to Labour members. So when 130 constituency parties submitted motions in support of Labour backing a new public vote on leaving Europe in the light of all the new evidence and facts available which were not known in 2016, it might be assumed that Corbyn and the Labour leadership would listen to the membership.

On the contrary, Labour's leadership displayed and deployed all the tactics of the Labour era of top-down control of party members. As Stephen Bush, the shrewd political correspondent of the *New Statesman*, wrote: 'On Brexit, the leadership found itself at odds with most members.' Trade union officials and Labour's top shadow cabinet lawyer went in to a locked room with delegates for eight hours to browbeat them into accepting the Corbyn line that a new referendum should be a far-off possibility only once a general election was held.

On television, Labour shadow cabinet members rubbished the idea that Labour wanted a new vote as a priority, or indeed that Brexit should be challenged and the politics of Brexit rejected and defeated. As part of the process of MPs inserting themselves into the Brexit process by way of so-called indicative votes, two Labour MPs, Phil Wilson and Peter Kyle, tabled an amendment calling for a confirmatory referendum on any final deal between the UK and the EU. Corbyn had little choice but to go along with this, but several Labour MPs, including the party chair, Ian Lavery, voted against the whip, thus helping to ensure a defeat for the idea of a confirmatory referendum. Lavery, a former mineworker close to Corbyn, suffered no rebuke or sanction after his decision to vote with Conservatives and against the official Labour line. There are always arguments about timing in a parliamentary process and with a solid phalanx of Conservative and DUP MPs voting against a new referendum, its chances of winning a Commons majority were slim. But once again Corbyn's failure to define an effective policy against the string-pullers of pro-Brexit Labour forces made him look lost and unable to offer leadership to the nation.

Indeed, at the time of the third anniversary of the Brexit plebiscite there was still no settled view on how it should be handled by the main political parties. Andrew Adonis, a Labour peer who had emerged as a determined champion of Remain, speaking and writing with more verve and passion than the entire Labour official leadership could muster, wrote in the *New European* that Corbyn's principal spokesperson on Brexit did not 'want to change the weather. Since 2016 he had been a Brexiter . . . Consistently including this week [of the 2018 Labour conference] he talks about getting the best Brexit deal, not about stopping Brexit.'

Labour rank-and-file delegates were not allowed to take EU flags into the party's 2018 conference to wave during the Brexit debate, which ended with the deputy general secretary of Labour's largest trade union affiliate, Unite, trashing the idea there could a referendum on staying in the EU. But Palestinian flags were handed out to be waved during Jeremy Corbyn's keynote address. Saying yes to Palestine is a long-standing Labour cause. Saying no to Europe was gradually taking over the top ranks of Labour under Corbyn's leadership.

At a crucial moment in national history, Labour preferred to watch from the stand and not get down onto the pitch and fight to defeat the Trump–Farage–Johnson vision of a Europe in which Britain ceased to be a major partner, player and leader.

4

NEGOTIATING BREXIT

One of the first European leaders Theresa May met as she began tackling Brexit was the Danish prime minister in October 2016. Lars Løkke Rasmussen was again prime minister of Denmark, having replaced the social democratic Helle Thorning-Schmidt, married to the UK Labour MP Steven Kinnock, son of Neil Kinnock, the former Labour leader and EU Commissioner.

Rasmussen leads Denmark's main centre-right party (confusingly having 'Liberal' in its title), the closest Denmark has to England's Conservative Party. Like Theresa May, he heads a minority government and, like her, he has been in centre-right politics all his life, climbing the echelons of local government, then into the Danish Parliament to become a minister, and then as prime minister, first in 2009 and again in 2015. It is more than a hundred years since a majority government of just one party was formed in Denmark. Danes have compromise and coalition in their political DNA, even if their politics can be fierce and competitive, with strong values and opposing ideological beliefs on display. Indeed, in due course, after an election in June 2019 Rasmussen had to make way for a social democratic prime minister who was able to form a loose alliance of parties to replace Rasmussen.

An eyewitness at Mrs May's encounter with Rasmussen described how the Danish prime minister was nonplussed by his British opposite number: 'Mrs May sat there for an hour and said nothing. There was no communication.' Afterwards Rasmussen asked his diplomatic advisers if Mrs May was always like that.

Every Tory MP can tell stories of how difficult it is to talk to their now-retired prime minister. Opinions are divided on whether it is extreme shyness – though being shy is not normally a successful politician's trait – or whether Mrs May liked to play her cards so close to her chest she did not even know what was in her hand.

I once tried to chat to her in a Commons corridor after I had read that her summer holiday had been based walking in the Swiss Alps. Since I had been climbing in the Alps myself that summer, I was curious which part of Switzerland she had been in. I asked her politely and she completely clammed up. She was not rude. She did not blank me. But she gave no information away. Without being in any way discourteous, she just shut down the conversation as fast as she could. It wasn't because I was an opposition MP. Every Tory MP confirms that she says as little as possible.

When she returned to Copenhagen for a visit in April 2018, Mr Rasmussen got down to business. He asked her: 'Theresa, what do you want from the EU? What is the British government policy on Brexit?' She replied: 'Read my speeches.'

Everyone dealing with Brexit in Brussels or the EU27 capitals pored over Mrs May's three keynote speeches setting out her views on Brexit: at Lancaster House, London in January 2017; in Florence in September 2017; and at the Mansion House in the City of London in March 2018. But no one was any the wiser. In all three of them she produced wish lists of what she expected the EU should concede. These aspirations are not what anyone was able to negotiate. Downing Street's desires all assumed a special status for Britain that was not on offer from other member states. The UK demands would have required a rewriting of the international law in EU treaties to give Britain privileges no other EU member state has.

After the Lancaster House speech in 2017, she lectured Brussels and the EU27, claiming that the EU would be responsible for 'an act of calamitous self-harm', with many Europeans, including car exporters in Germany, farmers in France or fisherman in Spain, becoming 'poorer'. This patronizing arrogance was reinforced by her declaration that Britain remained a 'great, global nation'.

The speech in January 2017 was destined not for European but for domestic consumption. It was aimed at reassuring the hard Brexit wing of the Conservative Party that she stood with them. In fact, as numerous EU specialists – notably Pascal Lamy, the former EU Commissioner, ex-chief of staff to Jacques Delors as Commission president and former head of the World Trade Organization (WTO) – have pointed out, there is, strictly speaking, no negotiation that can readily take place between the UK and the EU. The EU could not change its law to suit English anti-Europeans.

As Ambassador Peter Ptassek, the senior diplomat in charge of Germany's handling of Brexit, told me in his Wilhelmstrasse office in the German Foreign Ministry, for Germans the EU is a *Rechtsgemeinde* – literally a 'community of laws'. Britain wants to leave this community of laws following its referendum. For the Germans, as seen from Berlin, far from the EU being a federal superstate, Europe has never had more democratic, market economy, rule-of-law independent members of the United Nations. They are grouped in an international treaty organization, the EU, which is a set of laws and rules which contracting parties – that is, the member states of the EU – agree to abide by and on the whole obey.

A moment's glance at the arguments and rows between national capitals and Brussels shows the emptiness of the claim that the EU has replaced nation states in Europe as the only source of power. On the contrary, the EU has only as much power as its constituent nation states have been prepared to share in order to achieve a wider common purpose such as building a single set of market economy rules. The Dutch political scientist and one of the most original thinkers on Europe, Luuk van Middelaar, has given his latest book the subtitle *Improvising Politics on the European Stage*, which captures just how far from a single power centre replacing the national politics of Europe the EU actually is in reality.

Mrs May in her three speeches set out different demands based on different lists of what she wanted. But at the heart of all three speeches was the view that the UK could stop obeying any EU laws it did not like – notably those covering the single market and customs union and non-discrimination in hiring workers on grounds of nationality – as well as stop paying contributions and yet at the same time keep economic access and other advantages and benefits enjoyed by EU member states that are willing to respect its laws and rules.

In July 2018, two years after the Brexit vote, the government finally wrote down on paper what its desired policy outcome was. This wish list was elaborated in the so-called Chequers declaration and then in a longer white paper.

These retained the core Brexit message of the UK leaving the EU single market and customs union and no longer accepting the supremacy of the European Court of Justice. Instead of regulating the UK labour market to lessen and control the impact of workers from the EU arriving to take up jobs offered by British employers, Downing Street insisted freedom of movement had to end.

EU leaders in the period after Brexit queued up to say that Mrs May could not cherry-pick, or have her cake and eat it, or pick and choose which bits of the EU she liked and reject those that the other EU governments had to abide by. In London there was endless talk about 'negotiations' or a 'deal', yet the only real negotiations taking place were within the Conservative Party or to some extent between Downing Street and the Ulster unionist anti-Europeans. The EU had set out its position very early on. There would be a withdrawal agreement, necessary when any signatory nation quits an international treaty organization. It covered the money Britain owed, the status of EU citizens in the UK and the commitment not to have a physical border in Northern Ireland. Mrs May accepted those three points in December 2017, but then spent the next year negotiating with her own party and DUP supporters. There were meetings between the chief UK Brexit civil servant, Olly Robbins, and between British ministers and Michel Barnier, the EU official serving as European chief negotiator for Brexit, but they were hardly negotiations.

Barnier told me in May 2017 that he had offered a tariff-free trade deal to the UK for two years after 29 March 2019, which at the time was assumed to be the date the UK would leave the EU so as to avoid taking part in the European Parliament elections of May 2019. No negotiations on a final settlement could begin until Britain had left the EU and become what is called 'a third country', rather like Japan or Canada. This simple and unchanging point was lost on the British journalists who reported Brexit for the BBC and newspapers. They fell over themselves having to report every day on what was happening on Brexit. But the truth was that very little was happening in Brussels or the capitals of the twenty-seven nations that stayed in the EU; Brexit negotiations took place inside Britain between British actors.

Few in British public life or the media could put themselves in the shoes of European leaders. The latter kept their views private but, in conversation with any of them, they could barely contain their bitter dismay at Britain's assault on the EU after a fifteen-year-long campaign of political-media hostility to EU membership. In parallel Tory politicians indulged in open crude insults against European heads of government or the men they named to run Brussels institutions. Late in 2018, Amber Rudd, a Tory pro-European MP, described the president of the European Commission, Jean-Claude Juncker, as 'ghastly' following Mrs May's postponement of the Commons vote on her deal with the EU which would have been voted down, as indeed it was, in January and March the following year. Ms Rudd's childish insult was a crude bit of pandering to Tory rank-and-file members who dislike Europe. It was unworthy of a serious politician, but for a Europe-bashing headline in the *Daily Telegraph* or *Daily Mail* there was little the average ambitious Tory MP would not say. This culture of denigrating Britain's partners in Europe had been stoked by politicians including Theresa May, with her endless denunciations of workers from Europe who had been offered jobs by British employers, notably state employers like the NHS.

Claus Grube is as about as friendly and pro-British an EU expert official as it is possible to find. He was Denmark's ambassador to Britain and his nation's top EU official. But he spells out why the whole of Europe is united in not giving the Brexiters what they claimed they could easily obtain:

> If Brexit is to make sense somewhere, it only does so if you can improve your competitiveness by deregulating and distorting competition for goods, services, capital and qualified labour with [non-EU] rules, state aid, lower labour costs and/or reduced regulatory costs. Otherwise, why leave the EU/EEA? And that is what the EU fears will happen over time and why there will be strict limits to the 'creativity and flexibility' when it comes to securing a 'level playing field' as this will only amount to a transfer of resources from the EU to the UK to cover as much of the cost of Brexit as the UK can get away with.

Speaking on Europe, President Macron of France described the trio of threats of 'nationalism, identitarianism, isolationist sovereignism' – precisely the motor forces behind Brexit. He added: 'I will not cede anything, anything to those who promote hate, division and national isolationism.' He was talking of the far-right or illiberal authoritarian rulers of Hungary and perhaps Poland. Boris Johnson and other Tories in London are now sovereignist nationalists warbling about 'Global Britain'. They always insist they would seek good relations with France post-Brexit. But for Macron and most of his fellow European leaders, the win for Brexit was a massive defeat for their idea of European partnership. The idea that the EU27 would seek to reward or accommodate London for Brexit was always far-fetched, even if many MPs, newspapers and the BBC constantly reported discussions with the EU in terms of 'negotiations' rather than a secession from and rupture with the rest of Europe.

On the contrary, it is vital for Macron and other EU leaders that Britain is not seen to benefit from Brexit. If Britain's repudiation of Europe and the Tory leadership's hard anti-EU interpretation of Brexit is seen to be a success, then other nations in Europe could also follow the same route, and national-ist politicians such as Marine Le Pen and Matteo Salvini could pray in aid a successful, happy, prosperous, harmonious Brexit Britain cut out of Europe as the model to follow. According to Professor Stefanie Walter of the University of Zurich, it has been European public opinion and not the wishes of political leaders that have been driving this hard line in the EU27 approach to Brexit. Together with other researchers, Professor Walter carried out an EU-wide online survey of 9,423 EU27 citizens conducted by Dalia Research in June 2018 and wrote:

> Almost every second person who responded said that the EU should take a hard or very hard line in the Brexit negotiations. In contrast, only about 12 percent wanted to accommodate Britain. People who responded also overwhelmingly support their national government's Brexit negotiation positions, most of which are very tough.

Negotiation implies or suggests an attempt to achieve a 50–50 or maybe 60–40 agreement between two business partners, or parties forming a coali-tion government, or trade unions and bosses deciding wage hikes, or perhaps a couple divorcing and haggling over alimony, ownership of property or access to children. Leaving the EU means repudiating laws which others live by. One cannot cherry-pick which laws one accepts and which laws one refuses to abide by in any known community.

But instead of spelling out those truths to the public and in a sense begin-ning a process of negotiating with all parliamentarians, and through them with economic and other actors in Britain, Theresa May and ministers such as Boris Johnson and Jeremy Hunt presented themselves as standing alone in an unending confrontation with Europe on behalf of the 17 million – out of a nation of 65 million – who gave their votes after a litany of lies about the EU. The rest of Europe saw Mrs May unable to offer leadership or win parliamentary backing for her demands. An internal paper prepared in April 2018 for the so-called T50 team of EU Brexit negotiators under Michel Barnier and Sabine Weyand – his formidably sharp German deputy, who studied at Cambridge University in 1986 and has two decades as a top negotiator at the European Commission, specialising in trade issues – noted that all the possible permutations for the withdrawal agreement and political declaration had one major problem: none of them could be assured of winning endorsement from the House of Commons because of Mrs May's weakness as a leader. The T50 team in Brussels were sharper in their analysis than the Westminster journalists writing in their papers or pontificating on TV. Mrs May was actually not very good at the core political art: building a majority for her policy.

Even her friend, the Danish centre-right prime minister, told her to her face at the joint news conference held after their meeting: 'We have to be realistic and realise there will be changes. Leaving the single market comes with a price tag. There will be more bureaucracy in future, unfortunately.' In fact, all the European states with coastlines opposite the UK are having to hire more customs officers and set up new customs control bureaucracy. The cost of Brexit falls on European taxpayers as much as on British ones.

Between July 2016 and November 2019, inch by painful inch Downing Street watered down the ultra-amputational 'Brexit means Brexit' hyperbole. To be sure, Mrs May's chief Brexit ministers and their supporters in Parliament continued to make foolish claims. Liam Fox said in July 2017: 'The free trade agreement that we will have with the European Union should be one of the easiest in human history.' This echoed the statement from Michael Gove in April 2016: 'The day after we vote to leave, we hold all the cards and we can choose the path we want'; or, as David Davis put it in October 2016: 'There will be no downside to Brexit, only a considerable upside.'

In fact, once talks started in June 2017 it was clear that Britain had no leverage. The EU announced that the issues that had first to be decided were the amount of money the UK owed the EU, the rights of EU citizens living and working in Britain, and the need to ensure that the Good Friday Agreement of 1998 that abolished the border between the Republic of Ireland and the UK province of Northern Ireland would be upheld. At Lancaster House in January 2017, Mrs May said: 'Because we will no longer be members of the single market, we will not be required to pay huge sums into the EU budget.' David Davis said in September 2017 that the EU had 'sort of made up' the figure of £40 billion which Britain was required to pay the EU as part of the 'divorce' settlement. At one meeting a junior British official made a twenty-three-slide PowerPoint presentation to prove that the UK did not owe the EU a penny.

Yet when I was in the French Finance Ministry in Paris in March 2017, I was told that on French calculations, the figure the UK owed to cover existing liabilities was up to €50 billion. It is hard to see on what basis Boris Johnson, the then foreign secretary, could tell MPs in the Commons that the EU27 could 'go whistle' if they asked Britain to honour its liabilities. In the end, Mrs May agreed with the EU estimate and Britain will pay up to €45 billion, with payments from London to Brussels continuing until 2064. This is just one more facet of Brexiternity. The idea that the 2016 plebiscite vote fully and finally settled the issue of Britain's relationship with the rest of Europe was always an illusion, as Britain will have to keep sending money to Brussels for decades to come. And if Britain wants to stay in EU agencies such as Europol, it will have to keep paying money and to accept the ultimate sovereign arbitration of the European Court of Justice if a dispute arises.

The European Court of Justice will have oversight on how EU citizens are treated in Britain. Ireland has exercised a de facto veto with its insistence that no hard border be reintroduced in order for customs controls to take place between the UK, including its six Northern Ireland counties, and the rest of the island of Ireland.

In January 2017, David Davis said: 'I believe we can get a free trade and customs agreement concluded before March 2019.' This soon gave way to Britain asking for a two-year transition period after April 2019. For some reason Mrs May kept calling it an 'implementation period', except there is unlikely to be anything very much to implement. Robin Niblett, the director of Chatham House, London's venerable foreign affairs think tank, argues that the UK will have a 'vassal' status in this period. The image of being a 'vassal' state, or of 'vassalage' in the metaphor used by Jo Johnson MP in his resignation statement as a minister, was used by both supporters and opponents of EU membership as they attacked the deal the prime minister brought back from Brussels. Dr Niblett is right, but that is a consequence of Brexiternity.

In September 2017, Mrs May called for a transition period of 'around two years'. In February 2018, the government was even more ambitious, as it described an open-ended transition period after April 2019. In a formal paper, the government asserted: 'The period's duration should be determined simply by how long it will take to prepare and implement the new processes and new systems that will underpin the future partnership.' This Whitehall-ese worthy of Sir Humphrey underlines the era of Brexiternity Britain has to embrace.

But Brussels was having none of this. Britain was offered a twenty-one-month transition period running out on 1 January 2021. Even that was subject to acceptance by EU27 governments and to ratification by MEPs in the European Parliament, where there is very little sympathy for the Brexit ideology that won out in Britain. So all the transition period does is to extend the uncertainty, especially for business. In the final political declaration, the EU offered an extension of the transition for a further undetermined period. This adds further to the Brexit uncertainty. Most trade deals take years to negotiate. The EU began negotiating a trade deal with Japan in 2013 but it was five years later that the president of the European Commission and the Japanese prime minister signed the JEFTA free trade deal.

In the second half of 2019, a new team of EU Commissioners with new presidents of the Commission and the EU Council representing the heads of government, plus new MEPs will have begun their five-year cycle of work. Negotiating Brexit will be important, but so will many other EU priorities. Michel Barnier assured me that his T50 team negotiating with Britain will stay in place into 2020 and longer if needed. In fact, the chief negotiator, the exper-ienced EU trade official, Sabine Weyand, has left the T50 team following her promotion to director general of EU trade policy. So we may find that at the end of twenty-one months in January 2021, nothing final has been achieved, and so Brexit negotiations go on and on. The alternative is that Britain walks away with 'no deal' permitting access on previous terms to EU markets.

Politicians in the EU27 are also fed up with the endless insults directed at Michel Barnier – by ministers in the British cabinet, the DUP leader Arlene

Foster, or senior Conservative figures such as Iain Duncan Smith and Michael Howard. Thus there is no appetite to help Britain in any way whatsoever, even from natural centre-right political allies in Europe. At a meeting with her fellow heads of EU government, Mrs May read out newspaper articles she had published in European papers her fellow prime ministers had already read.

Another Brexit claim that has evaporated was the one made by David Davis soon after entering Mrs May's cabinet in July 2016, when he declared: 'Within two years, before the negotiation with the EU is likely to be complete, and therefore anything material has changed, we can negotiate a free trade area massively larger than the EU . . . The new trade agreements will come into force at the point of exit, but they will be fully negotiated.' This was also nonsense. One or two countries hinted that they were open for a trade deal with the UK on the basis of dumping hormone or chemically treated food or, in the case of India, on the basis of allowing visa-free travel to Britain, but no new trade deal was actually completed. At best, some countries such as South Korea were willing to continue trading with the UK on the basis of existing EU trade agreements. It was not much of an achievement for the Department of International Trade, set up with great fanfare in 2016, that all they and their noisy anti-European minister, Liam Fox, could produce were mouse-dropping agreements to keep trade links open on the basis of EU negotiated arrangements. In any event, Britain accepted the EU's ruling that 'the UK may negotiate, sign and ratify international agreements entered into in its own capacity in the areas of exclusive competence of the Union provided those agreements do not enter into force or apply during the transition period, unless so authorised by the Union'.

A ROLE FOR THE EUROPEAN COURT OF JUSTICE

As Prime Minister May and David Davis insisted, there would be no role for the European Court of Justice once Britain left as a signatory to the EU Treaty. Mrs May declared in October 2016: 'The authority of EU law in this country has ended forever . . . We are not leaving only to return to the jurisdiction of the ECJ. That's not going to happen.'

However, in the agreement with the EU of December 2017, Mrs May rolled over – or, if you prefer, u-turned – and accepted that:

> During the transition period, the institutions, bodies, offices and agencies of the Union shall have the powers conferred upon them by Union law in relation to the United Kingdom and natural and legal persons residing or established in the United Kingdom. In particular, *the Court of Justice of the European Union shall have jurisdiction as provided by the Treaties.* (my italics)

So the ultra-strong language from Mrs May beginning in 2016, especially at the Conservative Party conference, softened after her strident Lancaster House speech in January 2017 to become more accommodating to the EU's endlessly repeated position that 'Leave means Leave' and the UK could not expect to pick and choose those parts of the EU it wanted to keep and spit on the rest. Even if Michel Barnier or any EU27 leader wanted to help Mrs May, it was not legally possible to allow a special status for Britain. By the spring of 2018 Mrs May had shown this lady prime minister *was* for turning, as she accepted the arguments that while Britain could do as it pleased, the EU was bound by its own laws and mutual obligations. The new prime minister has to decide to accept the climb-down on the ECJ Mrs May agreed to, or once again huff and puff and threaten a unilateral rupture with commercial partners in Europe. Looking at the three-year record of her handling of Brexit, it is hard to decide if this was a slow retreat by Mrs May or perhaps a more strategic policy of delaying and avoiding giving any final battle to the EU so that her hard-line Brexit cabinet colleagues stayed within the fold.

Britain's Fabian Society was named after the famous Roman general Fabius Maximus, who defeated Hannibal in the great campaigns by the Carthaginian warrior to conquer Rome in the third century before the common era. Fabius Maximus was called Cunctator, the Delayer, as his strategy was to avoid any full-on confrontation with Hannibal. He delayed and delayed, allowing Carthaginian troops to exhaust themselves and run out of enthusiasm and energy until finally they gave up and Rome was saved. The Fabian Society was so named to underline the virtues of gradualism and gaining final objectives without destructive battles that rarely guarantee success.

So was Mrs May a modern Fabiana Maxima Cunctator – sounding warlike but determined to avoid confrontation that can end disastrously in a complete lose–lose outcome? If so, her strategy did not work and Britain now has a new prime minister even more hostile to Europe than any of his predecessors.

5

THE ECONOMIC CONSEQUENCES OF BREXIT

Brexit is bad for British capitalism. The City is seeing a slow haemorrhage of financial jobs to Frankfurt, Dublin, Luxembourg and Amsterdam, with investment fund managers cutting by half their hiring in London since the Brexit vote in 2016, according to a report in the *Financial Times*. Paris is making every effort to win London business with special tax breaks and even a special commercial court that will conduct hearings in English, as France's President Macron insists he wants to make Paris a European and global finance hub.

Macron's efforts to rebrand France and Paris as a centre for global finance capitalism took a knock when protests against his tax cuts for the rich in France were challenged by the *Gilets jaunes* (Yellow Vests) movement, which at times turned violent in the time-honoured French manner of demonstrating against the government of the day. Yet Macron, as a former Rothschild banker, knows of what he speaks. The City's rise to pre-eminence on a par with Wall Street is entirely due to Europe. The Single European Act of 1986 provided that if a firm or bank is licensed to do business in one European country, it could do business in all EU member states. Nearly 350,000 so-called banking and financial service 'EU passports' have been issued to traders, dealers and salespersons in the City.

The British financial industry employs 7.3 per cent of the UK's working population, totalling more than 2.2 million people. UK financial services constitute the country's largest tax-paying sector, contributing 11.5 per cent of the total tax take.

Since Margaret Thatcher, in her pro-European days, pushed through the creation of the single market in Europe, every bank and finance house in the United States, Japan, Switzerland, China, Russia, India, all of Asia, Latin America and Africa came and opened up in London to get automatic, unfettered access to the European single market of 500 million middle-class consumers. The British speciality of trading and clearing euros is a $120 trillion–volume business that will now leave London, as EU finance ministers and European Central Bank governors have made it clear that legal supervision for trading in the world's second-biggest currency would have to take place within the EU.

Many British businesses, healthcare services, tourism, catering, and many niche skilled jobs depend on European citizens – described routinely by the media and politicians using the value-loaded word 'immigrants' – including half a million Irish citizens, the second-biggest category of EU workers in Britain after Poles. Collectively, immigrants from India, Pakistan, Bangladesh and Sri Lanka far outnumber all the EU citizens in Britain. They often face the same xenophobic political and media hate attacks from the Europhobe right that Europeans have encountered this century. If Britain starts to discriminate against European citizens by imposing immigration controls such as travel, work, or residence visas on Europeans, then it will be impossible for Britain to retain the advantages of open trade within the single market.

Both during the original campaign and ever since, much of the Brexit debate has turned on economics. Yet despite endless articles in business pages and many speeches, the economic discussion has failed to catch fire.

At the time of writing, Brexit has not yet happened. Major firms like Airbus, Nissan, Jaguar Land Rover and Unipart have all expressed concern that losing access to the single market, both in terms of exports and the loss of just-in-time delivery of components, will lead them to reconsider their investments in Britain. Their press releases obtain a headline in the business pages of serious papers, but few major manufacturing facilities have shut down. Some big City firms, such as Lloyds of London, have announced partial relocations to EU capitals, but jobs always move in and out of the City so the impact of their announcements was limited.

Moreover, while the macroeconomic data have been poor – low growth, rise in inflation, reduction in incomes, lower tax receipts obliging the government to borrow more – these overall figures may make headlines but they have not yet had an impact on people's lives. Britain has been transformed into an employment-rich but pay-poor country. Never have there been so many people in work, yet never have there been more beggars on the streets or food banks so central to the existence of millions. The Soviet Union claimed it abolished unemployment as millions lived in poverty. Britain has created many jobs, but millions are so badly paid they need to be topped up by taxpayer subsidies or, like 800,000 workers on zero hours contracts, are offered no guarantee of a living wage. Many have to take a second or even a third job to make ends meet.

The leading economist Professor Vicky Pryce has pointed out that the increased growth in the global economy, and especially the surge of growth in Europe, has cushioned the impact of Brexit. She writes:

The UK has been helped by a strong recovery in world trade and a pick-up in exports, particularly to the rest of the EU, which is enjoying the fastest growth in years. Nevertheless, Brexit uncertainty is being blamed for the UK growing at the slowest rate in the G7 group of large industrialised nations. Before the referendum, we were the fastest growing.

Exports are helped by the devaluation of the pound following Brexit. But the sugar rush for exports that always follows a devaluation brings its own hangover as imports become more expensive, especially in essential items like food and energy that poorer people cannot avoid buying. Moreover, by 2018 it was clear that the mini-manufacturing boom that followed the Brexit devaluation of the pound appeared to be over. Manufacturing, if it includes direct output, supply chains, linked servicing contracts and the spending power of directly and indirectly employed workers, amounts to 23 per cent of GDP, according to research by Oxford Economics for the Manufacturing Technologies Association. In November 2018, car production fell by 19.6 per cent, following a 10 per cent drop in the previous month. Despite the devalued Brexit pound, UK car exports have dropped, and business optimism in the sector is the lowest it has been for twenty-seven years as Brexit

uncertainty takes its toll – all this in the period well before the UK has formally left the EU.

The devaluation of the pound has led to higher prices, which leads to
reduced retail activity. Inflation, as measured by the consumer price index
used by the Office of National Statistics, stood an annual 0.3 per cent in June
2016. By spring 2018 it was 3 per cent – a tenfold increase – technically one
of the swiftest surges in inflation ever seen in recent UK history. Because it
started at such a low rate, the inflation rate of 3 per cent may not seem too
high, but if it feeds into higher interest rates, anyone with a mortgage, a car
loan or other repayment loans based on the inflation rate will learn how costly
Brexit is going to be. It should not be forgotten that the state, in the shape of
the Treasury and the Bank of England, moved quickly in the summer of 2016
to boost the economy by throwing out of the window the normal prudence of
fiscal and monetary policy associated with recent management of British
economic affairs. The Bank of England bought vast quantities of government
bonds through its quantitative easing programme, which is modern parlance
for printing money and pumping it to the economy. This was one of the
contributors to the higher inflation the UK has compared to other leading
economies, but at least helped to keep the economy turning over.

British service industry firms could still be located in EU member states,
as they are in many countries around the world, but they would no longer be
based in Britain, exporting from Britain, with the British-based staff – UK
and EU citizens alike – paying tax or spending wages on consumption within
the British economy.

As Sam Lowe of the Centre for European Reform explained in a December
2018 report:

> Once outside the single market, fewer services would be provided
> cross-border from the UK, and more would be provided via the estab-
> lishment of a commercial presence within the EU-27. This would inev-
> itably lead to some well-paid jobs migrating to the EU-27 from the UK
> and lower British tax receipts. Leaving the single market could lead to
> a drop in exports of financial services (minus insurance and pensions)
> to the EU of up to 59 per cent, and declines of up to 19 per cent in
> insurance and pensions services, and 10 per cent in business services
> (including law, accountancy and professional services).

It is not difficult to see why. Britain is, par excellence, a trading economy. We buy and sell with gusto. Napoleon was reported to have mocked England as 'a nation of shopkeepers', but commerce is the foundation of most national wealth – commerce and trade in physical and immaterial goods and services. From the earliest of times British well-being has been built on selling – within Britain but, to make serious money, to nearby Europe: wool in the Middle Ages; coal and textiles after the Industrial Revolution; big and small metal goods, from Birmingham screws to Sheffield cutlery, in the nineteenth century. Today it is Airbus wings and automobiles and a great deal of online buying and selling. It is personal services, from trainers taking out their clients to get fit in public parks to endless cafés, restaurants, bars and clubs. Britain has fought long and hard to lower barriers to trade, not increase them, as Brexit inevitably entails.

A total of 47 per cent of all UK exports are sold in the European single market compared to 9 per cent into the Commonwealth. The UK exports more than four times as much to Europe as to the US and twelve times as much to Europe as to China. Exports from Britain represent a little over a fifth of the UK's GDP, with services representing more than half. Business services like banking, management consultancy, insurance and retail – especially the new online retail sectors – earn as much for Britain's national income in export value as the top twelve industrial sectors. The UK exports nearly as much to County Cork in Ireland as it does to all of South America.

No free trade agreement covers services which need a painstaking one-by-one market access negotiation, unlike Europe where British services make most of their money. The World Trade Organization, for example, covers neither services nor aviation. Both economic sectors need bilateral agreements between governments or between the EU and third countries.

That's how the EU's single market works, and leaving it will kill the industry. It's easy for these firms to up sticks and move to another city in order to keep selling in the EU without hindrance after Brexit. The UK's Creative Industries Federation has warned that £36 billion of exports from the sector – 5.2 per cent of total UK exports – may be at threat. It is not just exports to Europe. A survey carried out by the federation revealed 80 per cent of industry leaders fear Britain 'will not maintain its global reputation post-Brexit'. It is difficult to see how it can. Since the single market came into operation in the early 1990s, there have been no customs checks or requirements to pay duty or any kind of tax on goods moved into or out of the UK. Perhaps equally importantly, firms have been able to move workers at a moment's notice to where they can best add value as technical experts or problem solvers. British professionals and other workers can work and live freely wherever their employers need them in Europe.

Components, particularly in the automotive, chemical, pharmaceutical and aerospace sectors, often cross national boundaries several times. Airbus, the four-nation European aircraft producer, reckons that a million components come into the UK each year. It has been estimated that each car manufacturer currently in the UK – all of them now owned in Asia, with no special loyalty or attachment to Britain – would need some 15,000 rules of origin certificates, at a minimum cost estimated at £15 each. Airbus sends 80,000 technical expert teams a year to solve problems in its different factories in Europe. If those who come and work on wing or satellite production in Britain have to fuss around with entry work permits or visas, the attractiveness of doing business in the UK will drop quickly.

There are around 150,000 British firms that trade with the EU, either as exporters or importers. The vast majority have no need to make customs declarations. That will change after Brexit, if the UK leaves the customs union. The number of customs declarations is estimated to be in the order of 250 million forms each year – a mountain of new paperwork, especially for smaller firms already burdened with form filling for VAT and other declarations required by government.

A minimum of 5,000 new customs bureaucrats will have to be hired at considerable cost to the taxpayer. Far from the UK saying goodbye to the Eurocrats, for trading firms the dreaded Eurocracy has saved them endless form filling, especially on rules of origin certificates that are essential in order to trade from one customs zone to another. Once again, managers will have to discover the pleasure of paperwork in order to conduct business with suppliers or clients across the Channel.

Jon Thompson, head of HM Revenue and Customs, puts the cost of filling in customs declarations at £14 billion per year, but the management consulting firm Oliver Wyman puts the cost even higher, at £27 billion. In their analysis this could lead to 65,000 small companies whose only export market is the EU just giving up as the paperwork becomes so onerous, costly and time-consuming.

Britain will also have to set up a new regime to deal with state aid in order to avoid accusations of protectionism which led other countries to challenge the UK at the World Trade Organization. A new bureaucracy called a Trade Remedies Authority will be set up and firms with complaints about products coming into Britain being produced at below cost and therefore being dumped into the UK market can appeal for tariffs or other measures to protect domestic production. All this is currently handed reasonable efficiently (if not to every complainant's satisfaction) by the trade experts of the EU in the Brussels Commission. In duplicating this area of EU expertise, the British taxpayer will have to hand yet more money to government bureaucrats with no guarantee – rather the reverse – that firms will export more and consumers will get the cheapest possible products and services.

Technology cannot offer a frictionless solution to border controls. The need for formal product standard approvals, hygiene checks, advance security declarations, VAT calculations and payment, and the inevitable delays at the border cannot be wished away.

SAYONARA TIME FOR 1,000 JAPANESE FIRMS IN UK

Over 1,000 Japanese companies in the UK employing some 140,000 people are in Britain because of free access to the wider EU market, not simply the smaller UK home market. The 2,000 German companies employing 370,000 people with €110 billion of direct investment are part of seamless pan-EU supply chains.

In the chemical sector, for example, 60 per cent of UK exports go to the EU, and 75 per cent of imports come from the EU. The Institute of Fiscal Studies reckons that two-thirds of UK exports to the EU are components, partly treated chemicals or other intermediate inputs into to wider supply chains, as are 55 per cent of imports here from the EU. Investment to build these supply chains will be at risk if UK-based firms can no longer access the single market on equal terms. Half of the £1 trillion stock of UK foreign direct investment comes from EU-based investors. Will they invest in the future in a country that has turned its back on Europe?

The competitive ethos of the single market has provided cheaper imports for businesses as well as consumers. This single market competition has forced

UK firms to improve their performance or go out of business. By restricting firms' access to the biggest unfettered market of 450 million middle-class consumers in the world and ending participation in EU-negotiated trade deals which cover another 12 per cent of UK exports, as well as telling firms there will be new barriers to accessing skilled, qualified, highly educated workers, the full amputational Brexit urged by hard-liners in the government can only damage the global competitiveness of the UK economy. After Brexit, Britain's reputation will change from being the most open major European country to being the most bureaucratic.

Can these disadvantages be remedied through new bilateral trade deals with the rest of the world? It is right to look seriously at the alternative markets that may open to the UK outside the EU, some fast-growing. There is little evidence, however, that leaving the EU customs union and single market will lead to greater UK trade with third countries. Germany exports to China more than four times as much as the UK does and achieves this from inside the EU customs union and single market. It is, for example, unclear why third countries such as China, India or the United States should agree to negotiate bilateral trade deals with the UK that favour Britain's comparative advantage in the service sector. They will instead seek acceptance by the UK of their own national regulatory, environmental and technical standards as part of even a limited trade deal.

Given the reciprocity which runs through trade negotiations, third countries will also be aware that any concessions made to the UK will be expected by other trading partners, and the degree of their interest in the UK market will be strongly influenced by how far UK-based firms continue to enjoy competitive access to the much larger European market. Will firms in Asia, the Americas or the Gulf want to invest in the UK if they know that setting up in Britain or trading via will no longer guarantee unfettered, frictionless access to 450 million consumers? In trade negotiations, size does matter. Even a 300 per cent increase in total services trade with China would not equal a fifth of the UK's current services exports to the EU single market.

The EU as a trade negotiator has the economic weight to deal with China and the US as trade equals. The UK does not. The European Commission has negotiated trade deals with over fifty countries, most recently with Canada, Korea and Japan, and continues to engage with the US. Some £55 billion of

UK exports – 12 per cent of UK trade – benefit from these third country agreements.

Of course, the UK could unilaterally remove all tariffs and quotas, which would reduce prices of agricultural produce, textiles and steel. This would undermine the viability of many UK producers, particularly in farming. In the unlikely event that the UK took this step, other countries would maintain their own restrictions in both goods and services markets. UK suppliers to Europe would therefore still face barriers.

The iron rule of trade is that proximity equals profit. Most companies start exporting to neighbouring markets with similar rules, which for the UK usually means European Union members, then look further afield. If exports to the Netherlands or France become more expensive and complex, the hope that sales to more distant and challenging markets will become easier is not realistic. Changing specific third country rules which hold back exports, for example intellectual property theft of branded goods, is something the EU with its massive trading footprint can do more effectively than the UK.

Trade requires a competitive economy. Competition thrives on openness and a large domestic market with shared rules, particularly in the service sector. Leaving the customs union and creating barriers within the single market that takes around half of our trade must by definition move the UK economy away from openness and thereby reduce the ability of UK firms to attract investment, compete and export globally. Measures to maintain open labour markets, focus on entrepreneurs and innovation, and support exporters can mitigate but not remove this competitive handicap. That is what the facts tell us.

In today's globalized economy, policy choices reducing competitiveness can have long-lasting effects on living standards, innovation and investment. The question is therefore how far the undoubted economic harm to UK jobs, growth, tax revenues and public services caused by moving away from full EU market access can be justified on wider grounds.

6

BREXIT AND BRITAIN'S ROLE IN THE WORLD

Barely discussed in the daily news and comment articles on Brexit or the books written by Westminster journalists on Britain leaving the EU is the threat Brexit poses to Britain's standing as a geopolitical player. It is a truism that modern media coverage, like the phone-ins on radio stations, has become less and less interested in what is happening in the rest of the world. Nowhere is this more apparent than in the failure to examine the unprecedented weakening of the UK as a global policy player and influencer. For centuries, Britain expended blood and treasure to ensure Europe was open for British commerce, that no dominant continental power, ideology or faith took over, and that liberal, democratic, rule-of-law values dear to Britain spread across the continent.

In recent decades, Britain has had a seat, a vote and a voice in all the big-ticket decisions on Europe's direction of travel. British diplomats, other officials, stellar leaders like Margaret Thatcher and Tony Blair magnified their influence by cajoling, persuading, nudging the rest of Europe in a desired direction for Britain. This meant building alliances and accepting some push-backs, but Britain has had more power and influence in Europe in the last few decades than at any previous time in history. In every world capital, at the WTO and other international bodies, British diplomats would meet with fellow EU colleagues and try to push an agenda close to desired British interests.

All this comes to a dead shuddering stop upon Brexit, irrespective of whether it is hard or soft. The United Kingdom reverts to bilateral diplomacy. Britain overnight becomes an international policy player that has to cool its heels in the waiting rooms of EU deciders from the Council of Ministers to the European Commission.

In 1964 Britain made a historic geopolitical decision to withdraw all its military presence east of Suez. The once-great global British power handed over to the United States the leadership role in the Middle East and Asia-Pacific region which Britain had built up since the eighteenth century. Today, it is China, a communist dictatorship, that is the first power in Asia-Pacific, with its neighbours such as India and Australia, both Commonwealth members, as well as Japan, Korea, Vietnam, Taiwan and the Philippines worried at the rejection of multilateralism and embrace of isolationist protectionist measures by President Trump.

In his biography of his ancestor, John Churchill, the Duke of Marlborough, Winston Churchill described the 'feeble, divided condition of Europe' in the late seventeenth century from which 'the small island [Britain], beginning to gather to itself the empires of India and America, stripping France and Holland of their colonial possessions would emerge victorious, mistress of the Mediterranean, the Narrow Seas, and the oceans'. This grandiose last hurrah for English might and imperialism was published in 1933 and already by then Winston Churchill was musing on a united Europe as the best guarantor of peace and security for the British people.

It is true that since the process of European unity began in the 1950s, no external power or menace has threatened Britain. In June 2108, Justin Welby, the Archbishop of Canterbury, said that the European Union 'has brought peace, prosperity, compassion for the poor and weak, purpose for the aspirational and hope for all its people'. Archbishop Welby was repeating a truth that leaders in France and Germany, among other European nations, have dared utter, but rarely – if ever – a British political leader since the days of Churchill. Britain has had more than its peace secured by the European Union, along with multilateral treaty organizations such as NATO, the European Court of Human Rights and the Council of Europe, and other international treaty arrangements to limit nuclear arms developments or set up international courts to deal with war criminals.

The constant presence of a British prime minister and foreign secretary, helped by talented diplomatists, in all the foreign and security council meetings of Europe have added immeasurably to Britain's geopolitical weight and reach.

After the notorious assertion in 1962 by the former US secretary of state, Dean Acheson that 'Britain had lost an empire and not yet found a role', it was possible, as the twenty-first century began unfolding, to see a new role for Britain as the most effective of the bigger EU member states in pushing forward on foreign policy and multiplying British weight and influence in so doing. Acheson, one of the several great secretaries of state that America produced in the twentieth century, was clear that Britain's future lay as one of the leading powers in a European partnership: '[Britain's] attempt to play a separate power role, that is a role apart from Europe, a role based primarily on a "special relationship" with the United States, a role based on being head of the Commonwealth [is] played out.' There have been nine British prime ministers in Downing Street since Acheson told his blunt truth in 1962. None of them has spoken as clearly and honestly as the American statesman.

AFTER BREXIT, BRITAIN CEASES TO BE A EUROPEAN POWER

Brexit is throwing Britain's global role into the wind. Speaking at an Asian security summit conference in June 2018, Singapore's defence minister, Ng Eng Hen refused to describe Britain as 'a European power. I don't know what you are now', a puzzled Mr Ng told British participants as the nations of Asia – many, like Singapore, staunch Commonwealth members – tried to work out what Brexit Britain was going to turn into.

Unknown to the outside world, early every morning in Geneva a group of ambassadors from some of the richest and most powerful countries meet behind closed doors. The session is called 'Coordination' and consists of the UK and France, both permanent members of the UN Security Council, Germany with its economic clout, Spain with its Latin American network, and the other European Union ambassadors to the UN and related agencies in Geneva such as the World Trade Organization, the World Health Organization, the International Labour Organization and the UNHCR, the

UN refugee agency. The ambassadors draw up a common position in the name of the EU on issues that are on the daily agenda and where the EU has to relate to the United States, China, Russia, India, Japan and other major players or regional blocs.

British embassies in the 193 UN member states are now quite thinly staffed and working with EU member state embassies, as well as EU missions, gives UK diplomats an extra edge. At the end of 2017, the Foreign and Commonwealth Office (FCO) announced that it was reducing Britain's overseas diplomatic presence in order to increase staff at smaller UK embassies in Europe before Brexit. Even the British mission in Bern is getting two more staff, as the Swiss are increasingly interlinked with the EU, having reversed their 2014 referendum banning freedom of movement. The Bern–Brussels relationship is full of scratchy irritations, but few in Switzerland think the kind of rupture with Europe promoted by Brexit ideologues in England makes much sense.

There is no evidence that putting more UK diplomats into Britain's embassies in Europe has made any difference to the approach of national governments in the EU27 or European Economic Area (EEA) capitals to Brexit. But if Brexit is consummated, London will require a massive permanent presence in Brussels and increased diplomatic presence in EU capitals to handle all the bilateral negotiations which up to now have been done by ministers and officials based in London who have the right to attend, speak and vote in all the EU meetings that decide policy. Unless the Treasury finds a major increase in the FCO budget, this means that in order to staff the UK presence in Brussels as well as in bilateral embassies, diplomats will have to be withdrawn from embassies elsewhere in the world. Brexit will almost certainly mean British candidates will be less likely to get top international jobs, as they will no longer have the support of the EU for such positions.

In Paris, the British embassy was reduced to sending out diplomats to attend public meetings at which speakers from Britain discussed Brexit. If there was any criticism of Brexit, up would stand the hapless British diplomat to read out an official message in support of Britain cutting links with the EU. I witnessed talented ambassadors at public meetings in Europe having to parrot Whitehall lines about Global Britain and how Brexit would 'turn out OK'. Since to a man and woman they all thought Brexit was foolish, they had to force through clenched lips words they did not believe in for a moment. It was cringe-making to witness, such was the sad status to which British diplomacy was reduced.

EU embassies in Asia, the Americas and Africa are now often better staffed than their British equivalent. In Tokyo, the EU mission had more fluent Japanese speakers than the British embassy. If Foreign Office officials are part of a bigger team, this all adds value to British reporting back to London. Post-Brexit, that relationship between Foreign Office mission and the European External Action Service, the EU's foreign policy arm, stops.

NATO NEVER CREATED A MARKET FOR BRITISH GOODS

For the past half-century British foreign policy has been boosted thanks to the relative integration of the UK in the European Union. NATO has played its part, but NATO never opened a frontier, created a market for British goods, or allowed Britain to shape broader European foreign policy.

Even a so-called 'soft Brexit' means that the prime minister and foreign secretary will no longer participate in EU Councils, while British officials in Brussels will no longer help shape foreign policy. It will be a major loss of influence. It is in these gatherings that policies on sanctions against Russia after the annexation of Crimea, or imposing a travel ban on Robert Mugabe and his henchmen, or refusing to allow Croatia to enter the EU until it delivered war criminals to The Hague, or other foreign policy lines and positions are adopted.

When a military-grade Russian nerve agent, Novichok, was used to poison a former Russian military intelligence officer, Sergei Skripal, who had defected to Britain and now lived in Salisbury, along with his daughter Yulia, who at the time was visiting him from Moscow, Britain's network of EU foreign policy partners was mobilized. They agreed with London to fashion a common programme of sanctions and expulsions against the Kremlin. This was done, speaking as twenty-eight member states of the EU, to send a message that Russian agents could not travel to Britain to seek revenge by poisoning a man they considered a traitor.

Britain's foreign secretary attends, as of right, the monthly meeting of all EU foreign ministers and can convene a special meeting if necessary. Cathy Ashton, a British politician and EU Commissioner, was named as the first

EU high representative – in effect the EU foreign minister when the post was set up in 2009.

As Peter (Lord) Ricketts, a former national security adviser, ambassador in Paris and Britain's most senior diplomat as permanent under secretary at the Foreign Office, has pointed out:

> Once Britain is outside the European Union, we will no longer be at the table to leverage European support for our foreign policy priorities, as we have done many times in the past, most recently over sanctions on Russia following the annexation of Crimea. The EU itself has major choices to make, between continuing integration or accepting greater diversity, and between a focus on its region or taking on a wider foreign policy role. We will play no part in those choices, but will be affected by them.

Andrés Ortega, the Spanish and very Anglophile foreign affairs comment-ator in Madrid, has said 'Global Britain', which is meant to rise phoenix-like from Brexit, is a 'mirage'. British universities that have European studies departments will lose out. London can hardly keep its place as Europe's centre for influential policy debates on international affairs once British ministers and officials have the same role and weight in deciding European foreign policy as Mexican or Canadian diplomats have in shaping US foreign policy decisions.

This sad farewell to the Foreign Office as one of the architects and script writers of European foreign policy has gone broadly unnoticed. It reflects the inward-looking, nation-firstism of MPs and journalists that helped produce the Brexit decision. For British diplomacy, it is the end of an era.

Britain overnight will become an international policy player that has to cool its heels in the waiting rooms of EU decision-making bodies, from the Council to the Commission to the European External Action Service. There will be no point anyone in Washington, Beijing, Delhi, Lagos or Brasilia asking the British ambassador or visiting minister what Europe is going to do or say on key global issues, as the answer can only be 'Search me!'

Yes, this enfeebled post-EU Britain will have its seat as a permanent member of the UN Security Council. London can join the queue from Berlin, Paris and Warsaw in seeking an audience with the US President. The Commonwealth will be always with us. Britain will remain in NATO, the

Organization for Security and Co-operation in Europe and the Council of Europe – all worthwhile organizations, but none with anything like the importance of the nations of Europe working in concert on a permanent institutionalized basis as EU members.

But in the playing field upon which it has sought to be present, exercise influence, shape the rules and ensure core interests are defended, Britain will henceforth be left on the touchline. From Islamist terror, to environmental politics, to protecting the region's borders, deciding policy on Russia, Iran, Turkey, China – to name but four key nations whose behaviour impacts on our security – Britain will be disconnected from all the main EU players. Of course, there will be polite welcomes for the prime minister and foreign secretary, but the UK's 'third country' status means London's envoys have the same status as those from, say, Mexico or South Korea. Britain has asked for continued collaboration and information exchange with the rest of Europe in the common struggle against global crime and terrorism. But the European Arrest Warrant, full access to Europol and instant data exchange are all based on EU Treaty obligations, accepting the ultimate authority of the European Court of Justice, which the advocates of Brexit reject.

London will cease to be the foreign policy discussion centre of the world outside of Washington. The London foreign policy outfits such as Chatham House, the International Institute for Strategic Studies, the Royal United Service Institute, or newcomers like the Centre for European Reform and the European Council on Foreign Relations have high reputations. They will become less relevant and attract less global funding as the UK amputates itself from working as the most important EU foreign policy player because its foreign ministers and officials are no longer locked into the core European policy-making decisions. University departments teaching and researching Europe foreign policy will lose EU funding.

Already, the European Council on Foreign Relations, under its dynamic director, Mark Leonard, has relocated about half its work and staff to Berlin. The Centre for European Reform has excellent contacts with British officials and ministers who, until Brexit, played an important role in determining European foreign policy. But now London will be an outpost and the views of British ministers, MPs and senior government officials on Europe will be on a par with their colleagues in Turkey as Britain opts out of geopolitics as a major EU player.

As an FCO minister I met regularly with EU opposite numbers and was able to report to Tony Blair on the politics of what was happening in Europe, as political reporting is not always what bilateral embassies are good at. Fifteen or twenty-five years ago, it was fair to say that the EU was not Europe, but today, in practical terms, the EU, the EEA (the EU member states plus Norway, Iceland and Lichtenstein) and Europe are coterminous. Outside the EU, Britain is outside Europe. We will be looking in as EU member states get on with deciding everything from European policing and justice to which troubled regions of Africa or Arab countries an EU armed intervention may be needed and justified.

Brexit is the biggest status- or influence-reducing move ever seen in Britain's history of international relations. It is astonishing that the UK foreign policy establishment has not expressed more concern. The exclusive focus on trade and immigration has sidelined the coming loss of British influence without precedent in British history. The former foreign secretary, (Lord) William Hague and ex-NATO secretary-general, (Lord) George Robertson have called for the UK to have observer status at EU foreign policy meetings. But why not Turkey, Norway, Switzerland or indeed the United States? This is precisely the cherry-picking approach the EU27 reject. If Britain does leave the EU as a treaty organization, it will have no say and little influence over the future geopolitical direction of travel of its region of the world.

This will be particularly true at the United Nations, where Britain's departure from Europe leaves France as the only EU permanent member of the Security Council – this at a time when the Trump administration is rejecting British and EU international policy objectives on global warming, the Middle East and human rights. China and Russia seek to use the UN to lessen a focus on human rights and social justice or to stop any final settlement in the West Balkans by allowing Kosovo to take its place as a UN member state.

There is always a temptation, sometimes a tendency, for the UK to pootle along behind the United States as part of the myth of the so-called special relationship between London and Washington. If anything, Britain has been useful to Washington, as the English-speaking big power in the EU can act if not as a bridge, at least a friend in explaining US policy priorities to more suspicious foreign policy establishments across the Channel. Now Britain will be a stand-alone member of the UN structures not just on the Security

Council but in other key UN agencies such as the WTO, the World Health Organization, the UN refugee agency, the International Labour Organization and other UN agencies covering property rights, meteorology, or trade and development.

Britain will no longer be a key partner and policy decider in Team Europe at the UN, but will have to find its own resources to cover all these fields of international policy and, in some cases, law and conventions. As the European Council on Foreign Relations pointed out in a report published in May 2018:

> Brexit comes at a bad time for Europe at the United Nations, as the United States, Russia and China are challenging the liberal internationalism that the EU promotes. The United Kingdom has been an anchor of EU policy at the UN providing expertise and diplomatic leadership. Brexit has the potential to upset Franco-British cooperation as the Security Council, and broader European coordination on development and human rights across the UN system.

In the Government White Paper on Brexit (July 2018), London proposed:

a tailored partnership with the EU covering:

a. consultation and regular dialogue on geographic and thematic issues and the global challenges the UK and the EU face;

b. mechanisms to discuss and coordinate the implementation of existing and new sanctions;

c. arrangements to enable cooperation on crisis management operations, including using civilian and military assets and capabilities to promote global peace and stability, where it is mutually beneficial;

d. commitments to support a collaborative and inclusive approach to European capability development and planning;

e. commitments to continue to work together to address global development challenges, supporting a cooperative accord between the UK and the EU on development and external programming;

f. continued cooperation on EU strategic space projects, including their secure aspects; and

g. a Security of Information Agreement that facilitates the sharing of information and intelligence.

This is a laudable wish list – but still only a wish list. Once Britain loses its right to speak and vote in EU meetings that decide policy in the areas London thinks important, UK influence will fade. The Political Declaration section of Mrs May's withdrawal deal had several paragraphs on continuing cooperation between the UK and the EU on foreign and security policy issues, but scattered throughout the text were qualifying phrases like 'where appropriate' or 'where relevant'. In plain English, the EU will invite in UK ministers when its suits Brussels.

London loses all right to initiate or lead on common foreign and security policy as British minsters have done since the time of Margaret Thatcher. A British prime minister meets major country leaders in fora like the G7, G20 and the September meeting of the UN General Assembly. Britain was happy to support the European Defence Initiative launched by France's President Macron in 2018, which was a coalition of EU member states willing to cooperate on military interventions. It was parallel to both NATO and the EU, though neither organization opposed the French initiative. London eagerly signed up for it and there is no reason to suppose that a post-Brexit Britain will not have plenty of bilateral foreign, security and defence policy areas where it can collaborate with the EU as useful partners.

It should not be forgotten that foreign and defence policy has been carefully safeguarded as a national prerogative within all EU treaties. No country is yet willing to accept that its soldiers should be sent to fight and possibly be killed on missions or interventions decided by a majority vote in Brussels. As the EU foreign policy expert, Professor Richard Youngs has written: 'To some extent, flexibility and diversity have been allowed space in the [EU] foreign policy realm, which lies outside the more rigid institutional procedures of many domestic policy spheres. However, European governments and EU institutions have made only limited steps towards a qualitatively different way of doing foreign policy.'

Youngs is correct, but Britain has been one of the drivers, and occasionally the necessary brake, on the forward march of a common European defence and foreign policy. UK ministers and officials have been able to do this by always being present at the creation of any EU foreign or defence policy initiative. The French have a saying *Les absents ont toujours tort* – it is always a mistake not to be in the room.

British ministers and officials will no longer sit of right with a voice, vote and veto in every room where EU geopolitical decisions are made. The giants of British foreign policy – the two Pitts, Canning, Palmerston, Grey, Curzon, Churchill – would have given anything to exercise the influence that Britain has enjoyed in the last few decades thanks to being present in every council chamber where Europe's supranational affairs were discussed and decided. Now our ministers and diplomats will sit outside with the Brazilians, Turks, Nigerians, Indians or Japanese. By any definition, Brexit is a turning point in Britain's role and influence in the world.

The loss of foreign policy influence played no part in the debates leading up to the Brexit vote and the political-media elites in London have paid no attention to this reduction in Britain's geopolitical heft upon quitting the EU treaties. But future historians may decide Brexit was the moment when Britain quietly closed down as a global policy maker and went into decline as a country of influence over the decisions the world will have to take this century.

7

EUROPEANS IN BRITAIN, BRITS IN EUROPE

We Brits are, to put it mildly, in a muddle and very confused about immigration. I have lost count of the doors I have knocked on looking for support in elections for myself or for Labour friends when voters denounced 'immigration' as their most burn-up issue. The concern was expressed about Pakistanis and Afro-Caribbeans in the 1970s and Poles and Lithuanians forty years later. I am sure canvassers from other parties would report the same phenomenon.

As a student I worked in university holidays in the kitchen of the canteen at Ealing Police Station in West London. One Sunday a constable came in, slapped his truncheon on the counter, looked at the menu and announced he would like 'grilled herrings'. The chef was a Nigerian medical student from University College Hospital. He seemed to know how to fry, grill, or boil all the dishes on offer for the police officers as they enjoyed their break, gossiped with fellow cops, and filled up on the very cheap subsidized food. I shouted back into the kitchen 'herrings!' and turned to pouring a cup of tea and buttering some bread for the constable. In no time a plate with two well-grilled herrings appeared, and I called the policeman to the counter to get them.

He took a look at the fish. 'You've got a wog in there, haven't you?' he said, not exactly in an ugly manner — more the open, casual racism prevalent in the 1960s.

'Well, eh,' I stammered, 'as it happens we do have a very distinguished Nigerian, soon to qualify as a doctor and at the same time a fine cook who has consented to be our police canteen chef this Sunday.'

'Yeah, I knew it was a wog because an English chef would cut off the heads of the herring whereas the wogs always leave the fish head on,' said the police officer.

Now, for today's younger readers, the term 'wog' (thought to come from either English imperial racism and meaning 'Wily Oriental Gentleman' or perhaps from the stencil 'Working On Government Service' on the shirts of Indian, African or Arab labourers in the nineteenth-century British empire) is a foul, ugly epithet – a bit like 'nigger' in the United States of old.

I would like to be sure that such casual remarks have disappeared, but when I was a Labour MP in South Yorkshire from 1994 to 2012, I would hear derogatory remarks on the doorstep or casually from voters about 'Pakis'.

From about 2000 onwards, the term 'immigrant' was the description of any European citizen who came to Britain to work. It wasn't applied to French or Italian bankers in the City, or usually to the dedicated doctors and nurses recruited by the NHS in Poland or Portugal to do the jobs the medical professions and health ministers refuse to train British citizens to do. I worked for fifteen years in Geneva and was never once called an 'immigrant'. But the word, with all its negative connotations, began to be applied by the right-wing, anti-foreigner press and especially by Conservative MPs from the 1990s onwards to all the Italians, Spaniards, Poles and others who came to work in Britain.

Many of these European 'immigrants' were out of sight – working at dawn in cold fields pulling out vegetables so that British rather than imported fruit and vegetables could be on sale in German-owned low-cost supermarkets. Others were outside towns in big warehouses or hangar-type buildings making the sandwiches which became the staple lunch for so many. Or perhaps putting books into packages along with all the other products we buy online and then have conveniently delivered, usually by a non-British-born worker, to our front door.

A fishmonger friend in London with shops and a stall selling quality fish tells me he can't find Londoners willing to do the work of filleting, cutting up, preparing and selling the fish. 'I pay £500 a week, maybe up to £30,000 a year, but I have to hire from among EU workers.'

Another friend who ran a successful building business in Rotherham told me he tried so hard to get local young men to work. 'They come in at 8 a.m. on Monday and at 8 a.m. on Tuesday and then moan: "Is it 8 tomorrow, gaffer?" I offer weekend work at good overtime rates, but the English don't want to do it. The Poles and other Europeans, they work hard. A lot of them have technical qualifications from the way they are trained in school in Poland which we have given up. I would have had to move the firm offshore without these lads.'

Yet to read the *Daily Mail, Daily Telegraph* or *Sun*, consult anti-European organizations like Immigrant Watch or listen to UKIP, BNP and many mainstream politicians, to be found in the ranks of Labour MPs as well as among Tories, all these Europeans who pay taxes, in the case of Catholic east Europeans fill up half-empty Catholic churches, rent flats or houses from British property owners, spend their money in British supermarkets, pubs and shops constitute an unwelcome alien presence.

According to the Office for National Statistics, non-British citizens who have arrived from the rest of the world into the UK far outnumber all the Europeans who came to work after the two EU enlargements of 2004 and 2007. In the food manufacturing sector, 11 per cent of jobs were done by EU workers from the countries that joined in the twenty-first century and 26 per cent by citizens who entered the UK from elsewhere in the world. In the clothing sector, just 3.3 per cent of workers come from east Europe but 25 per cent from the rest of the world. In the residential care sector, 17.3 per cent of employees come from the rest of the world compared to just 2 per cent from the ten new EU member states.

Since 1945, Britain has had to import workers to do the jobs the sturdy white Englishman didn't want to do. After the Second World War, 200,000 Polish ex-soldiers were sent down coal mines. Windrush generation Afro-Caribbeans and immigrants from the former Indian empire shaping today's three-million-strong British Muslim community did vital public service work or worked in textile mills and foundries. More than a million Irish citizens came to rebuild Britain and work in all sectors of the economy in the years after the Second World War until Ireland joined the European Community and started to prosper as an independent European nation.

There were the Cypriots who transformed the restaurant offer in London and other cities. All these immigrants were rejected to begin with. Window posters saying 'No Coloured. No Irish. Dogs Welcome' could be seen on boarding houses in the 1950s. Britain's homegrown 1930s fascist leader, Sir Oswald Mosley stood for Parliament in the 1960s and claimed immigrants were coming into Britain to take jobs, housing or advantage of the welfare state and the National Health Service – all the arguments used this century against European workers. A Conservative MP was elected in 1964 in the West Midlands having campaigned on the slogan 'If you want a nigger neighbour, Vote Labour'.

ANTI-IMMIGRANT HATE AT THE HEART OF BREXIT

In the years leading up to the Brexit campaign the anti-immigrant story flared into life. The vocabulary of Enoch Powell's xenophobic populism was used to denounce incomers from Europe, culminating in the notorious Leave poster showing Britain invaded by a snaking queue. As the Tory commentator Matthew d'Ancona noted:

> Powellism found its purest expression in the 2016 EU referendum result, which enshrined the convergence of two of his great fixations: hostility to immigration and opposition to Britain's membership of the EU. Since the referendum, we have heard Tory ministers suggesting that companies should keep lists of foreign workers, that doctors born overseas were elbowing aside British teenagers who might otherwise read medicine, that foreign students should not aspire to settle here.

In March 2018, 12-year-old girls with French parents were on a bus in London when they were abused by older boys because they were overheard speaking French. They were told to speak English. One of them was punched and pushed. It was a small scene and their mother did not want to make a major fuss. But it conforms to endless reports of unpleasantness directed at European Union citizens – usually identified upon speaking their language.

A month later, a 49-year-old German woman, an expert in German military history, was gardening in front of her house in Wilmslow, the affluent Cheshire town. John Smart, a 72-year-old retired Manchester University lecturer, was walking past her and she said: 'Good morning.' He turned and sneered: 'You're that German, why are you still here? Go back!' Two months later, she was again in front of her house when Smart asked her: 'You still here?' She burst into tears at this Brexit-induced hate and collapsed in bed. In

March 2019, a young European mother of two got out of her car in Doncaster, to be attacked by young teenagers. They beat her to the ground, kicked her in the face, saying: 'You Polish cunt, you deserve a lesson' and that she should 'fuck off to her own country'. The Swedish Europe Minister Ann Linde said in January 2017 that she was shocked by the xenophobia experienced by Swedes in the UK since the referendum. There are 100,000 Swedes living and working in the UK. None had experienced hostility before. Who, after all, dislikes Sweden or a Swede?

At an Oxfordshire fishery open to anglers, a notice went up stating 'NO POLISH OR EASTERN BLOC FISHERMEN ALLOWED'. The freshly painted board telling European citizens keen on fishing that they could not sit alongside Brits to cast their lines was published in a newspaper in 2018. It caused little stir. One wonders how our media would react if British children at a school somewhere in Europe were abused and punched when overheard on public transport speaking English or notices were put up saying 'NO BRITISH ANGLERS ALLOWED' at a popular trout fishing pond used by anglers in France or the Netherlands?

There is still no clear outline of what will be the future status of the up to two million Brits who live permanently or for a good part of the year in other areas of Europe. The British government has been obliged by the EU not to start removing existing EU citizens in Britain, though there are many ugly anecdotes about European wives of British citizens, often with children born in Britain and a record of work in the public sector, being denied residency. London has been forced to concede that the European Court of Justice will have a role in safeguarding the EU citizenship rights of Europeans in Britain in the first years after April 2019.

But even assuming that to begin with there will be no major change, the pro-Brexit MPs, including many in Labour, seem to welcome with relish the idea that new immigration controls will be introduced. Different ideas are put forward, but they are all based on ending the right of European Union citizenship and with it the automatic right to live and work in other European Union countries, providing the incomer has a job to cover social security and healthcare insurance.

Different schemes are proposed by different actors in the Brexit debate. They are all based on bureaucratic control: the granting of a limited number of work or residence permits, the creation of a *Gastarbeiter,* seasonal status, special passports to work in the City, quotas in different economic sectors, a minimum salary of £30,000 which is far above what many workers in healthcare, agricultural work and the hospitality sector are paid, or fixed-term jobs for Europeans in Britain. Such discrimination against fellow Europeans will inevitably lead to reciprocal discrimination against British citizens already living or hoping to live, work or retire on the continent.

The centre-right think tank Resolution Foundation recommended that the government should publish 'a green paper setting out its vision for what the new immigration system aims to achieve by the end of 2017'. The Resolution Foundation said the UK should allow 'migration by EU/EEA nationals with a job offer in a shortage occupation'. It added that 'new temporary worker schemes will have to be created' and that the taxpayer should find £1 billion to pay for Home Office enforcement of such schemes.

Not since the wartime economy has there been such enthusiasm for manpower planning complete with a major bureaucracy to issue permits, enforce them and deport anyone who works longer than his or her original permission.

If any of the Resolution Foundations schemes are adopted – and the think tank is chaired by the former Conservative minister, Lord David Willetts, who presumably understands the mentality of his former colleagues – they will be reciprocated across the Channel. The days when a young Brit could try his or her luck bumming around Europe picking up work as and when will be over.

Global Future, a London think tank, estimated employers, big and small, would have to find an extra £1 billion to pay for visas and work permits for non-UK employees, mainly from Europe. The London Chamber of Commerce and Industry pointed out that 25 per cent of their members' workforce did not hold a British passport. Global Future estimated the private sector would pay £805 million and the public sector £337 million to the monolithic, cumbersome immigration bureaucracy both the Tory government and the Labour opposition believed necessary to make it more difficult for EU citizens to work in Britain. Far from leaving the EU lessening economic burdens, the costs of immigration bureaucracy falling upon private firms and the taxpayer would be part of a new Brexit tax all would have to pay.

It is unlikely the EU27 prime ministers will accept discrimination against their voters. Speaking for the European Parliament, Guy Verhofstadt told the

BBC's Andrew Marr that if the UK threatens to treat EU citizens as second-class residents in Brexit Britain, MEPs will not support a deal and Britain will crash out of existing trade links with Europe.

ANTI-FOREIGNER SENTIMENTS IN TORY PARTY

The latest census in Hungary showed a little over 5,000 Muslims living in the country – 0.057 per cent of the population. Yet the nationalist Hungarian leader, Viktor Orban, campaigned for election on the basis that he alone would keep Hungary free of Muslim immigrants. He later put up giant posters with pictures of George Soros, the Jewish philanthropist linked with Jean-Claude Juncker, which are reminiscent of antisemitic propaganda of the 1930s. As Oxford University's Professor Timothy Garton Ash notes, Orban has 'effectively forced out the Open Society Foundation of George Soros – the Jewish philanthropist against whom Orban's regime stirs up hatred, with propaganda imagery recalling the worst periods of European history'.

If Viktor Orban's objection is to Muslim immigrants and even the presence of American Jews in Hungary, the ire and fire of Boris Johnson, Nigel Farage and Theresa May was turned on European immigrants. As many commentators have noted, they rarely used the same language about non-EU immigration into the UK. This made little sense in the rest of Europe, where people movement across European frontiers has been the norm except in times of war and barbed wire dictatorships. Young Greeks came to England as the corrupt Greek governments up to 2000–15 were unable to offer jobs, but Greece accepted hundreds of thousands of Albanians, who do the low-paid fruit and vegetable picking, old-age caring or construction work east Europeans do in England.

Many Polish families have a Ukrainian nanny or cleaner, just as many British families have Poles who do such work. The nationalist-Catholic government in Warsaw opposes allowing any refugees from the conflict zones and destroyed states of the Middle East and North Africa, but has an open door policy to Ukrainian immigration, as Poland's booming construction industry cannot find enough Polish nationals to do the necessary jobs. Nearly two million Ukrainians are now working in Poland doing jobs native Poles won't do. More than a quarter of the construction workers in London are EU citizens and the UK's building firms keep putting out press releases saying they cannot survive without European workers for both unskilled and craft jobs. The bosses of these firms have been moaning since the referendum, but have refused to mobilize to put effective pressure on MPs and ministers over Brexit.

As government ministers were mulling the exact machinery of future restrictions on EU citizens living and working in the UK, British expats living in France turned up to meet the UK ambassador in Paris, Ed (Lord) Lewellyn, to ask about their future rights in France after Brexit. Lord Lewellyn, the former chief of staff to David Cameron, a Francophile pro-European and a former aide to Chris Patten, the spokesman of earlier Tory Europhiles, was unable to give any concrete replies that reassured the British expats they would be looked after by their own government and not fall victim to Brexit. The *Guardian* reporter, Lisa O'Carroll, described how one British passport holder, married to a New Zealander,

> expressed fury that the rights of his family, including children born in New Zealand but now living in France, had been thrown up in the air. 'You say May is looking after our interests,' he told the ambassador. 'If she is stripping us of our rights, that is demonstrably false. She is happy to flush my rights down the toilet as long as it saves the Tory party.'

In La Rochelle on France's Atlantic coastline in March 2019, I met a British couple, teachers from Oxford, who had taken early retirement and moved to France in 1998. Now they were older. The man had suffered from cancer. They were looking into the future and were concerned about their last years. Brexit means they would no longer have the same status as French citizens.

There were other questions put by British citizens to the hapless ambassador in France, who was simply unable to answer them. Taking away the right of EU citizenship from British expats living in twenty-seven other EU member states will alter their status and lay them at the mercy of different national immigration policies, just as Windrush British citizens and EU citizens in the UK have no clarity on their own status in the years after Brexit.

IMMIGRATION JOBSWORTH BUREAUCRATS

The Home Office has an atrocious record of handling applications from foreigners who want to live in the UK. Some asylum cases have taken more than twenty years to be resolved. When I was an MP dealing with constituents who wanted to marry someone from outside the EU, the casework could take years, with lawyers ratcheting up fees and individuals helpless in the face of the slowness and often arbitrary decision making of Home Office immigration officialdom. It is not that the Home Office official is mean or vicious as a human being, but there is a jobsworth mentality inherent in all immigration bureaucracies.

The government has announced that it will register EU citizens by alphabetical order. Given there are roughly 600 Polish surnames that begin with the letter Z, the poor Poles at the back of the Brexit registration queue may have to wait quite a while. The European citizens in the UK have also been told they should register online. Computer literacy may be no problem for a French banker in London or a Portuguese nurse in Liverpool, but there are many EU citizens who have no better skills in speaking foreign languages than the average British citizen living in an expat community in Spain. Many who work in low-paid, unskilled jobs digging up vegetables or picking fruit or working as a care assistant looking after helpless elderly men and women in residential homes are not likely to have online registration competences.

In October 2016, when the Brexit process started, the Brexit cabinet minister, Liam Fox said that EU nationals in the UK were the 'main card' London could use to extract concessions from the EU27. This concept of people living among us as bargaining chips was typical of Fox's mentality, but Theresa May did not take the opportunity to make a clear, definitive offer by assuring all EU nationals they were welcome to stay in Brexit Britain.

Instead in its white paper in July 2018, the government said it would use the 1971 Immigration Act as the basis for legislating the rights of EU citizens and not include guarantees of their status in the withdrawal agreement with Brussels. This means that all Europeans are now lumped in with immigrants from any other country. The 1971 Immigration Act cannot be amended or debated by Parliament, so any problems arising from it in terms of treatme of EU citizens in the UK leaves MPs powerless to defend the interests of any European nationals who turn to them for help.

In addition, the white paper revealed that there had been no negotiations with member states of the European Economic Area, including Norway and Ireland, or EFTA, such as Switzerland. Swiss and Norwegians enjoy existing freedom of movement rights and in turn extend those rights to British men and women.

The withdrawal agreement did include language about EU citizens living in Britain: they would not face deportation, but there was no guarantee that if they left the UK temporarily they could come back. There was no certainty about future family members joining a household. The home secretary, Sajid Javid, himself the son of immigrants from Pakistan, published a white paper in December 2018 which sought to limit the number of European citizens who could come to work in Britain. It was an odd patchwork, implying there would be a quota for unskilled workers who could enter for a given time if employers needed them, with more possibilities for employees paid £30,000 or more. To anyone who knows the history of Europeans moving across frontiers in Europe after 1950, Mr Javid's confused proposals harked back to an era of seasonal or temporary immigrant workers, often living in almost third world housing, as landlords do not like renting to tenants who have no security of employment.

The Swiss sought to have quotas of seasonal workers during the period 1950–75, but these fell foul of the European Convention of Human Rights ruling on families living together. In London, to demand that an employer pays £30,000 a year to hire a worker may be the going rate. In poorer areas of the north of England, Wales and Scotland, where housing and other costs are lower, few firms are able to pay £30,000 for an employee doing standard work. Thus the government's proposals to handle immigrant workers will attract far more to London and far fewer to the poorer regions of the UK where British workers willing to do long hours for low pay are hard to find.

In her haste to throw a bone to anti-immigrant Tory MPs in the hope of persuading them to approve her deal, Mrs May told the EU that Britain would repudiate the core four freedoms of intra-European movement at the very heart of the EU's existence. It was difficult to see what kind of a favourable trade deal based on easy access to the EU market Britain could obtain. Jeremy Corbyn and his ally, the shadow home secretary, Diane Abbott, went along with the government's anti-free movement immigration policy, thus indicating that Labour was not really interested in securing full, unfettered access to the EU market for firms based in Britain. In 2015, Labour under Ed Miliband had campaigned to win power by promising 'Controls on Immigration'. Labour lost. But under Corbyn, the party tried to have its freedom of movement cake and eat it, as Corbyn declared: 'We are not wedded to freedom of movement for EU citizens as a point of principle . . . nor do we rule it out.' If that was just another example of Corbyn fence-sitting, other Labour MPs insisted publicly that freedom of movement had to end.

In the midst of the confusion and uncertainty that pervaded all the Brexit talks with the EU Commission after 2016, there was no energy left to fashion a workable regime for European citizens in the UK. Instead, old legislation drawn up to stop too many Commonwealth citizens arriving in Britain was taken off the shelf, dusty files were opened, and fifty-year-old laws that have often shown themselves to be discriminatory were henceforth to be applied to French or Dutch or Greek nationals working in the UK.

This was very bad news for British citizens living in EU nations. Instead of an encompassing generous offer for nationals from EU27 countries (other than Irish citizens, who were to be allowed to maintain existing freedom of movement rules that long predated the UK and Ireland entering the European Economic Community), the British approach was mealy-mouthed and last-minute in nature. The whole point of freedom of movement is that it is about movement. No one knows what will happen to an English woman who falls in love with a Swedish man or a German woman and wants to build a life and home in Britain. Will a Polish couple currently living in Britain and who may obtain 'settled status', but who have sent a child, perhaps with learning or other difficulties, back to Poland to live with a grandparent who can provide full-time care, be able to bring the child to live within the family settled in Britain?

It is one of the oddest aspects of the Brexit saga that no one on the left – Labour MPs, trade unions, left think tanks – has sought to develop a policy matrix that first, controls freedom of movement without breaking EU law, second, increases jobs for British workers, and third, develops workplace rights to control hiring.

Elsewhere in the EU, freedom of movement is hemmed in with restrictions. It does not apply in an unfettered way to state or public sect

employment, even if one of the biggest employers of EU citizens in the UK is the NHS. It is based on work, not living off benefits. It allows tough registration rules. It requires that health, unemployment and old-age care insurance is taken out. There is even an emergency brake provision if a sudden wave of immigration overwhelms public order or social infrastructure. If after three months a European citizen in another country has not found work, they can be sent home. None of these control measures has ever been used by a British government, even after the enlargement of the EU to include poorer ex-communist countries in 2004.

CONTROLLING IMMIGRATION IS POSSIBLE UNDER EU LAW

The myth persists that the UK decision not to impose a seven-year transition period in 2004 before admitting EU citizens from new member states made a major difference to anti-immigrant feeling in Britain. In fact, the Conservative Party and UKIP had already been cranking up anti-immigrant pressure from the start of the century. Hundreds of thousands of Poles and other east Europeans were already in Britain after the UK and other EU member states correctly opened their doors to visitors from ex-communist countries following the end of Soviet overlordship. By making their presence legal, they paid tax, and the Migration Advisory Committee reported in 2018 that the average contribution of an EU worker to government revenue was £2,400 more per year than the average contribution from a British-born worker. Germany nominally imposed a seven-year transition period, but a 2004 German law called the *Zuwanderunggesetz* allowed so many exemptions permitting employment of east European workers that it made no difference. Today there are nearly seven million non-German workers from EU member states who live and work in Germany, double the number in the UK. Other EU members quietly let the seven-year transition period fall into irrelevancy. Unless European governments were willing to impose visas for all visits, including tourism, it was impossible to stop arrivals. President Sarkozy's government, 2007–17, offered Romanians €300 and a free bus ticket to return home. Many Romanians in France took advantage of the offer for a visit back home and then came back to France.

Key EU laws now strengthened under pressure from France's President Macron stipulate that workers sent by their employer from one country to another have to be paid the local rate for the job. In Britain after 2004, employment agencies were set up to offer cut-rate agency workers from poorer EU member states, despite the fact that the EU mandated that they should be given staff employment after a given period. However, no British government has enforced this directive. The employer federations, including the CBI, British Chamber of Commerce and Institute of Directors, lobbied as fiercely as they could to keep the UK labour market open to as many low-paid workers as possible. Business opposition to any effective regulation of a Wild West gangmaster hire-and-fire labour market stoked up the hostility to Europe of many British workers and voters.

David Cameron and Theresa May had six years after 2010 to recast Britain's administration of new foreign arrivals to the UK labour market. Mrs May did nothing. Indeed, her first move was to abolish identity cards, which at least allowed Britain to know who was who in the country and where they lived. As Europe minister in 2004, I set up along with the then home secretary, David Blunkett an EU workers' registration scheme so that the government would have some details of EU workers offered a job by British employers. In 2013, Mrs May abolished it.

The concern over the volume and velocity of arrivals of new workers from Europe was real. But it could have been dealt with by rethinking the way the UK's internal labour market failed to train local citizens and tilted the balance towards often unscrupulous, exploitative bosses.

The British apprenticeship system – or what is technically called vocational educational training (VET) – is the worst in Europe. To take one example, the Construction Industry Training Board says there is a shortfall of 31,600 qualified construction workers every year. Building firms make up for the absence of British training workers by bringing in skilled building workers who have gone through proper apprenticeship training in other EU member states. Young British men and women might like to go on apprenticeship training, but so poorly managed is the current UK apprenticeship scheme that the number of applicants dropped by 61 per cent in 2017. In the rest of Europe, apprenticeships are linked to proper qualifications – often requiring as much hard work and absorbing technical details as a university degree course – and involve employers who offer jobs to the young men and women emerging at their culmination.

In the UK in 2017, over 200,000 youngsters were put on so-called construction courses that left them without even a low-level National Vocational Qualification (NVQ) and no job. These are a way of parking young school leavers, but utterly useless in terms of real added value to the modern economy. The disaster of the apprenticeship and other vocational educational training schemes under successive Conservative, Labour and Liberal Democrat ministers left employers with no choice but to look to Europe to get the qualified skilled workers they need.

In March 2018, on the BBC's *Panorama* programme, the news presenter, Nick Robinson went to Mansfield in the deindustrialized heartlands of the once flourishing north Nottinghamshire coal regions, where the vote in favour of leaving the EU in the referendum was a thumping 39,927 over 16,417. He asked two questions to residents he met in the town centre. The first was: Did they think there were too many Europeans in the town? Everyone said 'yes', with one couple insisting they were benefit scroungers.

OK, said Robinson, moving to the next question: Which categories of immigrants should not be allowed in? He held up what he jokingly called Happy Family cards – showing a lorry driver, or a fruit picker, or a chef, or a care home worker. The Mansfield residents who were certain that there were too many European immigrants were reduced to a stuttering lack of certainty. Yes, Europeans working in care homes were needed and welcome. Yes, they were useful as lorry drivers. Well, yes, fruit picking and winter harvesting of root vegetables is arduous, so maybe it was work Europeans might do. There was a pause when the BBC man held up a picture of a chef. Should Europeans be allowed in to cook for Mansfield residents who liked to go out to restaurants? There was a pause and then agreement that perhaps specialist cooks coming in from Europe might brighten up the food offer in Mansfield.

The *Panorama* programme would be funny were it not so sad that this kind of basic exposé of the core contradiction about foreigners from Europe coming to work in Britain was never covered on the BBC before the referendum. Robinson interviewed employers, all of whom said they would face major difficulties in running their businesses if they could not hire enough workers from Europe.

This reality can be seen across Europe. Most big EU member states like Germany, France, or Spain have more people from other EU countries living and working as a share of their total population than does the UK. There are up to an estimated 900,000 Brits living full- or part-time in Spain. Few have made an effort to integrate in the sense of speaking Spanish and conforming to Spanish social practices and customs. As a share of the total Spanish population of 46 million, the number of Brits with a base in Spain is higher than the number of Poles in the UK. And like the British in Spain, the Polish in Britain shuttle between Britain and Poland, as anyone who has taken one of the innumerable flights from British to Polish cities in the last two decades can testify.

Poles make up 1.7 per cent of the total British population. In Ireland 4 per cent of the population is Polish. Yet despite having a tradition of nationalist populist political discourse in politics and the media, there is none of the open hostility in Ireland against east Europeans that has been commonplace in Britain's tabloid press or from the mouths of British anti-European politicians. There may be sour remarks in Dublin pubs about the number of Poles or Lithuanians in Ireland, but no politician or newspaper editor has turned these anti-immigrant feelings into a massive political issue in the manner of many MPs, mainly Conservative, and the offshore-owned press across the Irish sea in England.

To be sure, if you ask many people anywhere in Britain, it is easy to hear remarks about immigrants and, as we saw in the Brexit referendum, given a chance to vote in a plebiscite to stop arrivals from outside their country, voters will take it. When Mrs Thatcher in the 1979 election said Britain was in danger of being 'swamped' by immigrants, she won many extra votes. Anti-immigrant populists in most elections this century have done well. In Denmark in 2001, the Social Democrats, who had won the most seats in Danish elections since 1924, lost to conservative and populist right-wing parties insisting the Danish centre left was too lax on immigration.

In the 2019 Danish national election, the Social Democratic party hardened its profile by proposing tougher controls on immigrants. But no potential governing party in Denmark would propose shutting down existing access to fellow European citizens, as the two main UK parties call for. In the German and Austrian elections of 2017 and then the Italian election of March 2018, the question of immigration was central, though the term 'immigration' on the continent usually refers to refugees and economic migrants from conflict-destroyed Middle Eastern states, not well-educated Catholic Poles or Portuguese, as in England.

Nigel Farage, with his ugly remarks about not wanting an east European family to move in next door or saying he no longer heard English spoken on commuter train journeys, denies he has the slightest tinge of xenophobia in his make-up. As he boasted to a City audience when I was on a panel with him, no one could accuse him of being anti-European as he was married to a German.

Let us accept at face value not so much the insistence but the self-righteous belief of those who whipped up anti-European passions over many years that they are not animated by hostility to Europeans, but by higher, purer motives of national sovereignty or a belief that Britain will be a better, stronger nation once disconnected from its European Union partners.

As the Nick Robinson's *Panorama* interviews showed, voters can hold contradictory emotions or views simultaneously. They feel too many European citizens have come to work in Britain, yet agree that their contribution as workers is useful and productive. By early 2019, 45 per cent of the UK population said they were positive about immigrants and in March 2019, Professor Matthew Goodwin tweeted: 'British public concern over immigration falls to new low in the post-referendum period. Only 22% now say it is a top issue, leaving it 5th, behind Brexit, crime, health and the economy.'

Is it too late? Must Britain create a new bureaucracy for our fellow Europeans that issues work and residence permits, perhaps in order to stop people arriving without visas and then disappearing into the informal labour market, even travel visas, as well as seasonal or regional quotas of workers? As we begin discriminating against the rest of Europe, then public opinion in those countries will demand that similar action is taken against us. Thus the existing right of the British people will be reduced. Is that really a good idea?

NO ONE KNOWS WHO LIVES IN BRITAIN OR WHERE

Can British policy makers use the crisis of how to handle Brexit as an opportunity to rethink the management and structure of the internal labour market?

For a start, it would be useful to know who is in the country and where they live. The identity cards system introduced by the Labour government in 2010 shortly before being replaced by the Conservative–Lib Dem coalition arrived far too late to become rooted in. It was easy for the new government to simply abolish the ID cards which are common elsewhere in the continent in countries with much stronger constitutional protection for citizens' rights than is the case in Britain. As a result, the basis of knowledge about who is working in the country is haphazard, based on unreliable surveys at airports.

Instead Britain might look at the Netherlands. There, every Dutch and EU citizen has a BSN (*Burgerservicenummer*) which is obligatory if you plan to live and work in that country for more than three months. It is obtained from the local authority where you register when you first arrive. It is necessary to get access to public or health services, to take a job, pay taxes or vote in local elections. It is possible to obtain an identity card based on the BSN. A similar system of registration in Britain would reassure all citizens that the number of non-nationals was known. It helps stop any abuse of the welfare system and is needed for any recourse to healthcare. A side benefit would be the elimination of voter fraud, as the BSN has to be produced in order to vote.

A national UK registration scheme avoids the neuralgic objections to ID cards. The Dutch have an outstanding record of personal liberty and civic rights. But the Dutch, as a founder member of the ECSC in 1950, see freedom of movement not as a problem of immigration, but a necessary mechanism to keep borders open both ways. Nearly half a million Dutch citizens live elsewhere in Europe. Together with their neighbouring nations of Belgium and Luxembourg – the so-called Benelux grouping – employers there have welcomed European citizens as workers because the Dutch and Belgians have proper registration systems for residence and work which apply to all within their frontiers. This does not eliminate racist and anti-immigrant populist politics, but at least gives local citizens a sense that the authorities know who is in the country, and they are properly registered for employment, taxes, housing and access to public services.

Ending freedom of movement, as the proponents of Brexit demand, means bringing in consequent checks on cars, buses and other vehicles. The Netherlands has hundreds of roads crossing into Germany and Belgium. There is even one small town where the Dutch–Belgian border runs down the town centre. Freedom of movement is about allowing normal commercial traffic to move without let or hindrance. It has none of the xenophobic pathology of the British debate on freedom of movement. The Dutch would no more think of imposing strict controls on people movement between the Netherlands and Belgian Flanders than the UK would on crossing the border between England and Scotland.

Similarly, for Germany, with eight borders with its EU neighbours (nine with non-EU Switzerland), the idea of giving up freedom of movement would simply be seen as bizarre. Nearly half a million European workers cross into Germany to work every day from their own towns in neighbouring countries. Bringing in all the panoply of visa, work and residence immigration bureaucracy proposed by many in Britain, including Labour MPs, would be seen as reverting to a mid-twentieth-century or even pre-war Europe.

FOR GERMANY, EU FREEDOM OF MOVEMENT IS ECONOMIC COMMON SENSE

Germany, like the Benelux nations, needs open borders for economic reasons. Germany has a wider interest. It requires a stable neighbourhood, especially in the former Soviet bloc nations that joined the EU this century. Berlin encourages investment in these countries, not only for the advantages of cheaper labour until economies catch up, but also to assure the 75 million citizens living in the EU ex-communist countries that they can stay in their own countries while always having the possibility, if desired, to come and work in Germany.

Early in 2019, the German government said it needed about 250,000 immigrant workers to come into Germany every year just to fill existing and expected vacancies in the labour market. Freedom of movement allows German employers to match workforce needs with the evolving nature of their businesses. In a sense, Britain wisely adopted this system after Ireland became an independent sovereign state after the 1920 war of independence. But the big difference with the UK is that in the Netherlands there is a comprehensive registration system which assures all Dutch citizens that no one can enter and stay in the Netherlands on the basis of accessing benefits.

The Germans have Europe's most rigorous apprenticeship system, often dating back centuries. If England respects a monarchy because of its deep historical roots, so too does Germany respect the concept of apprenticeship – a system that not even Hitler dared to tamper with.

Brexit could be an opportunity to reform the UK labour market and modernize the way inhabitants are counted and registered in Britain for the purposes of residence, work, access to public services and to take part in democratic processes. It could also be the moment to enact a major reform of apprenticeships and other means of training the essential future workforce. It is not too hard to work out how many doctors, nurses and other medical staff are needed now and over the next period. Thousands of young British students work so hard for four or five top-grade A-levels, hoping to become doctors, only to find that the closed-shop medical profession seeks to control and limit the number of medical graduates. Instead the NHS hires doctors from Europe. Why not train young British men and women to become medical professionals instead of bringing in so many from Europe or, indeed, sucking out doctors from poorer countries when their services could be put to use where they were born and studied?

These questions were not much discussed or even advanced in the years before the Brexit vote, during the campaign itself and in the period since June 2016, as Britain tries to work out what kind of Brexit it wants or needs, assuming that Brexit there must be.

Enthusiasts for Brexit, including spokespeople for both the government and opposition, made much of the need to control European citizens coming to Britain. Yet one of the most dramatic changes following Brexit was how fast was the emigration of EU citizens from Britain back to their home countries. In 2018, more east, central and south European citizens were leaving Britain than entering. The number of workers from the eight new EU member states went down by 89,000 in 2018. By contrast, the number of non-EU workers allowed into the UK in 2018 rose by 130,000. According to the Office of National Statistics, there were 184,000 fewer Poles, Slovakians, Romanians and other east Europeans working in the UK at the end of 2018 than at the time of the 2016 plebiscite. Different factors explain this dramatic turnaround. There are many more jobs now available in east Europe as Poland, the Czech Republic, Slovakia, Hungary, Romania and Bulgaria have used EU membership and the single market to attract foreign direct investment. The economies of Portugal and Spain and, to a lesser extent, Italy and even Greece have recovered strength. Unemployment has dropped rapidly in new EU member states. They are also seeing a drop in birth rates, so need to bring in foreign labour or welcome back citizens who went to the UK in the years before the Brexit vote and subsequent unpleasant remarks and even attacks on EU citizens reported in the UK after June 2016.

European unemployment April 2019 by % of population	
Czech Republic	2.2%
Germany	3.3%
Netherlands	3.3%
Hungary	3.4%
Malta	3.5%
UK	3.7%
Poland	3.8%
Romania	3.9%
Ireland	4.4%
Slovenia	4.5%
Bulgaria	4.5%
Austria	4.7%
Estonia	5.0%
Denmark	5.1%
Slovakia	5.4%
Luxembourg	5.7%
Lithuania	5.8%
Sweden	6.3%
Latvia	6.4%
Cyprus	6.5%
Portugal	6.6%
Finland	6.8%
Croatia	7.0%
France	8.6%

Italy	9.9%
Spain	13.6%
Greece	18.1%
EU28	6.3%

(Source: Eurostat)

GDP growth in Poland in 2017 was 4.6 per cent, in the Czech Republic 4.3 per cent and in Hungary 4 per cent compared to 1.7 per cent in Britain. The income that European citizens working in Britain from east and south-east Europe or the Mediterranean EU member states were earning has dropped thanks to the Brexit devaluation of the pound sterling, so those European workers who were remitting part of their wages from Britain back home to families have seen a 20 per cent drop in remitted earnings. All these factors have led to a remarkable reversal of arrivals from the EU since Brexit. The freedom of movement issue that was a major factor in producing the Brexit majority may have solved itself.

In fact, freedom of movement cannot be stopped unless Britain brings in a full visa regime, with every tourist or visitor coming to the UK being required to have a visa granted in order to get onto a plane, to take a bus or train, or use a car to visit Britain. Any such measure would also hit the 73 million Brits who fly abroad each year and would not be politically popular with British voters, who have been lied to that freedom of movement is something that European citizens like as it allows them to come and exploit the British. In fact, millions of British citizens take advantage of freedom of movement rights, from young people just doing a gap year in a European country to their grandparents who retire to a warmer climate and see their UK pension going a lot further with cheaper food, wine and heating bills.

Under present rules, any EU citizen can enter the UK without a visa, as can citizens from fifty-six other countries. Once inside Britain, as there is no registration system, they are free to do what they want. Many work for cash payments in the so-called informal or black labour market.

Controlling people movement by effective management of the internal labour market, including empowering those who are not going via university into professional, executive or administrative jobs, is a more sensible solution than erecting new border controls and 'jobsworth' immigration bureaucrats.

The government should learn from its recent experience. In 2003, the Labour government said a new 'e-border' system would be fully operational in 2011. £340 million was spent developing the scheme, before Home Office immigration bureaucrats abandoned it in 2010. The next home secretary, Theresa May had to pay out £150 million in legal damages to contractors. Mrs May was determined to reinforce failure and a further £303 million was spent trying to create another digital e-border system. In 2015 the National Audit Office denounced the scheme as a failure.

Yet somehow the officials so utterly incapable of bringing in an e-border and who wasted nearly a billion pounds in their fruitless efforts are meant to have the ability to magic into existence new 'frictionless' systems to allow entry and exit into the UK across the Channel or the border with Northern Ireland. As an MP, I had to deal with immigration cases on a weekly basis. At any given moment in the 1990s and first decade of this century, the Home Office had 700,000 cases pending, as people were entitled to appeal and the heavily lawyered proceedings in tribunals and courts could take years. The Home Office margin of error was up to 10 per cent in such cases, so if Whitehall's worst bureaucracy has to process up to 3.5 million cases of EU citizens who will seek to have their right to live in Britain confirmed after Brexit, it implies that as many as 350,000 individuals will face months, if not years, of anxiety. As it is, the fee to apply for residence status is £65 for an adult and £32.50 for a child. Calculations suggest that the Home Office will make a profit of £44 million if all EU citizens applied to keep living in Britain after Brexit. This is ugly politics opening the way to much human misery. It will also invite reciprocal and equivalent action against British citizens living on the continent.

When I spoke to the head of the *Abteilung Brexit* (Brexit Department) in the German Foreign Office in 2017, he explained how David Cameron had come to Berlin before the referendum to explain to Angela Merkel the intolerable strains being put on Britain by the arrival of so many Europeans. Cameron said they put too much pressure on housing, social services, schools and GPs. The Germans listened with concern. They did not dispute the British prime minister's assertions. They simply asked if Downing Street could furnish the German government with a list of all these troublesome Europeans: details of where they lived, worked and problems they caused British public services. As the top Brexit diplomat in Berlin's Foreign Ministry in Wilhelmstrasse said to me: 'We are still waiting for the list.' He did add that when Berlin reminded Downing Street of the request for some details of EU citizens in the UK that were causing so much difficulty, Cameron's team sent over a *Daily Telegraph* article written by a retired UK ambassador to Saudi Arabia, who set up an unpleasant organization called Immigrant Watch which regularly produced reports lapped up by the populist press about the problems of European (but not Irish or Australian or American) citizens working and paying taxes and social security in Britain.

In fact, it is possible to feel sorry for David Cameron. No British government in recent time has much idea of who is in the country. Over decades, the biggest single contingent of 'immigrant' workers from a foreign country have been the Irish. Ever since the creation of an independent Ireland in the 1920s, Irish citizens have come and gone freely to mainland UK as well as into the six counties of Northern Ireland. No one has ever asked an Irish citizen if they were entitled to be in the UK, work here, buy a house, found a business, marry and have a family. But Cameron – as indeed Gordon Brown or Tony Blair before him – could have looked at ways of controlling freedom of movement by changing the internal management of the UK labour market to lessen dependence on low-paid workers from Europe and setting up a registration system so that everyone can feel secure that we know who is in the country and thus have immigration under better control than has been the case in the past.

Such policy measures based on national variations of freedom of movement are compatible with staying in the single market, which Norway has adopted and which Switzerland has accepted in order to keep market access open. Might it be possible to lift the thorny issue of freedom of movement out of the toxic post-2016 Brexit debate? Could the CBI and TUC or a Royal Commission be tasked with coming up with proposals so that British employers were less dependent on immigrant workers? Instead of staring at each other in reciprocal hostility across the Brexit divide, could MPs of different parties make joint recommendations on how a registration system would allow the British people to know who was living in the country?

8

HOW THE BREXIT AND ORANGE CARD FUSED

In 1844, the young Benjamin Disraeli rose to define a major new problem that MPs in the House of Commons would have to deal with. He described the problem thus:

> A dense population, in extreme distress, inhabit an island where there is an Established Church, which is not their Church, and a territorial aristocracy the richest of whom live in foreign capitals. Thus you have a starving population, an absentee aristocracy, and an alien Church; and in addition the weakest executive in the world. That is the Irish Question.

It took nearly a century before the Irish question was partly answered when the island of Ireland was partitioned in 1922 and the majority population of Ireland finally gained most, if not total, sovereign control over their affairs.

In fact, the Irish question was not fully resolved until 1998 when a dense thicket of 140 agreements between London and Dublin located within the mesh of legal obligations inherent in being a signatory member of the EU treaties finally stopped violence, abolished borders, and allowed the nationalist Catholic citizens of the six counties of Ulster, still ruled from London, to feel that they were at one with the majority of their countrymen and women on the island of Ireland.

One of the paradoxes of Brexit is that the loss of the right to live, work, travel, settle, retire in any EU member state enjoyed by 65 million British citizens by virtue of our European Union citizenship does not apply to British citizens who live in Northern Ireland. They can all obtain an Irish passport and retain access to European free movement. Indeed, an estimated 500,000 UK citizens in Northern Ireland out of a total population of 1.87 million have done so. The Northern Irish MP, Ian Paisley Jr, a member of the hard-line protestant Democratic Unionist Party founded by his preacher-politician father Ian Paisley, tweeted to his constituents after the Brexit vote was announced: 'My advice is if you are entitled to second passport then take one. I sign off lots of applications for constituents.'

Ian Paisley Jr, like other DUP MPs, was being simultaneously honest and hypocritical. Honest in that his voters would be cutting of their noses to spite their faces by rejecting the offer of EU citizenship and travel rights and he is not going to tell them to be so foolish. Hypocritical in that in his speeches and votes as a Westminster MP, he does everything to deny to British citizens living in England, Scotland and Wales the rights he says his own constituents should enjoy and take advantage of.

The concept of collateral damage was a famous euphemism dating from the Vietnam War. It meant serious harm done to innocent bystanders as a result of military action. It re-emerged as a euphemism in the various wars involving Iraq and Afghanistan in the last thirty years. Whether collateral damage is deliberate or unintentional is irrelevant. Once the button is pushed to unleash the missile, many uninvolved people get badly hurt.

This is surely a metaphor that can be fairly applied to Ireland, which is set to be the biggest collateral victim of the way the government in London has handled Brexit.

For many, the Irish question dates from the Battle of the Boyne in 1690, after the English protestant ruling elites invited in a European immigrant, William of Orange, to rule over Britain in the name of protestant supremacy. For others, the Irish question goes right back to 1169, when William the Conqueror invaded and handed Irish lands over to his followers.

The Irish question is also bound up with English protestantism. When he was defeated as prime minister in 1874, William Gladstone spent his first months in opposition writing an 800-page tract called *Vaticanism* denouncing the Catholic faith and accusing the Catholic Church of 'an utterly hopeless and visionary effort to Romanize the church and people of England'. In language reminiscent of the Reverend Ian Paisley, who, as an MEP, attacked Pope John Paul II and called him 'the anti-Christ' when the Pope addressed the European Parliament in 1988, Gladstone accused the nineteenth-century Catholic Church of adopting 'a policy of violence and change in faith . . . when no one can become her convert, without renouncing this moral and mental freedom, and placing his civil loyalty and duty at the mercy of another'.

The Democratic Unionist Party avoids both the Gladstonian and Paisley ranting against Catholicism and the Pope but remains ardent in its historic interpretation of ancient protestant prejudices against gays, against women's rights and above all in rejecting cooperation with Ireland on the basis of mutual respect and shared identity.

The Irish question was partly solved between 1920 and 1922 with a short war of independence followed by a vicious civil war. It flared up again in 1968 with the so-called Troubles – the violence between extreme Irish nationalists, on one hand, and the British state and Ulster protestant unionists who had denied civil rights to Catholics in the part of Ulster under British rule, on the other. Terrorism, killing of innocents and torture by the IRA, Ulster unionist paramilitaries and police and even army units of the British state took place. It took until 1998 and the Good Friday Agreement for hopes to arise that the Irish question might finally be answered.

In France for the Easter weekend of 1998, I noted how important the Good Friday Agreement was for Europe:

10 April 1998

Good Friday and the news of Tony Blair's success in Northern Ireland dominates all the French papers. He has really pulled off something. If common membership of the European Union dissolves through economic and other contact developments the barriers between north and south so much the good. This has every chance of being the equivalent for Tony Blair what Algeria was for de Gaulle or what the Falkland Islands were for Margaret Thatcher. Once again a British Prime Minister is a huge international star. The French papers show a photo of Blair shaking hands with Bertie Ahern. It looks like a London–Dublin deal over the heads of the factions in Northern Ireland. But Dublin is as opposed to Sinn Fein and the IRA as London, so the deal itself does not represent a victory for the ultra Republicans. Gerry Adams may have as many difficulties as David Trimble.

Today, with hindsight, we can see that the peace in the six counties is bought with a religious, communal and identity divide that shames the elected DUP and Sinn Fein politicians in charge. Each summer, protestant unionists march in parades and burn bonfires to celebrate the Battle of the Boyne in July 1690. Ever since 1691, Northern Ireland protestants have paraded with their distinct orange sashes – the colour of the Dutch William of Orange imported by English protestant elites as a new anti-Catholic king – and have done so by marching into Catholic communities of Northern Ireland like an occupying power.

In July 2018, as the row intensified over how Northern Ireland politicians were handling Brexit, bonfires in Derry and Belfast had placards attached to them to go up in flames with the slogan 'K-A-T'. This means 'Kill All Taigs' – the ugly protestant unionist derogatory term used to describe Irish Catholics. Irish nationalist republicans also seek to provoke with marches in Belfast and the two decades since the Good Friday Agreement have not brought the two communities together in unity. But it is at least peace and the abolition of the border with no customs control or any kind of check, as both the UK and Ireland were in the same customs union, and the single market has given Ireland, north and south, the best decades in the island's history.

Now all this is under threat from Brexit. The most obvious threat is the end of the common customs union between the UK and its EU partners, including Ireland. There is nowhere in the world where two different customs systems exist side by side without some physical control on goods passing between them.

Turkey is in the EU customs union except for agricultural goods. Switzerland is in the Schengen zone and generally waves through cars at frontier checkpoints on the main roads between Switzerland and its EU neighbours. But lorries crossing from Turkey into the EU can wait up to thirty hours to have the customs carnets checked. While any EU citizen, including the British until Brexit bites, can cross frontiers with as much wine, beer or food as they wish from another EU member state, it is a crime to cross into Switzerland with more than 1 kg of meat – about four good steaks – or 5 litres (seven bottles) of wine without declaring the imports to customs at the Swiss–EU border crossing posts. The Swiss have 22,000 customs officers to enforce their customs duty rules.

There has been no need for any kind of customs or border checks within Ireland, since both the UK and Ireland are members of the same customs union and single market. There is no physical border or visible checkpoints along the 500 km frontier between the UK province of Northern Ireland and the Republic of Ireland. Crossing between the two countries is like crossing from England into Scotland or from Canton Geneva to Canton Vaud in Switzerland.

If the UK leaves the common customs union within the EU that Ireland and Britain are both members of and changes any single market rules and regulations, the World Trade Organization mandates checks at the border as happen on the Swiss and Turkish borders with EU member states. In the peaceful Nordic world there are customs checks on lorries and vans crossing from Sweden in the EU customs union into Norway outside it.

So if Northern Ireland is outside the EU customs union, then controls there will be, enforced by agents of the state in uniform at a frontier crossing post. There is no magical technological solution – whether by drones, or pre-clearance, or checks carried out away from border crossings. It will be a night-mare for Irish lorries crossing through England to reach ferry ports on the east coast linked to Europe.

The Dutch Parliament has produced a report saying that an extra 750 customs officers will be needed to check goods coming from the UK. That is for the relatively small Netherlands. London will have to get taxpayers to fund a giant new bureaucracy to deal with customs checks. A first estimate suggests 5,000 extra customs officers may be needed, but this is almost certainly on the low side. The UK National Audit Office reckons that customs control checks just on non-EU goods will go from 55 million a year to 255 million.

The terms 'customs union' and 'single market' were not on the referendum ballot paper and it is doubtful if a single British MP or political journalist in 2016 even knew what 'a' or 'the' customs union was. Of seventy speeches made in the 2016 Brexit campaign by MPs and MEPs supporting a Brexit vote, just one mentioned the customs union.

In March 2018, Mrs May made a big speech in Munich on the UK and EU security after Brexit. It was more about policing than security in the broader sense, but it was revealing that she did not mention Ireland – except in a two-word reference to the European Arrest Warrant. At least those two words were two more than her then foreign secretary, Boris Johnson uttered when he made what was meant to be a defining speech on Brexit on 14 February 2018 in which the word 'Ireland' did not even appear.

In the 1950s, the so-called 'Border Campaign' was initiated by Irish nationalists who believed in a single united Ireland, not the partitioned nation with six Irish counties in Ulster still under British rule. The Irish nationalists attacked border posts and other symbols of British rule. Eighteen people were killed and thirty-six wounded. The Border Campaign ended in 1962 after tough repression by security forces including mass internment ordered by Dublin. Six years later, in 1968, the so-called 'Troubles' began as a three-way conflict between Irish republican paramilitaries, Ulster unionist protestant death squads and the British state in the form of its army, police and security services. The violence lasted three decades; 3,600 people were killed and up to 50,000 wounded or injured and 400,000 British soldiers had to be deployed to this tiny corner of Europe.

Those who forget history are condemned to repeat it. The collective political amnesia in Whitehall, Parliament and the media about how the Irish question can turn violent is extraordinary. The pro-Brexit Tory MP, Jacob Rees-Mogg said that imposing new frontier checks in Northern Ireland meant that people could be 'inspected' in the same way as 'we had during the Troubles'. His casual reference to a thirty-year armed conflict in which so many people were killed, wounded and tortured produced a retort from the Irish Tánaiste (deputy prime minister) and foreign minister, Simon Coveney that it was 'hard to believe' a politician of Mr Rees-Mogg's seniority would be 'so ill informed' about the Irish border. But Mr Rees-Mogg, who has an Eton and Oxford education, knew exactly what he was saying. For him and for the hard rightist anti-Europeans in his Orange Brexit wing of the Conservative Party and their DUP allies, Brexit is the opportunity to roll the clock back and overturn the Good Friday Agreement.

There was a sharp confrontation in the House of Commons in Easter Week 2019 when Rees-Mogg and other Brexit extremists met the speaker of the US House of Representatives, Nancy Pelosi, the third most senior elected US political leader after the president and vice-president. Following the mid-term victory for Democrats in November 2018, she now controls the law-making agenda of the US Congress. Together with other senior US legislators she was visiting the UK and Ireland to look at the impact of leaving the EU customs union and single market. Ms Pelosi made clear that there was no question of a swift UK–US trade deal if Britain cuts existing trade links with the EU, as Mrs May's deal indicates as well as the hard Brexiters' desire for a full rupture with EU trade rules. Speaking to Ireland's parliament, the Dail, and flanked by powerful Irish-American politicians, Ms Pelosi said Mrs May and pro-Brexit politicians in England should not think 'for one minute that there's any comfort for them in the fact that if they leave the EU they would quickly have a US–UK trade agreement'. It is the US Congress that decides American trade policy, not President Trump. Ms Pelosi added: 'We treasure the Good Friday accord because of what it says is possible for the entire world and the reason to hope that in every place the dream of reconciliation is possible for them too.' Backbench pro-Brexit MP Mark Francois told Pelosi that she did not understand the issues at stake. She snapped at him: 'Don't condescend to me or to us.'

I served on many delegations of UK MPs to the US Congress or joined in receiving American politicians in Westminster. I cannot recall such a sharp pointed slap-down of a British MP by a senior US member of Congress. Whatever else a future of Brexiternity may bring, better relations between anti-European politicians in London and their opposite numbers in Washington is not one of them.

Nigel Farage added fuel to the fire by telling *The Times* that the EU's Brexit negotiator, Michel Barnier 'would like the IRA to become active again' and accusing the former French foreign minister of 'almost encouraging Republican terrorism'.

The BBC radio news political journalist, Nick Robinson interviewed the Archbishop of Armagh, the head of the Catholic Church in Ireland about his concerns if customs controls were reintroduced on the border in Northern Ireland. He asked Archbishop Martin about visiting a well-known Irish town between Dublin and Dundalk, which Nick Robinson mispronounced as 'DROGG HEEDA' (Drogheda). Robinson wouldn't pronounce the name of the English city Worcester, 'WORK ESSTER', but so many of the BBC and other journalists who are great professionals when it comes to London politics are on terra incognita elsewhere in Europe – even a neighbouring English-speaking EU member state like Ireland.

Perhaps the very success of the Good Friday Agreement means that English politicians and the London media have not had to think hard about the Irish question for twenty years. The monopolization of elections in the six Northern Ireland counties by the DUP and Sinn Fein means that compared to the years of a John Hume or Gerry Fitt, or even a David Trimble, there is very little intercourse between English MPs and their elected colleagues in Northern Ireland.

Sinn Fein, of course, refuses to play a role as elected MPs to the House of Commons, which means that in the entire debate on Brexit the views of the Northern Irish nationalist community have never been heard in the Commons or on the airwaves. In the 'normal' general elections of 2010 and 2015, the DUP obtained just 25 per cent of votes cast. This went up in the Brexit general election of June 2017, as the identity politics unleashed by Brexit squeezed all other Northern Irish parties bar the two most extreme ones: the DUP and Sinn Fein. (One moderate and pro-EU Ulster unionist MP was returned but took little part in debates over Brexit.)

In England the Orange Card has emerged from the bottom of a dusty drawer to be played again as the hard-line Tory MPs whip up as much anti-Dublin feeling as they can, rather than give an inch on the utility of staying in the customs union. They dismiss the threat to the Good Friday Agreement as being of little consequence compared to the ideological purity of a full amputational Brexit.

HAS THE GOOD FRIDAY AGREEMENT OUTLIVED ITS USE?

For Owen Paterson, the former Northern Ireland secretary and a strident anti-European, the threat to the Good Friday Agreement is of little consequence. In a tweet he wrote: 'The collapse of power-sharing in Northern Ireland shows the Good Friday Agreement has outlived its use.'

The alliance between obscurantist ultra-protestant loyalist politics and English Toryism is not new. As the late nineteenth-century Tory prime minister, Lord Salisbury put it: 'I would no more give the vote to the Irish than to the hottentot.' That was a long time ago, but it is interesting to note that one survey showed a majority of practising Anglicans – once known as the Conservative Party at prayer – voted for Brexit. Boris Johnson displayed all the curled-lip condescension of English protestant Toryism when he mocked the sensitivities over ending the Good Friday Agreement by supporting the restoration of a physical customs border upon the UK's exit from the customs union and single market. Speaking to Tory activists in his campaign to replace Mrs May in Downing Street, Johnson said of the 300-mile-long border: 'It's so small and there are so few firms that actually use the border regularly, it's just beyond belief that we're allowing the tail to wag the dog in this way.'

In Ireland, memories of the Troubles are still strong. The conflict in part was caused by the existence of a border dividing the island of Ireland. Johnson's buffoonish remark was seen as just the latest in a long line of rabid anti-Irish insults by English politicians who have always treated the Irish with at best condescension, and often almost disdain.

The return of a divided Ireland with a border in the north to check that any agricultural products, goods or components are fully and legally in compliance with EU regulations is implicit in the version of Brexit that DUP Ulster unionist politicians and the Brexit Orange Conservatives in England want to see become operational.

A survey carried out by academics at Queen's University, Belfast and published in 2018 showed support for 'illegal or extreme protests against any North–South border checks, especially amongst Catholic and Sinn Fein voters'. If some kind of border control presence was re-established following Brexit, the survey reported:

1. Over one-fifth of Catholics (22%), and 36% of Catholics who vote for Sinn Féin, would support protestors blocking traffic.
2. Nearly one in ten Catholics (9%), and 15% of Catholics who vote for Sinn Féin, would support cameras being vandalized.
3. One in ten Sinn Féin supporters would support border infrastructure or installations being attacked.

To anyone who knows how tense politics in Northern Ireland is, this willing-ness to contemplate violence against any semblance of a return to the borders that existed prior to the peace settlement of the Good Friday Agreement of 1998 should come as no surprise.

One of the Catholics surveyed, aged between 18 and 29, a Remain voter in the ABC1 category (i.e. reasonably well-off), said that protests 'would start peaceful and then if they don't get anywhere they would just escalate it'. An older protestant in the C2DE social category (i.e. working-class) said: 'I think the ceasefire would go.' Half of those surveyed (49 per cent) said they would prefer a soft Brexit along the lines of the UK leaving the EU Treaty but remaining in the customs union and single market. But that was not acceptable to the Brexit wing of the Conservative Party headed by Boris Johnson and Michael Gove, as they insisted their interpretation of the Brexit referendum meant Britain would leave both the customs union and the single market. Jeremy Corbyn and Labour spokespersons also insisted the UK must quit the single market. Downing Street agreed as long ago as December 2017 that the EU and UK agreed:

> the achievements, benefits and commitments of the peace process will remain of paramount importance to peace, stability and reconciliation. They agree that the Good Friday or Belfast Agreement reached on 10 April 1998 by the United Kingdom Government, the Irish Government and the other participants in the multi-party negotiations (the '1998 Agreement') must be protected in all its parts.

Downing Street went further: 'The United Kingdom also recalls its commitment to the avoidance of a hard border, including any physical infrastructure or related checks and controls', and added:

> In the absence of agreed solutions, the United Kingdom will maintain full alignment with those rules of the Internal Market and the Customs Union which, now or in the future, support North–South cooperation, the all island economy and the protection of the 1998 Agreement.

In the best traditions of Perfidious Albion, Mrs May began trying to wriggle out of that agreement as soon as she could. She had little choice. Her majority in the Commons depended on the ten DUP MPs who made common cause with the extreme Brexit Tory MPs who wanted a full amputational Brexit with a complete rupture with the customs union and single market. The Labour Party went along with this line, as Jeremy Corbyn whipped Labour MPs to vote against proposals which had support from moderate Tory MPs to either stay in the customs union or seek a relationship between Britain and the EU similar to that enjoyed by non-EU members of the European Economic Area such as Norway or Lichtenstein.

To the dismay of Dublin and the disappointment of Brussels, the solid commitment of December 2017 to accept fully the rules of the customs union and single market (called 'internal market' in EU jargon) for the protection of the Good Friday Agreement and the all-island economy of Ireland became the subject of intense internal party controversy for Conservative MPs during 2018.

Theresa May tried to square the circle in her Chequers statement and subsequent white paper. Thanks to Labour MPs, she defeated efforts in the Commons which would have supported the December 2017 agreement. Instead Mrs May proposed an eccentric, untried and implausible scheme of British customs officials collecting EU tariffs on goods crossing from the UK into Ireland and vice versa and then generously forwarding the receipts to Brussels. It was all meant to happen thanks to computers or possibly drones and was described as 'magical thinking'.

In the end, the EU Brexit supremo, Michel Barnier told Mrs May's replacement Brexit minister, Dominic Raab at their first meeting:

> Maintaining control of our money, law and borders also applies to the EU customs policy. The EU cannot and will not delegate the application of its customs policy and rules, VAT and duty collection to a non-member who would not be subject to the EU governance structures. Any customs arrangements or customs union – and I have always said that the EU is open to a customs union – must respect this principle.

Raab is one of the hard ideological anti-Europeans who decided to establish his profile once elected as an MP in 2010 by non-stop denunciations of Europe. He is ideologically on the ultra-free market wing of the Tory Party and wants to see many public services handed over to profit-extracting private firms. He called for withdrawal from the European Convention on Human Rights and from the European Arrest Warrant System. These were cranky positions but played well to a certain hard right-wing grouping in English politics.

Raab is not associated with the Dublin-hating unionist protestant supremacists in Conservative politics and it could be argued that his ambition is greater than his ability. His short tenure as Brexit secretary ended after just a few months as he decided Mrs May's future was not guaranteed, but he failed to win much support in the Tory leadership contest to replace her. But Raab made his contribution to Brexit's collateral damage to Ireland, as once again the Orange Card is played in Tory politics.

Business in Ireland is moaning and complaining about Brexit but not campaigning. The thousands of Irish firms and scores of thousands of Irish citizens in leadership positions in England have not so far coalesced into an effective campaign to delay or suspend Brexit. Around 50,000 Irish citizens are directors of British companies and there were 1,200 Irish-owned businesses in Britain with a turnover of £32 billion in 2015. They, like their British counterparts in the Confederation of British Industry, the British Chambers of Commerce, the major City and industrial or trade federations, refused to campaign against or challenge Brexit. In the words of Yeats, 'the best lack conviction while the worst are full of passionate intensity'. On the subject of Ireland, political zeal trumps economic interest; the worst may yet happen and we may see a full amputational rupture between England and Europe. Ireland has solid support in Brussels and in the EU27 capitals, but throughout history not many Tories have over-worried about the impact of their ideology upon Ireland.

The pro-Brexit elites in England refused to contemplate how big the impact of Brexit will be on Ireland. For ultra-Irish nationalists now with a new party, Saoradh, which believes Sinn Fein has betrayed Ireland, the pleasure of taking a pot shot or exploding a bomb at a British customs checkpoint has never gone away. If customs officials are attacked, they have to be protected by the police and when the police are shot at, the army moves in. On the 102nd anniversary of the Irish independence uprising on Easter Sunday 1916, when Irish patriots were summarily put to death by a British Army general, thousands marched in Belfast behind a paramilitary 'honour guard' in combat fatigues.

The New IRA is also committed to using violence to bring about a united Ireland. They exploded a car bomb in Derry in January 2019 as Mrs May was insisting on ruling out Britain staying in the EU customs union, which obviates the need for a hard border in Ireland. No one was injured, but it was a sign that there are some in Ireland willing to take up the gun and the bomb just as the 1968 generation of anti-British Irishmen and women, for whom driving out any expression of British presence in Ireland is a passionate intensity of faith and feeling. If a border with customs posts and stop-and-searches of vehicles returns, it provides the very physical expression of the British state that offers a target to people of violence.

In April 2019, the New IRA killed a 29-year-old Belfast journalist, Lyra McKee, when they opened fire on security forces carrying out searches in Derry. There was an outpouring of anger and grief, as there was when similar atrocities took place in the 1970s or 1980s. For the New IRA, Brexit – and the hard Brexit approach of the DUP with its refusal to respect the clear view of the majority of voters in Northern Ireland that the UK should not leave Europe and the DUP political manoeuvring with Tory anti-European allies in the Westminster Parliament – had opened new possibilities for their ultimate goal of reuniting Ireland and ending the presence of the British state.

A New IRA spokesperson explained:

Brexit is an English construct devised by the Tory Party. There is an awakening of issues concerning the presence of the border now. Brexit has forced the IRA to refocus and has underlined how Ireland remains partitioned. It's put the border on the agenda again. We would be foolish not to capitalise on the fallout when it happens.

As English Tories were stating that the Good Friday Agreement was now out of date, big meetings were held in Cork and elsewhere calling for a renewed campaign for a United Ireland. Irish leaders of all parties and from sectors of the nation made protest after protest about the danger to Ireland of a return to a hard border upon Britain leaving the customs union. But for the ideological anti-Europeans, a full rupture with Europe was essential for their vision of what England had to become. Sacrificing Ireland for the English Tory elites was of no more consequence today than at any time in past history.

9

ALTERNATIVES TO EUROPE – THE ANGLOSPHERE? COMMONWEALTH?

Is there an alternative to Europe? A constant refrain over a number of years from those who oppose Britain working as a European nation and partner is that we have alternatives in the form of the Commonwealth or the English-speaking world. Cabinet ministers including Andrea Leadsom and Priti Patel, along with Jacob Rees-Mogg, published a report late in 2017 urging Britain to reject Europe and replace it with better economic ties with the Commonwealth. The report, co-authored by the pro-Brexit Tory MP James Cleverly and Tim Hewish, policy director of the Royal Commonwealth Society, called for a return to 'free trading principles' and accused Whitehall of neglecting the Commonwealth. Instead Britain post-Brexit should embrace 'the benefit of trading with nations that share a common language and culture'.

In one of his last statements before he resigned as foreign secretary, Boris Johnson rhapsodized about the Commonwealth in contrast to his hated European Union: 'We remember what happened in 1973, we made this historic choice to get into the Common Market. But we made a terrific mistake. We turned our backs on trade with Commonwealth countries [which] went off a cliff.' Now, he argued, the UK is ready to 'rekindle the lost relationships. I think we're going to have a lot of fun and it will be, I hope, a really exciting period for the Commonwealth'. In Buckingham Palace, Johnson is not recalled as a big Commonwealth fan. Courtiers recall his 2002 article in the *Daily Telegraph* in which he wrote that the Queen supported the

Commonwealth 'because it supplies her with regular cheering crowds of flag-waving piccaninnies'. The offensive term for a black child was also used by Enoch Powell in his 1968 'Rivers of Blood' speech, the moment when open racist contempt for immigrants living in Britain was introduced into mainstream British political discourse.

Invoking the Commonwealth against Europe is very old hat for anti-Europeans. In 1963, the Labour leader, Hugh Gaitskell cited the sacrifice of New Zealand soldiers in the First World War as a reason to reject joining the European Economic Community. Shortly before the Brexit vote, the anti-European Tory MP David Davis proclaimed: 'We must see Brexit as a great opportunity to refocus our economy on global, rather than regional, trade. This is an opportunity to renew our strong relationships with Commonwealth and Anglosphere countries.'

In her first trip to three African countries – South Africa, Kenya and Nigeria – in August 2018, Theresa May proclaimed that a radiant post-Brexit future beckoned in terms of trade and investment for Britain and Africa. She declared that, by 2022, 'I want the UK to be the G7's No. 1 investor in Africa'. The sound bite was meaningless. The combined GDP of South Africa, Nigeria and Kenya was about the same as the Netherlands and investment into these Commonwealth countries from the UK had fallen as a result of falling commodity prices and political corruption allegations, notably in South Africa. According to the Office for National Statistics, sub-Saharan Africa accounts for about 1.5 per cent of all Britain's trade compared to the EU, which accounts for around 45 per cent of UK trade. According to the UN's international trade body, UNCTAD, while investment from France into Africa increased from 2011 to 2016, investment from the UK went down. France's President Macron had made eleven visits to nine African countries since entering the Elysée Palace in May 2017. Mrs May had not been able to find time to go to Africa in her first two years in Downing Street.

Moreover, the EU and South Africa (along with five other nations in the South African Development Community [SADC]) had signed a free trade deal which came into force in 2016. Yet under this, South Africa had only taken up 44 per cent of an increased wine quota and 7.8 per cent of a new increased quota for sugar exports offered by the EU. Assuming the UK disconnects from such free trade agreements, London will have to start all over again negotiating a trade deal with South Africa.

The first EU–SADC agreement was initialled in 1999 and took fifteen years to be fleshed out into a full trade agreement. It is still hampered by non-tariff regulations, especially on food safety. There are zero tariffs for most agricultural imports from Africa into Europe, so when the UK minister Harriet Baldwin told the BBC that following Brexit 'there is scope for UK consumers and African exporters to benefit', she had been very badly briefed, as there is no advantage to any African country in the UK leaving the EU. Moreover, given the UK has said it will transpose these food and product safety rules into UK law, there will be no incentive for South Africa or other African nations to conclude any special deal with London just because Britain ceases to be an EU Treaty member.

But these practical points, made by trade economists and officials who are expert in negotiating trade, have no impact on the faith of those who believe that once delinked from Europe, a new chapter of English-speaking history opens.

In his 2014 book *The English and Their History*, Oxford University Professor Robert Tombs, a strong academic supporter of Brexit, wrote: 'Since the 18th century England, Ireland and Scotland have sent millions of migrants around the world creating what has been called the Anglosphere. Similar people, activities, associations and buildings took root in North America, South Africa and Australia.' In the first two Anglosphere nations he lists, it required a civil war and decades of racist oppression and conflict plus the emergence of two great leaders – Martin Luther King in America and Nelson Mandela in South Africa – before all US and South African citizens were able finally to bury the central political core of historic Anglosphere politics, namely white racial supremacy and second-class political status for non-white citizens in the Anglosphere. To be sure, it is history, but the colonization of nations such as Australia and New Zealand, let alone North America, was on the basis of ugly exterminationist or what today would be called ethnic cleansing methods. This is still within the living memory or family folklore of millions for whom the invocation of the Anglosphere or the glories of British rule recall humiliation, forced movement, or open conflict.

At times it is better to deal with the assertion of European or Anglosphere supremacy or contemporary relevance with a light touch. As South Africa's Archbishop Desmond Tutu liked to joke: 'When the white Europeans came to South Africa we had all the land and they had all the bibles. They said to us "Let us kneel and pray to God" and when we got up they had all the land and we had all the bibles!' When Gandhi was asked: 'What do you think of British civilization?' he replied: 'Ah, that would be a good idea.'

DEBATES ON BRITISH EMPIRE GO ON FOREVER

There can always be found professors in Oxford and Cambridge – two universities which benefitted the most from the wealth of English imperialism repatriated back to Britain – to defend the benefits of imperialism. They are thinner on the ground in Africa and Asia. The notion of a world filled by 'English-speaking peoples', as Churchill called his four volumes of Anglosphere promotion literature, still has a hold and resonates in British politics.

But are there reasonable alternatives to working in Europe? In Washington and most Commonwealth countries, the presence of the UK over the last four decades as a senior EC then EU nation has been seen as a positive. Despite President Trump's rambling tweets describing the EU as a 'foe', most serious American policy makers do not share President Putin's wish to see a Balkanization of Europe into competing rival nation states.

Over many years of visiting Washington from the Oval Office to Capitol Hill as a political activist, journalist, FCO minister, invited university or think-tank speaker, an MP on NATO or Council of Europe parliamentary delegations, I have never, ever met a single American involved in US foreign policy who has asked about or mentioned the Commonwealth. The same is true of any European capital city when I meet minsters, elected politicians, policy makers and opinion shapers.

It is not difficult to see why. The idea of the Commonwealth as an important political or economic institution does not exist outside a narrow London circle baby-boomer generation – those who have lived the same era as Prince Charles (born 1948) and Princess Anne (born 1950). The Commonwealth has given the British head of state, Queen Elizabeth II, a certain global standing and presence not commensurate with Britain's weight in the third decade of the twenty-first century, when southern powers such as China, Brazil and Nigeria will be the most populous states and, in China's case, the biggest economic power and soon a military giant. In her reign, the Queen has been to Canada, with a population of 27 million, twenty-five times and to India, the most populous nation on earth with its 1.37 billion citizens, just three times.

There is a large Indian diaspora in Britain, but they are British first, Hindu, Sikh or Muslim second, and feel no more connected to India than the Tory politician Michael Howard feels connected to Romania, the home-land of his parents, or Sadiq Khan, the mayor of London and Sajid Javid, the home secretary feel Pakistani because their fathers emigrated from Pakistan. India is the biggest member of the Commonwealth, but Britain puts many obstacles in the way of Indian citizens coming to work, study, live or do busi-ness in Britain in comparison to the easy access British citizens have to living or working in Europe under EU Treaty obligations.

In no way can the Commonwealth be compared to the European Union or be seen as a replacement. There are fifty-three Commonwealth member states, nearly twice the number of EU member states. There are 2.4 billion Commonwealth citizens – five times the size of the EU27. Commonwealth countries vary greatly in size: India accounts for over half of the Commonwealth's population with a population of 1.34 billion; two Commonwealth members, Tuvalu and Nauru, have only 10,000 citizens; and five Commonwealth coun-tries have a population of under 1 million. In 2019, Australia and Singapore have a GDP per capita of over $55,000 while six Commonwealth countries have a GDP per capita of less than $1,000.

Most Commonwealth countries are former British colonies, though none other than the EU member states of Malta and Cyprus have the common rights to live, work or retire in Britain that all British citizens enjoy in the European Union. A British citizen can travel on a UK passport to Canada without a visa, but Australia demands payment of US$99 for a tourist visa. British citizens who want to work in Commonwealth countries or live or retire in one of them have to go through cumbersome immigration bureau-cracy. It is not possible to simply do business in any Commonwealth country (other than Malta and Cyprus) without going through national, state or local government formalities.

In 2016, UK exports to the Commonwealth were worth £48.5 billion; British imports from the Commonwealth were £45.9 billion. The UK had a trade surplus with the Commonwealth of £2.6 billion – a deficit in goods was more than offset by a surplus in services. The entire Commonwealth accounted for 8.9 per cent of UK exports in 2016. This is about the same as UK exports to Germany. UK imports from the Commonwealth are about the same as the imports from China. Overall trade between the UK and the Commonwealth has declined since 2011. UK exports to Ireland are worth £27 billion – more than half the total exports to all of the Commonwealth. Two EU member states in the Commonwealth, Cyprus and Malta, with a combined population of 1.6 million, take more UK exports than New Zealand, Malaysia and Nigeria, with a combined population of 221.8 million. The main demand from Commonwealth states such as India is for visa-free access to the UK for 1.4 billion Indian Commonwealth citizens.

So it is unlikely that the Commonwealth can in any serious fashion replace the EU in terms of trade and economic relations and denies British citizens the rights they enjoy in Europe of living, working or retiring. But the Commonwealth is far removed from the core British values that Europe defends.

JUDICIAL KILLINGS – A COMMONWEALTH SPECIALITY

In 2017, the United Nations secretary-general, Ban Ki-moon declared: 'The death penalty has no place in the 21st century.' And yet thirty-three Commonwealth countries keep capital punishment on their statutes. The Commonwealth's biggest countries in terms of population – India, Pakistan, Nigeria and Bangladesh – have all hanged prisoners in recent years.

In contrast, the European Convention on Human Rights was amended in 1983 with a protocol barring the death penalty. Abolition of the death penalty is a prerequisite for membership in the Council of Europe, so Russia had to declare a moratorium on capital punishment when it joined the Council of Europe in 1996. The EU's Charter of Fundamental Rights also bans capital punishment.

Thirty-six of the Commonwealth's fifty-three member states have ugly laws on their statute books that deny gay and lesbian people core human rights. In 2019 the Commonwealth member state of Brunei announced it would bring in Islamist sharia law to put homosexuals to death by lapidation – the posh word for stoning to death. In Bangladesh, Barbados, Guyana, Pakistan, Sierra Leone, Tanzania and Uganda there is a maximum sentence of life imprisonment for homosexuality. Malaysia adds its own homophobic twist, as LGBT Malaysians can be flogged and face up to twenty years' imprisonment.

From the first stirrings of European partnership and common laws and frontier opening measures, those suspicious of Europe have invoked the Commonwealth as an alternative. Part of this is kith-and-kin nostalgia and Britain draws status from the Commonwealth just as France does from the *Francophonie* – the association of French-speaking former French colonies. But we should remind ourselves again of what the US secretary of state, Dean Acheson said in 1962 – that Britain's 'attempt to play a separate power role, that is a role apart from Europe, a role based primarily on a "special relationship" with the United States, a role based on being head of the Commonwealth' is 'about played out'. Nearly sixty years later those words ring more true than ever. In fact, most Commonwealth countries welcomed Britain being an important EU player with a voice, vote and many officials working in Brussels. Membership of the EU and the Commonwealth complement each other. By leaving Europe, Britain is weakening the Commonwealth, which is not really an alternative to the EU. But is the Anglosphere?

There are 360 million people out of the world's total population of 7.5 billion who have English as a first language. But the countries they live in have little in common. There have always been dreamers who believe that somehow the world could be reshaped into an Anglosphere versus the rest. As Cecil Rhodes, who used military force to colonize parts of southern Africa to further his economic empire, put it:

The idea gleaming and dancing before one's eyes like a will-of-the-wisp at last frames itself into a plan . . . the furtherance of the British Empire and the bringing of the whole uncivilised world under British rule for the recovery of the United States, for the making of the Anglo-Saxon race but one Empire.

Race. Empire. Anglo-Saxon. United States. At about the same time, the Conservative politician Joseph Chamberlain was dreaming up his proposal for protectionist economics based on so-called imperial preference. Anglosphere economics only work on the basis of rejecting free trade. Chamberlain's economics led Winston Churchill and other Tory MPs at the beginning of the twentieth century to cross the floor to join the Liberal Party, which was committed to free trade. In 1920, Britain and Australia opposed clauses in the covenant of the League of Nations that outlawed racial discrimination, which Japan wanted to see inserted.

Churchill, of course, vehemently opposed independence for India and described Mahatma Gandhi as 'nauseating' and a 'half-naked fakir'. In 1943, as Britain's policy of hoarding rice and grain helped lead to the death of up to three million Bengalis in India, Churchill scribbled on a letter sent to the Viceroy of India, Lord Wavell: 'Why hasn't Gandhi died yet?'

RACE, EMPIRE AND THE ANGLOSPHERE

The Anglosphere had too many internal contradictions ever to take off. The most important was the founding of the United States of America as an anti-British entity. Kipling may have asked America to pick up 'the white man's burden', but throughout its history the US has been at odds with the United Kingdom, save for a brief period 1942–45 when they were allies to defeat Nazi Germany. It was Russian men and material that defeated the Wehrmacht. Russia suffered more than ten million military casualties compared to 387,000 for Britain and 407,300 for America.

As soon as the war was over, Washington turned the screws on London, imposing draconian economic policies and lending support to any British colony seeking independence. The US refused to support the 1945 Labour government policy of restricting immigration to Palestine, leading to the ugly antisemitic remark of the British foreign secretary, Ernest Bevin that the only reason the US supported the resettlement of Holocaust survivors in what was to become Israel was because 'they did not want too many Jews in New York'. America refused to share its nuclear weapons secrets with Britain, who went on alone to build an atomic bomb. In 1956, President Eisenhower called up the British prime minister, Anthony Eden to ask 'Are you mad, Anthony?' following the invasion of Egypt at Suez. Eisenhower then threatened to cut oil and other economic support for Britain unless Eden surrendered to the Egyptian leader, Nasser. The idea of an Anglosphere entente after 1945 was a chimera.

Harold Wilson refused President Lyndon Johnson's request to send a token number of British soldiers to fight with the US Army in Vietnam in the

1960s and when finally there was full-scale UK–US cooperation in the Iraq conflict in 2003, it turned into a geopolitical disaster for both countries. Every US president from Truman onwards until the arrival of Donald Trump supported European integration and construction. American banks welcomed Mrs Thatcher's abolition of national sovereignty vetoes to create the EU single market in the 1980s and moved en masse to the City to take advantage of selling into the EU's borderless single market. Mrs May insisted that Brexit would lead to a shining new future for what she called 'Global Britain' and what cynics in Whitehall called 'Empire 2.0'. The idea was rubbished in America and Australia.

In 1971 the historian Robert Conquest opposed British entry into Europe. He argued in *Encounter*:

> the direction in which Britain should seek closer ties is within its own tradition of language, laws and politics; that is, with the United States, Canada, Australia, New Zealand, Ireland and the Caribbean Commonwealth countries . . . I would also argue that a United Europe without us would be stronger and safer under the protection of a much larger and more powerful 'Anglo-Saxon' union.

Today's Anglosphere advocates have at least shed the arrogance of the earlier generation of anti-European right-wing intellectuals such as Conquest that the European Union would be much better off under the protective umbrella of an English-speaking global union, but the Anglosphere dream lives on. During the Labour government 1997–2010, many Tories who later became prominent in the Brexit campaign went regularly to the US to meet with right-wing Americans. They wrote in defence of British imperialism. Historian commentators such as Andrew Roberts and Niall Ferguson painted a picture of a Britain separated from Europe and relinked to America and English-speaking countries. They pointed to intelligence cooperation between the US, UK, Australia, Canada and New Zealand – the 'Five Eyes' – but the most useful contribution in combatting terrorism was when London justice officials used the European Arrest Warrant to bring back quickly from Rome one of the terrorists accused of the London Islamist terror bombings in July 2005.

Leading anti-Europeanists such as Michael Gove and David Davis painted a glowing picture of a post-EU Anglosphere for Britain. Davis said a Brexit vote would be 'an opportunity to renew our strong relationships with Commonwealth and Anglosphere countries. We share history, culture and language. We have family ties. The usual barriers to trade are largely absent.' Gove burbled about Britain having 'exported to nations like the US, India . . . a system of democratic self-government which has brought prosperity and peace to millions'. The response of the Australian government could not be more clear. In February 2019, Australia ordered twelve submarines for its navy. Did Anglosphere loyalties mean Australian ministers turned to Britain? The submarines, at a cost of 34 million euros, were built in and bought from France.

As Professors Michael Kenny and Nick Pearce conclude in their survey of *The Anglosphere in British Politics*, the hunt for an alternative to working in partnership with Europe cannot be dismissed too easily. Britain is still haunted by the Acheson question as to its role and identity. The original Anglosphere project – and arguably the only one to have worked well – is indeed the United Kingdom itself, with its four different nations and a global megalopolis in London. Britain has largely succeeded in integrating new citizens coming from different parts of the world with different cultures and different religious or racial backgrounds. Until the launch of the great anti-European campaign at the beginning of the twenty-first century, Britain was also home to many different European communities who lived harmoniously with British-born citizens. Then UKIP, the BNP, the *Daily Mail, Sun* and *Daily Telegraph* and other politicians seeking to win votes decided to depict European citizens in Britain as unwanted invaders.

Professors Kenny and Pearce are surely right that other countries in the so-called Anglosphere of nations around the world where English is spoken 'show no serious inclination to join the UK in forging new political and economic alliances'. Britain can turn its back on Europe, but the idea that there is a twenty-first-century English-speaking world in which we can lead and prosper is just another Brexit myth.

10

WHERE IS THE OPPOSITION TO BREXIT? THE SOLUTIONIST DEAD-END

If before the Brexit referendum there was a comfortable assumption that Leave could not win, in its aftermath there was a new complacency that the result could be easily overturned.

Initially, the sense of shock was palpable. 'You were only supposed to blow the bloody doors off!' the *Daily Mail* columnist Sarah Vine told her husband, the arch-Europhobe Conservative MP Michael Gove. Once the blood-letting over who would become the new prime minister ended and Mrs May incorporated a number of devout anti-Europeans into her cabinet, there was uncertainty about how to react.

But from all sides came protests and insistence that Brexit would be stopped, reversed, overcome. Politicians took to the airwaves or wrote for newspaper comment columns protesting about the iniquities of Brexit. Lawyers threatened all sorts of legal cases, going up to the highest courts in the land, the very highest.

Political grandees such as Ken Clark, Nick Clegg and any number of former Labour ministers fulminated. University vice chancellors insisted Brexit would be a disaster. Some economic actors – businesses – protested.

A march was held in London with furious denunciations by Alastair Campbell at a rally outside Parliament. Prominent journalists such as Henry Porter and Hugo Dixon organized meetings or, in Dixon's case, a daily online bulletin, *InFacts*, pointing out in dry, factual language the consequences of Brexit.

Membership of the pro-European Movement soared. Almost every other day there was a meeting or debate somewhere in England in which Brexit was denounced. Meetings filled civic halls and marches against Brexit went through city centres.

Yet as the months went by, all these attacks on Brexit appeared to have little effect. Why was this? The answer lay in the collective funk, not to say cowardice of the political class in Britain. One well-known Conservative MP, an ex-military man, popular in the Tory Party and liked in the House of Commons, told me in March 2019: 'I voted Leave. I support Brexit. I have always been critical of the EU. But Brexit is destroying my party and doing huge damage to the country. To be honest, if I woke up one morning, put on the BBC and heard the whole thing had been called off, no one would be more happy.' But, of course, my former parliamentary friend, while he might share his despair with me as an ex-MP, was never going to say anything to his party activists in his constituency or tell the *Daily Telegraph* or *Daily Mail* that it was time to bring Brexit to an end.

Labour MPs and trade union leaders publicly disagreed with each other. There was no core message from the Labour leadership as shadow cabinet ministers appeared confused and incoherent on television and radio. In the immediate aftermath of the 2016 vote it seemed as if the nation was in shock. All those who had complacently agreed with David Cameron that Brexit could not happen seemed speechless. There were many instant, spontaneous responses. Four million signed an e-petition to Parliament demanding a rerun of the referendum. In many countries it takes far fewer citizens to sign their names asking for a referendum – 100,000 in Switzerland or 50,000 in Denmark – but the four million signatories in Britain were ignored.

Two giant marches took place: one in October 2018 with 700,000 participants; and one in March 2019, when a million anti-Brexit protestors demanding a new referendum, dubbed a People's Vote, marched from Hyde Park to Parliament in one of the biggest-ever peaceful protests in post-war Britain. A new newspaper was launched called the *New European*, which bucked the trend that has seen news journalism go online and print media decline. The *New European* was lively and well written, produced by experienced professional journalists. The paper was sold in WH Smith and supermarkets and is still going strong three years after the vote.

For the anti-Europeans the referendum result could not be challenged. It was sacred, the holiest of holy events in the history of British democracy. 'The people have spoken', intoned David Dimbleby on BBC Television.

Eight anti-Brexit outfits took office space in Millbank Tower, close to Parliament and from where the Labour Party planned its election victory in 1997. Open Britain has 560,000 Facebook followers, which seems impressive, but is little more than 1 per cent of the UK electorate. The venerable European Movement, first set up when Winston Churchill launched the campaign for European unity, has significantly increased the number of branches, with 150 now in operation. They set up stalls in city and town centres to hand out anti-Brexit leaflets. Most of their membership and participants in meetings are closer in age to the European Movement's chair, the former Tory minister Stephen Dorrell (born 1952), and while there is evidence that students and young professionals are dismayed by Brexit, there has not really been a movement of pro-European youngsters using modern messaging of events, witty interventions on social media, or rock concerts to mobilize against Brexit.

EX PMs AND PARTY LEADERS RAIL AGAINST BREXIT – BUT WHO LISTENS?

The voices against Brexit include Tony Blair, Nick Clegg and Sir John Major. They are articulate, as one might expect from politicians who led their parties and rose to high government office. But they all come with major baggage. In Sir John Major's case, his enthusiastic endorsement in 2013 for David Cameron's proposed Brexit referendum opened the way to Conservative establishment support of a risky populist plebiscite which destroyed Cameron. Moreover, Major was seen as an unimpressive, poor prime minister after the glory years – in the eyes of the British right – of Margaret Thatcher. His weak and ineffectual inability to stand up to the mass slaughters and ethnic cleansing by Serbs in Sarajevo, Kosovo and above all Srebrenica compared unfavourably with his predecessor's leadership in the Falklands and initially against Saddam Hussein's invasion of Kuwait. Mrs Thatcher won three elections and left office with seven more Tory years in power ahead. Sir John Major was defeated by Labour in one of the most humiliating defeats in Conservative Party history, which ushered in thirteen years of Labour government.

Tony Blair came close to admitting that the failure of western policy in Iraq after the easy invasion and toppling of Saddam Hussein meant that the audience for his views on Brexit was limited. The invasion of Iraq was supported by Boris Johnson and Theresa May. Blair thought Saddam Hussein was another Slobodan Milosevic and using military force, which had stopped Milosevic's mass murder of European Muslims in Bosnia and Kosovo, would work in Iraq. He was wrong, but so too was David Cameron, who also supported use of military force to remove Colonel Gaddafi in Libya and Bashar al-Assad in Syria. Destroying the state structures in Iraq, Libya and Syria opened the way to a war of all and against all. Millions of Arab Muslim refugees, including some Islamist jihadi terrorists, poured out of these war-destroyed states and millions sought to escape oppression and poverty in sub-Saharan Africa through the 1,900 km breach in the southern Mediterranean or North Africa – security previously constituted by a properly controlled Libyan frontier.

Blair also made few friends in his party by the manner in which he made money after leaving office in 2007. The former Labour leader's business profile since stepping down as prime minister has earned him millions, much of which has been used to support his progressive centre-left research institute and charitable work. But Blair has been unable to recover from the after-effects of the Iraq invasion, just as Cameron will be remembered, other than for Brexit, as the prime minister who supported the destruction of the state of Libya, with consequences in terms of mass refugee and immigrant flows across the Mediterranean. Cameron has said nothing about Brexit in the three years since he lost the referendum he foolishly called and which he allowed to take place with none of the usual democratic safeguards when referendums are held.

Sir Nick Clegg will never be forgiven by millions of millennials for tripling student fees, leaving a whole generation with decades-worth of debt. He took a strong, confident Liberal Democratic party with scores of MPs and a strong presence in local government and made it into a poodle of the austerity and right-wing politics of David Cameron, George Osborne and Theresa May. In 2015, voters punished Clegg by voting him and most Lib Dem MPs out of the Commons. In European Parliament elections in 2019 the Lib

Dems had some success, but so did the Greens in 1989. A surge of protest votes in the low turnout of a European Parliament election rarely translates into seats in the Commons. It will take years for the Lib Dems to get back to their previous status when Clegg was elected leader in 2005. He drew the obvious conclusion that his career in British public life was over when at the end of 2018 he accepted a multi-million-dollar package to be a lobbyist for Facebook, the social media platform which has been the vector of non-stop pro-Brexit propaganda, often supported by foreign money.

Clegg's successor as Lib Dem party leader was Tim Farron, a little-known Cumbrian MP who got lost in the thickets of gay rights because, as an evangelical Christian, his church believed homosexuality to be a sin. His successor, in turn, was Sir Vince Cable, born in 1943 but sometimes looking older than his years, who had also been associated with the austerity politics of the 2010–15 government, the massive hike in student fees, and the failure of the Lib Dems in coalition to protest against David Cameron's decision to hold the Brexit plebiscite. He announced his main task was to convert the Liberal Democrats from a party with seats in Parliament into a nebulous movement. He, in turn, was replaced by Jo Swinson.

At times, it seemed as if the Lib Dems hoped to use the anti-Brexit campaign as a means to regain political strength and support. The director of the anti-Brexit campaign, James McGrory, a creative and energetic political operative, remained an adviser to Sir Nick Clegg until the latter's disappearance into Silicon Valley. At many of the European Movement and other anti-Brexit events, street stalls, social media campaigns or marches, Lib Dem activists were more widely represented than either Labour or Tory party members.

The Scottish National Party was anti-Brexit. However, its relentless focus on using Brexit as a reason to break up the United Kingdom played to its core belief base, but meant the rest of Britain took little interest in the admonitions against Brexit of SNP leaders Nicola Sturgeon and Alex Salmond. When Ms Sturgeon endorsed the action of Scottish government bureaucrats against Salmond over allegations about his behaviour when first minister, the two most prominent Scottish politicians this century found themselves publicly intertwined in a bitter personal dispute. Their chances of making an impact on the national Brexit debate became nugatory. Moreover, there was something incoherent about Nicola Sturgeon denouncing the break-up of the union with Europe and in her second breath demanding the break-up of Scotland's union with the other nations of the United Kingdom. EU good but UK bad rang Orwellian. The Welsh nationalists and the greens also opposed Brexit but had little sway.

BREXIT – A COUNTRY FOR OLD MEN

Normally, when a major political convulsion grips a nation, it throws up new political figures. But the cast list of the Brexit debates on television involved, in addition to Vince Cable (75), Kenneth Clarke (78), Nigel Lawson (86), Michael Heseltine (86), Norman Lamont (76), Michael Howard (77) and Sir John Major (75). Truly Brexit was a country for old men.

John Kerr, the legendary Foreign Office diplomat – who was UK ambassador to the EU, then the US, and finally head of the Foreign Office where he was the drafter of the EU constitutional treaty in 2004 and then its bastard offspring, the Lisbon Treaty, with its Article 50 language – describes himself, aged 76, fellow ex-diplomat peers who oppose Brexit such as David Hannay (82) and other peers such as the former Labour leader, Neil Kinnock (76), or Tory grandees such as Chris Patten (74) as a 'revolution led by Zimmer frames' in the House of Lords.

At times it seemed as if the charge against Brexit was a matter reserved for the House of Lords. Lords Adonis, Malloch-Brown, Falconer, Mandelson and others became the spokespersons against Brexit. They were articulate and fluent but, other than Peter Mandelson, suffered from the problem of never having been elected to anything and being very much part of a London elite network disconnected from provincial, working-class, insecure England beyond the M25.

The real question is: why was it so hard for 650 MPs and the two main political parties to come to terms with Brexit? For the Conservative Party, there was a dialectic between the new leader, Theresa May and her party. She promoted a succession of high-profile anti-Europeans to the cabinet, both immediately after the referendum and then after the 2017 general election. Was she giving the 1990s generation of Tory MPs opposed to the European Union, including Boris Johnson and David Davis, enough rope so that either they demonstrated Brexit would work to Britain's benefit or, if not, they could be dismissed? Certainly, the second anniversary of the Brexit vote came and went and there was no clarity or sense of policy and purpose from the government.

The third anniversary came amid the Conservative Party beauty contest to choose a leader and new prime minister. The electorate were the paid-up rank-and-file members of the Conservative Party. No one in the party could or would produce an independently audited list of these men and women who would decide the next prime minister. Figures ranged from 70,000 to 160,000, but there was no independent verification of these numbers. I wrote to the UK Electoral Commission asking about the size of Conservative Party membership, its age, and how many had joined in recent months from other parties. The Commission wrote back to say they had no such data about the men and women who would impose Britain's next prime minister on the country. I asked the Electoral Commission to provide me, for the purposes of this book, with an up-to-date number for Tory Party membership. They said no one knew the figure. Studies of the Tory Party membership suggested a predominately elderly profile of mainly white men and women well past retirement age. They were thought to be largely anti-European, with a third wanting to see capital punishment restored.

The Brexit debate inside the Conservative Party was dominated by a well-organized and well-financed group of anti-EU MPs. They were countered by the lively pro-European Tory MP Anna Soubry, a former regional TV journalist, who was fluent and feisty, but not a heavyweight inside her party. She eventually left to join the short-lived Change UK group of MPs. Other Tory MPs who made no secret, in private conversations with me, of their disdain for Brexit, such as Claire Perry or Mark Field, were promoted as ministers and had to toe the official Theresa May line that Brexit would be a success. Long-serving Tory MPs including Sir Nicholas Soames and Caroline Spelman were aghast at the idea of Brexit, but kept their counsel. Soames supported Jeremy Hunt, but Hunt was as keen on Brexit as Boris Johnson. Very few Tory MPs were willing to say in public what they freely admitted in private – that Brexit under any form was bad for Britain.

It is often said that the Conservatives' secret weapon is loyalty. After the shock result of the 2017 general election, the majority of Tory MPs who had voted Remain just huddled together and said as little as possible. Braver ones such as Dominic Grieve, Philip Lee, the Welsh Tory MP Guto Bebb and

Antoinette Sandbach spoke out against Brexit or supported a new vote, but they were outriders. Boris Johnson's brother, Jo, a junior minister, hit the headlines by resigning in protest at the sheer vacuity of Mrs May's deal and urged a new referendum. He won his weekend of headlines and prime time TV interviews, but at the end of 2018 the number of Tory MPs supporting a new referendum was not in double figures.

For Brendan Donnelly, a former Tory MEP and one of the best thinkers in his party on Europe,

> the governing Conservative Party is irredeemably split on the form that Brexit should take [between] those who believe that leaving without an agreement is at worst a manageable inconvenience; and those who have considerable doubts about the whole Brexit project but need to be reassured that the government is aware of the particular danger of leaving the EU in an abrupt and chaotic fashion.

He goes on to argue:

> As far as European policy is concerned, the Conservatives have lost any sense of shared political identity that would lead either to self-discipline or central sanctions accepted as legitimate in defence of a common project . . . the bitter conflict currently lacerating the Conservative Party . . . is a conflict between the traditional, pragmatic and cautious party of Philip Hammond and perhaps by inclination Mrs. May and the ideologically driven, iconoclastic and reckless party of Boris Johnson and Jacob Rees-Mogg.

All these are valid points, but the implication that the Tories have to split to find a way out of Brexit goes against three centuries of relative Tory unity as a coalition of different interests that at times can be at odds with itself – think free trade in the nineteenth century, Ireland, decolonization, and today Europe – but which ultimately wants to stay in power as the ultimate aim of political organization. Had Britain an electoral system based on proportional representation, there is no doubt that there would be more than one centre-right conservative party, just as there would probably be more than one left-leaning party. There can be splits away from parties, like the Unionists leaving the

Liberal Party at the end of the nineteenth century to oppose home rule for Ireland, or the Social Democratic Party breakaway from Labour after 1981. Yet the obligation to compose differences and win elections under Britain's majoritarian first-past-the-post system of voting is a powerful glue that holds parties together just as it does in the United States, where to hold any elected office from town rat-catcher to president requires standing on a party ticket. Unlike snakes shedding dead skin, political parties cannot slough off past identities even if more likely to lose than win elections.

So the Brexiternity we now face will undoubtedly pose serious problems for the Tories. It means that the governing Conservative Party has been out of play as a united force on Brexit since June 2016. Unlike the period from 1945 to 1985 when the Tories were relatively united on Europe and thus able to dictate and control the direction of travel of the UK's policy in relation to the continent, Mrs May had to deal with a weak, divided party base and has been unable to find any language or promote a new generation of Tory MPs willing to defend British interests on the question of Europe. In the end she threw in the towel as the fundamentalist ultras in the Tory Party refused to listen to her or follow where she wanted to go.

LABOUR SPLIT JUST AS MUCH AS TORIES

But what of Labour? In the two years following Brexit, the party settled into a huddled down, defensive posture, just hoping the Conservative divisions would be enough to damage the party and even bring about a new general election in which Labour would do well. The central problem remained that the two key Labour figures, the leader Jeremy Corbyn and shadow chancellor John McDonnell, had grown up as politicians in an age when the Labour left was vehemently anti-European. McDonnell told the *New Statesman* that the politician he most admired was Tony Benn, who spent the last thirty years of his career in Parliament denouncing Europe. Corbyn has voted against every EU treaty since entering the Commons in 1983. He learnt Spanish following two marriages to Latin American women and is knowledgeable about politics in Venezuela, Nicaragua, Bolivia, Colombia and Mexico, but indifferent to politics in Spain. His internationalism is about Palestine or the Polisario movement in the Sahara. On European socialism and progressive politics he had little to say. He looked to hard left parties in Europe like *Die Linke* in Germany or Jean-Luc Mélenchon's *La France Insoumise* in France. Both parties were in strident opposition to Labour's sister parties on the continent.

In December 2018, at a leaders' conference in Lisbon of the Party of European Socialists, the pan-EU federation of all democratic left parties in Europe, I witnessed first-hand the puzzlement of EU social democratic and socialist prime ministers as they tried to work out who Corbyn was and what he stood for. The European left does not quite know what to make of the Labour leader. His Bernie Sanders-type speeches denouncing austerity, cuts in the public realm and Trump go down well. People are confused, however, by his barely disguised indifference to supporting a social democratic Europe as a bulwark against the fused communist-capitalism of China, the 'America first' nationalism and protectionism of Trump, and the paring away of media and other core political freedoms in Russia, east Europe or South America.

Corbyn has often repeated his mantra that the Brexit decision of June 2016 could not be challenged. He repeated his call for Theresa May to move aside and let Labour negotiate a better, fairer Brexit deal but one which would still repudiate the EU's core values and principles, notably on the so-called four indivisible freedoms of movement: of capital, goods, services and labour. Corbyn attacked the EU as being responsible for Brexit, saying: 'EU support for austerity and failed neoliberal policies have caused serious hardship for working people across Europe' and the EU had 'damaged the credibility of European social democratic parties and played a significant role in the vote for Brexit'. These are the tired clichés than can be read in any right-wing anti-European article in the *Daily Mail* or *Daily Telegraph*.

Most European leaders think it was a fifteen-year-long right-wing xenophobic campaign led by senior Tories, UKIP, Rupert Murdoch, the Europhobe press like the *Sun* or *Daily Telegraph*, as well as crude quasi-racist anti-immigrant demagogy that led to Brexit. But now the Labour leader was blaming Europe. When he spoke to the European socialists late in 2018, Corbyn was in Portugal, a country run by a socialist-led party. Portugal was one of the hardest hit by the financial crash, but instead of adopting the flamboyant anti-European rhetoric of Yanis Varoufakis in Greece, the Portuguese left worked seriously and professionally with EU officials to get the economy back on its feet.

It was not the EU but northern European countries, including key EU member states led by social democratic leaders in power or in coalition, that insisted on financial orthodoxy. Corbyn's EU-bashing sounded little different from right-wing criticisms of Europe. There was no criticism from Corbyn of right-wing populism and identity politics. No criticism of Boris Johnson, Steve Bannon, Marine le Pen, Matteo Salvini, or any of the other new hard right politics like the AfD in Germany or VOX in Spain that got an immense boost from Brexit. No sense that Labour considered the increasing evidence of corrupt and criminal financing from outside the UK that helped win Brexit as worthy of condemnation. Instead Corbyn said: 'If the European political establishment carries on with business as usual, the fake populists of the far right will fill the vacuum. European socialists have to fight for a different kind of Europe.'

This was a reflection of the Labour leader's long-held belief since the 1970s that Europe was a problem, not an answer. European socialists are well aware that Corbyn has voted against every EU treaty since he was elected as an MP. There was no acknowledgement that Brexit was a major foreign policy win for President Trump, who calls the EU 'a foe', and President Putin, whose top-line foreign policy goal is to see Europe revert to disaggregated bickering nation states that Russia can deal with one by one.

Corbyn had no namecheck for Frans Timmermans, the thoughtful Dutch Labour politician, a vice president of the European Commission, who was chosen at the Party of European Socialists' 2019 conference to be the European left's lead candidate to be Commission president in the European Parliament election, nor any words of praise for the much-admired contribution of British MEPs to the centre left's combined work in the European Parliament.

While never an intellectual, Corbyn is not stupid. Having seen the damage caused by Labour's espousal of Brexit in its general election manifesto in 1983 when the party called for a negotiated withdrawal from the European Community, he knew that openly promoting separation from Europe was not a vote-winner for Labour. The Labour Party had a solid contingent of anti-European MPs whose doyen was the left-wing coal miner Dennis Skinner (87). His distaste for what he always described in snarling terms as the 'Common Market' as he denounced any and all EU measures in the Commons was passionate. I examined all the interventions Corbyn made

in the Commons on the EU between 2005 and his election as leader of the
Labour Party in 2015. He never took part in general EU debates which
allowed those hostile to the EU from both Tory and Labour benches to raise
demands for a referendum to quit Europe or to attack the UK's membership
of the EU. Corbyn asked focused questions of ministers about what the EU
was doing on issues and causes like Palestine, global warming, support for
refugees, or peace and disarmament. He was indifferent to the issues that
motivated other Labour MPs hostile to Europe – sovereignty, the euro, the
claimed power of Brussels officials – and as an open border internationalist
representing a constituency in north London encompassing many different
non-English communities, he had no problem with freedom of movement.

In the referendum campaign Corbyn endorsed Remain. I went to one
anti-Brexit campaigning session in London, but his speech focused on air
quality in London and he found no strong words to call on Labour supporters to vote positively against Brexit. In the 2018 local government elections
in London, I told Corbyn at a Labour campaign meeting he could galvanize
support in London with its massive pro-European voter base if he opposed
Brexit. He took no notice and Brexit and its impact on London was not a
theme in the election campaign. In consequence, Labour failed to gain
control of a single council in London. Unlike the previous four Labour
leaders – John Smith, Tony Blair, Gordon Brown and Ed Miliband – who
were at ease in discussing Europe and could see the advantages of their
country staying engaged in partnership with other European nations, Corbyn
had never in three and half decades of Commons membership shown any
interest in finding reasons to be positive about Europe.

Corbyn's shadow ministers were in permanent disarray. They contradicted
each other on how to interpret Brexit, on whether the UK might stay fully in
the customs union without the endless caveats enumerated by Corbyn, and
the extent of the immigration control bureaucracy that would have to be set
up, as no shadow cabinet minister was prepared to challenge the view that
freedom of movement had to end, which would mean telling the EU27
member states that Labour Britain could not remain even in an EEA relationship with the EU.

Labour announced tests that the EU27 would have to pass before a
Labour government would deign to continue a relationship between the UK
and the EU. The key test about any future arrangement with the EU was:

'Does it deliver "the exact same benefits" as we currently have as members of the single market and the customs union?' The sheer incoherence of Labour's proposition that the UK had to enjoy 100 per cent of the benefits of single market and customs union membership while simultaneously leaving both arrangements was baffling to most sensible people – rather like saying one could enjoy exactly the same satisfaction from sex or swimming while still remaining fully clothed.

Other tests Labour proposed to apply in judging any final Brexit deal included 'Does it defend rights and protections and prevent a race to the bottom?' and 'Does it deliver for all regions and nations of the UK?' This is the kind of language worthy of one of the spoof Ladybird books that have become popular. Alastair Campbell scathingly pointed out that none of the proposed deals can deliver 'the exact same benefits' as existing membership of the single market and customs union; that an attack on social regulations and a race to the bottom was precisely what neo-liberal Brexiters said should happen; and the government's own assessment papers showed that certain regions of the UK, notably in the north-east, would be very hard hit by Brexit. Labour's shadow trade secretary, Barry Gardiner summed up in one word his view on Labour's six Brexit tests by saying they were 'Bollocks'.

Gardiner was no more coherent himself, writing in the *Guardian* to declare that Labour could not accept staying in the customs union, only to find that Corbyn changed that line shortly after to declare Labour was in favour of a customs union with the EU post-Brexit. This was in contrast to Mrs May's adamantine refusal of such an arrangement, which would have soothed some business worries and concerns in Dublin about a return to the reintroduction of a border in Ireland to enact customs checks on meat, milk and other goods passing between the UK's six Ulster countries in the north-east of Ireland and the Republic of Ireland.

Most Labour MPs, like most Conservative MPs, just went with the flow of official statements from Mrs May and Mr Corbyn and did not challenge them, or even bother to question the internal logic or chances of being accepted by EU27 politicians and the EU Commission in Brussels.

There was anger among Labour supporters when Corbyn insisted that even if a new election were held and he became prime minister, Brexit would go ahead after he had gone to Brussels to try to get a better deal than Mrs May. It was a slap in the face for the 700,000 who marched for a new public vote two months before the Corbyn statement, or the six million in the spring of 2019 who signed an e-petition to Parliament calling for MPs to accept their national leadership responsibility and revoke Article 50. Labour MPs expressed a mixture of anger and frustration at their leader adopting a line little different from that of the Conservative prime minister. The then prime minister and leader of the opposition were in lockstep in insisting they would not challenge Brexit. The duty of Her Majesty's opposition, it seemed, was no longer to oppose.

ANTI-BREXIT LABOUR MPs ALSO CORBYN CRITICS

A significant factor was that many of the outspoken anti-Brexit Labour MPs had been the most strident in opposing Jeremy Corbyn's election as Labour leader, and some had resigned from the Labour front bench in protest at his leadership. Nothing makes MPs of all parties more resentful than seeing colleagues given preferential billing and treated as media stars by saying what the establishment media want to hear. Most of the pro-EU and anti-Brexit cohort of MPs were seen as anti-Corbynites on the right of the Labour Party spectrum after 2015. When the Labour leader caused months of negative headlines about Labour and the Jewish community in the summer of 2018, following his stubborn refusal to adopt a European-wide statement defining antisemitism, it was often the same Labour MPs who campaigned against Brexit who were vociferous in criticizing him.

Corbyn offered a concession on the antisemitism issue by accepting an international definition of antisemitism drawn up by the European democratic left after being urged to do so by major Labour Party affiliated trade union leaders. This token gesture still did not stop the Simon Wiesenthal Centre, an American-based human rights organization which researches the Holocaust, placing Corbyn fourth on its list of events, organizations or people who encouraged antisemitism in 2018. Even worse, the UK's Equality and Human Rights Commission launched a formal inquiry in May 2019 into whether Labour under Corbyn had unlawfully discriminated against, harassed or victimized people because they are Jewish. More than 100 Jewish citizens and Jewish organizations asked to give evidence to the inquiry.

Trade union leaders and Labour MPs alike sensed the votes ebbing away from Labour as Corbyn's lifelong commitment to the Palestinian cause had made him blind and deaf to genuine fears in the Jewish communities of Britain about the rise of antisemitism.

Many Labour MPs who were hostile to Brexit kept their heads down and repeated the mantra of respecting the June 2016 vote. It made for a more comfortable life in their working-class constituencies and avoided rows with the ardent supporters of the Corbyn line on politics who surged into Labour Party membership as a result of Ed Miliband allowing anyone to join the Labour Party for just £3 without ever demonstrating support for, or activity on behalf of the party. Labour MPs could see how colleagues who dared challenge Corbyn faced no-confidence votes in their local parties or motions to stand down or face a reselection ballot. It was all much easier just to keep quiet and hope for calmer times when again it might be possible to be open against Brexit and in support of Europe.

All MPs take their cue from the party leaders and prominent spokespersons. No one appointed to the shadow cabinet by Corbyn was willing to say there were serious question marks over the conduct of the 2016 plebiscite, despite excellent exposés in papers such as the *Observer* and the *Guardian* on the fines and police referrals by the Electoral Commission over illegal or improper behaviour by Brexit campaigners. In a general election, some of what the Electoral Commission uncovered – especially undeclared payments to sway the vote – would have led to the constituency election result being declared null and void and a new election ordered. But that seemed impossible to argue in the case of the Brexit plebiscite.

In 2018 the Labour opponents of Brexit (and the Liberal Democrats) changed tack and started to argue for a new consultation in which voters would be asked if they wanted to leave Europe for an uncertain future or indeed to risk the so-called No Deal crash-out Brexit with a complete amputation from current commercial and personal relations with the E.U. A number of anti-Brexit campaigners had already called for a new referendum. One of the earliest was the journalist, Hugo Dixon, who before the referendum had launched an impressive daily online bulletin called *InFacts* which corrected untrue or misleading statements put out by Boris Johnson, Michael Gove and David Davis. In a prescient statement published in September

2016 by the *Financial Times*, for which he had been a distinguished business correspondent, Dixon wrote:

> When businesses realise [the damage full Brexit entails], they may sound the alarm. When voters see they were lied to, they may change their minds. Pro-Remain politicians who have run for the hills since the vote may then agree that British people should be asked whether they really want to leave once we know what Brexit means. This is democratically the right thing to do and the way to fight hard Brexit.

Others took up Dixon's call. I had doubts, writing in the *Guardian* in August 2017 that if there were enough MPs to vote for a new referendum then there would be enough to postpone, delay or even drop Brexit; instead anti-Brexit campaigners should focus on grass-roots campaigns. I was wrong to assume MPs would emerge from their bunkers and foxholes into which they disappeared after 23 June 2016. A collective funk took over the political class. Mrs May never once sought to open a dialogue or produce a cross-party response to Brexit bringing in Labour, the Lib Dems and the nationalist parties.

As politics got more and more blocked, I changed my mind and saw a new referendum as the only way of cutting the Gordian knot and releasing Britain from the Brexit trap it had fallen into. Slowly throughout 2017 it became clear that despite triggering the Article 50 clause in the EU Treaty to leave the European Union on 29 March 2019, in good time before the European Parliament elections of May 2019, Mrs May was the prisoner of opposing groups in her cabinet and party. She had no room for compromise or to offer a Brexit road map that anyone could read, let alone follow. In the end she could not honour the deadline of 29 March 2019 and Britain stayed on in the EU, shrouded by uncertainty about how to end the Brexit nightmare.

The ever-darkening economic and business news – especially the warnings from foreign firms about relocating out of the UK in event of Mrs May's version of Brexit – began to have an impact. The anti-Brexit campaign organizations, notably the leftover Remain group now called Open Britain, plus the revitalized European Movement, and the punchy weekly tabloid, the *New European*, decided their main campaign focus should be on the need for a new vote. In the end, given the failure of MPs to take hold of the Brexit issue and restore the authority of Parliamentary representative democracy, it seemed that only a referendum could kill a referendum and therefore it was reasonable and legitimate to ask if a new referendum was needed.

Twice European nations had voted no to staying in the European Union – in Denmark in 1992 and Ireland in 2008 – by repudiating an EU Treaty. In both cases these referendums were reversed after a second referendum was held and Ireland and Denmark are today EU Treaty members, though both have certain opt-outs or caveats which were put in place to help win the second referendum.

In 1992 there was a narrow majority in a referendum in Denmark to reject the Maastricht Treaty, which would have meant Denmark exiting the European Union. The Danes, like the British, are a proud long-standing European democracy. Their election system based on proportional represent-ation is different from Britain's first-past-the post system. There has been no majority one-party government in Denmark since 1909. The government insisted that while accepting the clear expression of the will of the Danish people in the plebiscite, it invited the people of the nation to reflect on whether that was the final and only word and Denmark's future lay in being isolated from its European partners. But they were careful not to rush forward simply to reject the result and insist on a second referendum.

The chief Danish government official on Europe at the time was Joergen Oerstroem Moeller, the state secretary for European affairs. He argues that the immediate calls after the Brexit vote in Britain for a second referendum were misplaced and too early. Instead he argued that 'in two or three years, circumstances may be so messy that a referendum could be the most demo-cratic response to a number of unpalatable scenarios'.

Moeller makes an important point when he states:

> The main justification for the referendum would need to be clear and transparent: to enable a decision on known withdrawal terms, which was not the case in June 2016, it would be legitimate and reasonable to ask voters whether they wished to confirm or reverse their earlier decision. The poll would not be a 'second referendum' or a plea to repent, but a new consultation of the people on an eminently democratic basis.

The campaign for what was called a 'People's Vote' began to take off and gathered momentum in the months following the second anniversary of the

June 2016 plebiscite. Opinion polls began showing a clear majority for Remain in the event of a new consultation. As the second anniversary of the plebiscite came and went and even the most ardent press supporters of Brexit had to carry factual news reports about queues at borders, shortage of food and medicines, flight delays and even the police and army in talks about possible civil unrest in the event of a No Deal crash-out Brexit, the mood changed. By September 2018, Professor Sir John Curtice, the *capo de capos* of the polling world, reported that there was now a 59–41 split in favour of staying in the EU. He qualified it with all the sensible caveats of the professional pollster, but other surveys showed that Wales, which had voted Leave in 2016, now had a majority against Brexit: 80 per cent of voters aged 18–24 now wanted to stay in Europe and 2.6 million voters who supported Leave in 2016 had now changed their minds. Another survey found that 112 Labour constituencies which had Leave majorities in 2016 had changed to not wanting to leave Europe two years on.

Trade unions also came out in favour of a new consultation. As the TUC gathered for its 150th anniversary annual congress in Manchester in autumn 2018, a poll of 2,700 trade union members found that members of the UK's biggest union, Unite supported staying in the EU by 61–35 per cent and would welcome a new referendum. The second biggest private sector union, the GMB membership wanted the UK to stay in the EU by 55– 37 per cent, while members of the public service-based Unison said they wanted to stay in the EU by 61–35 per cent.

Jeremy Corbyn and the shadow cabinet had made much of the need since June 2016 'to respect the result of the referendum' in a well-worn mantra used by Labour MPs who were nervous of coming out openly to oppose Brexit. But union members much closer to economic reality, especially outside London, saw the Brexit picture differently. In the TUC poll, union members thought that standards of living would deteriorate after Brexit. Unison members reckoned Brexit would make them poorer by a margin of 61–16 per cent, Unite members by 55–11 per cent and GMB members by 49–11 per cent.

Three unions – the GMB, Community, which organizes steel and textile workers, and the white-collar transport union TSSA – came out for a new vote. Together they sponsored a total of 108 Labour MPs, including the chair of the Parliamentary Labour Party, John Cryer. These MPs represented a Britain far away from the London seats of Labour's leader, deputy leader and shadow foreign and Brexit secretaries. The TUC's influential and popular general secretary, Frances O'Grady, used the 2018 TUC to issue her own call for a new vote.

Labour grandees such as the shadow trade secretary, Barry Gardiner had contemptuously dismissed the idea of a new vote, saying it would lead to 'social unrest' and 'perhaps civil disobedience', but Labour's shadow chancellor, John McDonnell, while maintaining his preference for a new general election, stated he was open to the idea of a new public vote. When several Labour MPs left to set up a new party, the short-lived Change UK, Jeremy Corbyn hurriedly told the rest of his MPs that he now backed a second referendum. In due course this was qualified to say it would be a referendum on Mrs May's deal, not on the principle of staying in the EU. Corbyn, it seemed, could do the hokey cokey with the idea of a new referendum but much preferred sitting on the fence.

As Labour Party bickering intensified after its poor showing in European elections, the party chairman, Ian Lavery, a north-eastern Labour MP who had inherited the rump of the miners' union, denounced support for a new referendum as 'left-wing intellectuals' sneering at 'ordinary people'. In fact, it was parties who supported the right of the people to be consulted who outperformed Labour in May 2019, but Mr Lavery took no notice.

BUSINESS REFUSES TO CAMPAIGN AGAINST BREXIT

While the trade unions were grappling with Brexit, business remained mute. Business is the dog that is not barking on Brexit. The CBI, the British Chambers of Commerce or the Institute of Directors were willing to say a No Deal amputation from Europe would be bad for business, which is a statement of the obvious. But no major employers' federation or active CEO of a major firm was willing to go out front and say with style and punch that Brexit is a disaster. Most are Conservative voters who do not want to undermine the Conservative government and risk Corbyn arriving in 10 Downing Street to create 'Venezuela on the Thames', as his rightist critics put it. Yet in their refusal to challenge Brexit and in always seeking to cosy up to the Tory occupant in Downing Street, business leaders were making the arrival of Prime Minister Jeremy Corbyn all the more likely.

Thus there was no coherent opposition to Brexit from business. There were complaints and moans and comment pieces by the head of the CBI or British Chambers of Commerce in the *Financial Times* and other posh newspapers that were not propaganda organs for Brexit like the *Daily Telegraph*, but none of this ever coalesced into a coherent business campaign. There were several reasons for this. Business is close to the Conservative Party. Of course, business has to have good relations with any government of the day, but the natural, organic and perfectly normal leaning of business is to the conservative right.

Business leaders are like lost infants in the maze of political passion. Before Brexit they believed the comfort blanket assurances from David Cameron, his ministers, senior civil servants and the establishment press that Brexit would fail. After July 2016, business was lost, but above all it did not want to campaign against Brexit as that would have been seen as campaigning against the prime minister and the government of the day.

Ministers, civil servants and the prime minister politely received business delegations and listened to their concerns. But business refused to exercise any public pressure, talk to their employees, local communities and trade unions, or commission any serious work that would have challenged Brexit. In the City, fortunes were paid to legal and management consultancy firms to produce reports on what Brexit might entail. But these were as much use as cutting open a chicken on an altar to examine its entrails to see what the future would hold.

City outfits hired former ministers from the 2010–15 government to travel to EU27 capitals to ask local banks, investment funds, insurance firms and other financial services organizations to press their national governments to grant the City special status so that Brexit wouldn't mean Brexit. It was a complete waste of two years. Others argued that as German car firms or French luxury goods firms or Dutch horticulturalists liked exporting to Britain, they would back Brexit and lobby their governments to give in to Brexit demands from Boris Johnson and papers such as the *Daily Telegraph*, *Daily Mail* and the *Sun*. Again this was a delusion. It was also a political comfort blanket. Tory MPs and anti-EU journalists kept arguing that as, self-evidently, businesses on the continent that traded with Britain would suffer as a result of Brexit, they would force their local politicians to give in to London's demands.

The core UK demand remained a wish to have full or full-ish access to the EU internal market while simultaneously rejecting the common rules other EU member states agreed to abide by. In French, this is called *avoir le beurre et l'argent du beurre* (having the butter and the money you spent buying the butter) or in German *Rosinenpickerei* (cherry-picking). Unsurprisingly neither the governments of the EU27 nor their business federations thought this was a good idea. So out of touch with continental political and business opinion was the political and media class in London that they just kept repeating the line that the EU would bend to British demands. It allowed editorial writers in the anti-EU press to claim that Europe was at fault or Brussels was being intransigent. The battle of blame for Brexit was already well under way in 2018.

Usually, business tones down any criticism of a Conservative government as it wants to give no comfort to Labour. But after July 2016, Labour was on the same page as Mrs May, so it would have been possible for the CBI and British Chambers of Commerce and other trade and industrial federations to challenge Brexit and simultaneously challenge Jeremy Corbyn's pro-Brexit inclinations. I wrote to the Road Haulage Association, whose lorry driving members would be hard hit by customs and regulatory checks at Dover, the Eurotunnel, and any ferry boat port on the coast. I received a polite reply that while the RHA had concerns, it was not campaigning against Brexit. Similar responses came from other sectors such as chemicals and aviation or the British Chambers of Commerce, whom I contacted urging them to produce reports for their employees and the communities where their plants or offices were located to explain in strictly factual terms the damage Brexit would do to jobs, future investment and the firms' future. It was surreal. All these firms knew that Brexit in almost any form acceptable to hard-line anti-European Conservative MPs was very bad news for their bottom line. But they were not prepared to do anything to change public and political opinion. They were willing to complain but not campaign. Never was British capitalism so weak and feeble in the defence of its core interests.

'SOLUTIONISM' REPLACES SAYING BREXIT IS WRONG

In part, businesses were also let down by the network of policy think tanks in London or university centres on European policy. Their directors and researchers were not pro-Brexit – far from it. However, after the referendum result they decided to opt for 'solutionism', that is, proposing solutions to the various questions and policy options that Brexit threw up. They did not use their intellectual muscle to expose the damage that would be done to Britain. Most foreign policy think tanks are partly funded by business, establishment charitable foundations or by government and its funding agencies. They were naturally reluctant to chew off the hands that fed them. So there were numerous reports on what might be put forward as British negotiating policy but most were irrelevant, as no real negotiations could get under way until the British government adopted a policy outlining what it wanted from Brussels. This was only written down in July 2018 and the mountains of words produced by think tanks and university European study centres were not much referred to.

Worthy conferences and seminars were held in handsome conference rooms in Westminster, Pall Mall and the City, but collectively this was a form of angels dancing on the heads of pins and did nothing to generate intelligent opposition to Brexit. The think tankers and professors will argue that it is not their job to argue and organize for a change in political direction of travel. Yet this new *trahison des clercs* was curious, as think tanks like to wag fingers and decree what a government should do. On Europe they were unwilling to come out openly and say that Brexit would be bad for Britain across a range of issues of concern to them. Instead the language was 'If the government and EU could agree then we would live in a better world'. This Panglossian thinking failed to take into account political realities in Westminster or the absence of leadership in the two main parties or the unchanging determination of the EU27 to make sure Brexit did not lead to a weakening or sundering of the European Union.

Nor did the think tanks, policy foundations and university professors assess how much Brexit was a win for the Trump–Putin–Orban nationalist, illiberal and xenophobic world view and why many European leaders saw Brexit as a hard ideological project aimed at a fundamental destabilization of Europe such as it had developed since 1950. Think-tank directors would meet their friends and contacts in European capitals or at seminars abroad and interpret courteous, friendly language as meaning EU27 policy would change in the direction wished for in London. They held conferences for their staff or invited academics to produce papers, but they were all aimed at solutions based on accepting the premise of Brexit and not challenging it.

The historian Peter Neville, in his study of British appeasement in the 1930s writes: 'If appeasement needed an intellectual forum, Chatham House provided it.' After the Brexit plebiscite, Chatham House – or the Royal Institute of International Affairs, to give the foreign policy think tank its full title – was like other foreign policy outfits in that seminars or speeches took place about Brexit, but not with a view to changing public opinion by offering a greater understanding of its negative impact.

There were plenty of right-wing policy outfits like the Legatum Institute, Policy Exchange or the Institute for Economic Affairs which supported leaving Europe. They had been set up or funded by right-wing American billionaires opposed to the idea of a coherent European Union not subservient to the United States on global policy issues and especially averse to European ideas of social fairness and combatting inequality. Compared to the fact-based think tanks on Europe, they were often sleeker and had better media contacts in anti-European papers like the *Daily Telegraph* or *Spectator* or Eurosceptic BBC editors of programmes like Radio 4's *Today* who had long looked down their collective noses at Europe. The American-funded pro-Brexit think tanks also offered their own solutions. These consisted of pre-referendum positions calling for a rapid and complete amputation from current economic and other links with EU member states.

'Solutionism' failed. There is no evidence that Mrs May and her policy deciders paid the slightest attention to the solutionist prescriptions. Neither did any of her would-be successors, unless the think tank or academic in question was confirming their already well-established anti-EU prejudices. Of course, if the director of a policy outfit came back from a visit to a European capital to announce that Berlin or Paris or Warsaw or the EU27 ambassadors in Brussels were warming to some aspect of the No. 10 line on what should happen, then this was gratefully received and such musings made available to the press. But the referendum outcome was never challenged by the policy wonks and university professors who had been opining on Europe for years, if not decades, and their solutionist approach to Brexit had little impact.

11

BREXIT, BOOKS, AND THE PESSIMISM OF INTELLECTUALS

Brexit has been largely discussed in Britain in terms of English politics and, in particular, the twists and turns in Westminster politics. Most books now on Europe are about Brexit, often journalistic post-mortems by monolingual Westminster reporters. They are good reportage on the hothouse debates in Westminster, London political party meetings and Whitehall, but are neither history nor analysis, still less a guide to Brexit from the point of view of the national governments of Europe, still less the thinking of the EU Commission team negotiating Brexit.

Very few British journalists in London whose writing has filled pages since July 2016 have worked in a continental country, speak a European language, can turn a page in *Die Welt* or *Le Monde* to have an idea of what Berlin or Paris thinks. They rely for their information on what is produced in English for the London press, which knows much about Westminster party politics but next to nothing about European politics.

Yet it may be helpful to lift our eyes and see how the entire second decade of the twenty-first century in Europe has been gripped by a dark pessimism about national identity and the future of the nations of Europe faced with dramatic changes in capitalism or people movement. A look at the books on Europe published outside the UK shows this loss of confidence and pessimism in full flow.

Europe publishes 520,000 books a year. Price maintenance systems (*Prix du livre* or *Preisbindung*) mean that bookshops, not just big chains but individually owned bookshops, are a feature of many medium and even small towns in France, Germany and other EU member states. French supermarkets all have big book sales stands with latest editions, but books are seen as a creative and professional product, and not just another commodity to be sold as cheaply as possible.

The EU sponsors translations and helps keep writing in different languages available so that the giant GAFA (Google–Apple–Facebook–Amazon) English language steamroller does not crush everything that does not conform to London and Manhattan rules of publishing. The EU also has directives on copyright and there has been a battle going on between publishers, especially in Germany, and Amazon over price cutting. There are stringent EU rules on data protection and transmission. Small claims libel actions in court are possible, which might be welcome in the UK as a protection against vexatious libel claims but would also mean more stringent fact checking than is always the case in UK publishing.

Britain outside the EU would become a 'third country' rather as is the United States. This could mean that US publishers would ship their books directly for sale into the UK with a £ price sticker over the $ one, rather than selling rights to a British publisher who then brings the book out as a product designed and printed in Britain – i.e. the EU. It also means the EU becomes a contested territory; previously it was assumed the British publisher would have EU rights as well, but increasingly US publishers are seeking to retain EU rights and sell into that market themselves.

The European Commission has a special agency which funds translation from European languages into English. After Brexit, that funding channel to British publishers will dry up, and it is hard to see a British government composed largely of monolingual ministers who have spent fifteen years or more denouncing Europe finding the replacement money to support writers in the twenty-seven other member states being translated so we can read them here.

Big continental publishers like Hachette and Bertelsmann have become used to a constant interchange between British and European publishing executives and, of course, EU citizens have been a staple of book store employment. They are willing to work the long antisocial opening hours and for the low pay on offer from bookshops.

Many of the books published recently in continental Europe and Britain reflect the triumph of Brexit and Trump in 2016 and the time the economic picture in Spain, Italy and Portugal was bleak, Marine Le Pen and Geert Wilders were en route to power, the euro and even the EU were about to implode, and liberal, social democratic, green and broadly progressive political values had fallen into history's dustbin.

PESSIMISM OF WILL AND INTELLECT

Never has so much pessimism of will and intellect filled pages upon pages of European political literature. Recent publications include Etienne Balibar's *Europe, crise et fin?* (The end crisis of Europe?), François Heisbourg's *La fin du rêve européen* (The end of the European dream), Olivier Lacoste's *La fin de l'Europe?* (The end of Europe?), Eric Juillot's *La Déconstruction européenne* (The demolition of Europe) – and those are just French titles. Much of it is encouraged by European politicians, who seem to think that announcing imminent disaster prevents it from arriving. Is any of this justified?

When Jean-Claude Juncker took office as president of the EU Commission, he said it was a 'last chance' for Europe. At the same time, Martin Schulz, then the German Social Democratic president of the European Parliament, gravely warned that 'No one can say whether the EU will still exist in this form in ten years'. Mark Mazower, the historian of darker moments in twentieth-century European history, announced in 2016 that the 'EU is living on borrowed time', while the noted Greek chronicler of modern Europe, Loukas Tsoukalis, claimed that the EU is 'as fragile as a glasshouse'.

Mr Schulz is now out of European politics and Jean-Claude Juncker has presided over an EU 2014–19 that has overcome a financial crisis as serious as that of the 1930s without relapsing into mass unemployment and giving up democracy. To be sure, there are problems galore, notably Brexit. But as it approaches its eighth decade – taking the first supranational European community project of 1950 as a starting point – the EU seems better at surviving and even prospering than entering a political hospice to await its end.

In *After Europe*, Ivan Krastev, the Bulgarian liberal-pessimist politicologue normally full of brilliant insights, slumps into alarm at the arrival of foreigners and refugees in Europe. 'Europeans today are living at a moment when paralyzing uncertainty captures a society's imagination . . . a moment when what was until now *unthinkable* – the disintegration of the union – begins to be perceived as *inevitable*.'

Krastev sees massive people movement as dissolving the EU. He should have visited automobile plants in Germany, France, Sweden and Italy in the 1960s and 1970s and checked how many true-born Germans, Swedes or French were working assembling cars. John David Morley, the British writer, who lived in Munich from 1970 to 2018, reminds us, correctly, that surges of people in Europe are nothing new:

> Ten million refugees in 1945–46. All households commandeered for the next ten years to take in their allotment of refugees, packing them in by the dozen (two dozen in this house where I now live on my own). Not a family in this country that doesn't have a grandparent who remembers what those times were like.

Since the late 1950s, Britain, France, Germany, the Netherlands and Nordic Europe have taken in millions of Muslims, Hindus and Sikhs from Asia, North and East Africa, along with Christians from Afro-Caribbean nations as well as Turkey. Krastev likes to quote David Goodhart, who has published two recent books warning that Europeans working in Britain cause intolerable social tensions.

In addition to Krastev, the Italian political scientist, Raffaele Simone in his *Come la Democrazia Fallisce* (How democracy collapses) is obsessed with immigration. Simone's reference point is Thilo Sarrazin, the former German social democratic politician whose 2010 book *Deutschland schafft sich ab* (Germany is abolishing itself) was a long tirade against the presence of Muslims in Germany and against multiculturalism – '*Multikulti*', as it is called in German. In his *Mémoire de paix pour temps de guerre* (Memories of peace in times of war) Dominique de Villepin, the former French prime minister and foreign minister, points out that there has always been a project based on a monocultural Europe, white and Christian. 'The Nazi project was clearly a European project based on nationalist and collaborationist regimes like Admiral Horthy in Hungary, Belgium's Rexist party, Franco in Spain, Dmowski in pre-war Poland, or Doriot and Laval in France', he writes.

The obsession with people moving across frontiers is a staple in the current crop of books on Europe. Hans Werner Sinn, the leading German economics pundit, published *Der Schwarze Juni* (Black June) late in 2016 to denounce the policy of accepting refugees from the Middle East wars launched by European powers and the US, and to highlight what he calls the 'disaster of the euro' and Brexit. Sinn is also obsessed with the decision of the German constitutional court in June 2016 to approve the European Central Bank's quantitative easing programme. A year later, with every eurozone economy back in growth thanks to the sensible sub-Keynsian policy of the ECB and with the German export machine profiting the most from this return to growth, Sinn's classic monetarist ordo-liberalism orthodox seemed quaint.

Between 2014 and 2019 the EU's finance commissioner was Pierre Moscovici. He served as France's Europe minister in the Lionel Jospin government 1997–2002 alongside Hubert Védrine as foreign minister. The two Frenchmen were prompted by Brexit to write books with apocalyptic titles: *Sauver l'Europe*! (Save Europe!) by Védrine and *S'il est minuit en Europe* (If it's midnight in Europe) by Moscovici. For French socialist foreign policy expert Védrine, the problem with Europe is what he calls the '*Europeistes*'. These are not quite the same as those Jean-Marie Le Pen called '*les fédérastes*', which the arch anti-European Sir Bill Cash translated as 'federasts' in speeches in the House of Commons, but Védrine's '*Europeistes*' is a collective noun for anyone who thinks European cooperation and integration is, on balance, a good idea.

As with Claus Offe in his *Europa in der Falle*, published in English as *Europe Entrapped*, who begins with the cliché: 'The European Union is at a crossroads: either it moves to a dramatic improvement of its institutional structure or it will collapse', many of these dark accounts of Europe glide around the fact that the EU up to the moment of Brexit was a conglomeration of twenty-eight independent nation states.

But still the pessimists of Europe have to set up Védrine's *Europeistes* as straw men, which he then proceeds to denounce with gusto. His answer is a refounding conference for the European Union, bringing together political elites from all member states. The EU already tried that with its constitutional convention chaired by Valéry Giscard d'Estaing in the early years of the twenty-first century. The constitution drawn up was shot down in referendums in France and the Netherlands in 2005.

Pierre Moscovici argues that the French referendum on the EU happened in the form of the 2017 presidential election. He was writing before it took place and the name Emmanuel Macron does not appear in his book. It opens rather with his fear of Marine Le Pen becoming president of France – the scenario that seemed to have informed much of the black visions of Europe that underpinned so many of this generation of books.

Britain's *New Statesman* political weekly devoted seven pages in a March 2017 issue to Geert Wilders as the coming man of Dutch and European politics. In fact, he failed miserably, as did Marine Le Pen, and in the British general election of June 2017 the anti-European populist party UKIP scored just 1.8 per cent of the vote. To be sure, in the European Parliament election two years later, Nigel Farage's one-man Brexit Party did well, but only obtained 4 per cent more votes than Farage's UKIP party in 2014. Despite its promise, Geert Wilders's party did not win a single MEP seat. In 2015, commentators wrote that Farage and his UKIP party would enter the House of Commons; however, UKIP was eliminated as a political force in the general election in 2017 and the European Parliament election in 2019. Time will tell if Farage's Brexit Party will enter the House of Commons.

Right wing populists with their furious denunciations of sinister forces taking over the nation can command headlines and time on television. Nor should one underestimate their continuing strength, just as communist populists did well in France and Italy after 1945. Yet when voting for the serious business of government – taxes, jobs, policing, healthcare, education, pensions, war and peace – the mature democracies are loath to place any real and total trust in populist charlatans.

Moscovici does not believe in referendums as a sacrosanct means of government, whether in terms of EU developments or more generally. In contrast to Védrine's *Europeistes*, Moscovici pleads for Europe's *progressistes* (progressives) – as he dubs them – to come together. This may be wishful thinking. The late-twentieth-century left, which at the end of that century had its parties and prime ministers in power in thirteen of the then fifteen EU member states, is now in a sorry state. In France, the once-mighty Parti socialiste, Moscovici's own party, has all but disappeared in the wake of the Macron victories in the 2017 presidential and legislative elections. Germany's SPD struggles to make headway against their centre-right opponents under

Angela Merkel and won fewer votes than the German greens in the European elections of May 2019.

Greece's PASOK has been replaced by the populist leftists of Syriza which, in turn, was overtaken by the traditional centre-right New Democracy party. In Spain the once-powerful PSOE socialists have lost many of their votes to the populist leftists of Podemos, although PSOE staged a remarkable parliamentary coup in May 2018 under a new young leader, Pedro Sanchez. He secured a parliamentary vote about the deep corruption in the then ruling Partido Popular government, which led to the ouster of its leader and Spain's head of government, Mariano Rajoy. Sanchez's socialist party was evicted after thirty-seven years of ruling the big Spanish region of Andalusia when a new right-wing populist party, VOX, won a number of seats in the regional parliament. VOX, however, is not anti-European and an error – especially among monolingual commentators and some academics in England – has been to assume all populist politics shares the same obsession of Brexit politicians in England.

Spain, like the United Kingdom, has to face the problem of secessionist, separatist populism in the form of national identity political parties like the Scottish or Catalan nationalist and independentist parties. Yet far from being anti-European, both the Scottish and Catalan nationalists insist they want to keep the small nations they seek to lead out of the broader British or Spanish state into membership of the EU.

In many countries, coalition politics is the norm. Sometimes that has entailed alliances with racist or anti-EU nationalist parties. The democratic left barely exists in east Europe. Victories in 2017 for a nominally social democratic party in Romania (the party's adherence to social democratic values is questioned by the EU-wide centre-left Party of European Socialists) or Albania or Macedonia cannot compensate for disappearance from power elsewhere. Britain's Labour Party defied opinion poll expectations by winning seats in the June 2017 election.

Other books mainly from French authors offer bleak, sometimes dramatic perspectives on Brexit. Régis Debray thinks the problem is that Europeans 'have become Americans', as he puts it in his new book *Civilisation*. The turning point for Debray came in 1972. For the first time, he writes, the official selection of films at the Cannes Film Festival was made by the organizers and not decided by the French Foreign Ministry. Some might date the 1970s as the moment when Europe rediscovered its confidence and élan to wean itself off the US post-war Marshall Plan and NATO dependence. Debray trots out Harold Macmillan's Greece–Rome metaphor that as power slipped from Greece to Rome, so today power has slipped from Europe to America.

But what real power did Europe have during Debray's early lifetime (he was born in 1940)? Colonial wars, dictatorships in Spain, Greece and Portugal, and hateful treatment of women, gays and immigrants were the hallmarks of Europe in Debray's young adulthood. European integration and the arrival in 1992 of the EU has produced a springtime of nations, with their different cultures, cuisines, cinema, literature and other forms of identity. Europe produces more books than the United States and the European Commission takes on Apple and Google in a way that no individual European government would dare do.

MODISH PESSIMISM ABOUT EUROPE

Patrice Franceschi, a French writer and action man (he has flown around the world an ultralight plane and sailed in and out of most oceans) argues in *Combattre! Comment les Etats-Unis de l'Europe peuvent sauver la France* (Fight! How the United States of Europe can save France) that France should quit the EU and hold a referendum on the creation of a United States of Europe. The common language of this USE should be ancient Greek!

Most of today's books on Europe veer from the darkest EU pessimism, like any article in the *Daily Mail/Telegraph* stable, to surreal appeals for a 'polyphonic' non-EU Europe or for an instant federal Europe speaking the Greek of Pericles!

In 2016, an American professor, John Gillingham wrote *The EU: An Obituary*. It was published by a left-wing publisher in London, Verso, at about the same time as the *Guardian* was promoting the modish view of Lexit – left-wing exit from the EU advanced by leftist writers such as Owen Jones, the *New Statesman*'s economic editor Grace Blakeley, and the veteran Trotskyist *New Left Review* columnist Tariq Ali. Professor Gillingham writes of 'an EU in disarray, which is untrustworthy, falling behind economically, and unable or unwilling to deliver on its commitments'. He is based at the Harvard Center for European Studies and every source in his book is from an

English language publication. There is no anti-European cliché unused, especially that from the 1980s onwards Europe 'experienced an integration relaunch aimed at a European federal state'. The driving force for European integration in the 1980s was, of course, Margaret Thatcher and her enthusiasm for abolishing national vetoes in order to create the single market. By 2016, let alone in the years after the Brexit vote, Europe was less federal than ever, less looking like a superstate than ever, but for the good Harvard professor and his left-wing London publisher, the best story in the European town was to write a whole book promoting the UKIP and Rupert Murdoch agenda that Britain had to amputate itself from Europe and regain freedom to become poorer and less influential.

In 2018, Ian Kearns, a British European expert, published *Collapse: Europe after the European Union*. It was another in the unending litany of decline and fall of the EU literature. To be fair to Mr Kearns, he outlines seven reasons he believes are leading or can lead to the collapse of the EU. But he insisted to me that he was not a supporter of Brexit. But it is much, much easier to get published if the title the book is an updated version of the Oswald Spengler classic *The Decline of the West*, published just after the end of the First World War and which announced the end of Europe. *Is the EU Doomed?* is the typically apocalyptic title of Jan Zielonka's 2014 book-length essay. It articulates the classic British anti-European line that the EU is not Europe. That cliché may have been true in the late twentieth century and even in the opening years of the current century. But today the EU (plus the European Economic Area) corresponds to Europe.

If Britain stays economically linked to the EU even under specific tailored arrangements, it will be on the basis of living under core EU laws and in cooperation and conformity with structures the rest of Europe, including non-EU member states such as Norway and Switzerland, have come to accept. It is too facile to rubbish the institutions and laws and parliamentary work of the European Union but express the belief that if they are diminished, or other countries follow Britain's Brexit example and walk out of the EU, then the problems that give rise to legitimate criticisms of the EU will be solved.

Professor Zielonka argues for a 'polyphonic Europe' in which:

the European Council will become just one among several other decision-making bodies in Europe. Large cities and regions will have their own meetings and administration to coordinate common endeavours . . . In short, the EU may not be formally dissolved but it will become less powerful, relevant and coherent. In time, it will become toothless and useless.

His fellow thinker on what Europe is or should be, Richard Youngs, argues that 'an alternative EU must encourage more participative local level debate, but also combine this with democratic processes in which people show better consideration of citizens' interests in other countries'. It was hoped that bringing in a directly elected European Parliament in 1979 would result in stronger 'democratic processes [leading to] common endeavours', but it hasn't quite worked out like this.

These arguments may make sense in the dining hall and common room of All Souls College, Oxford, but are they based in reality? Brexit, if anything, seemed to lead to a reinforcement of the desire to stay in the EU. Politicians in countries such as Poland and Hungary won elections with Eurosceptic and outright Europhobe statements and accusations that Tory and UKIP politicians in Britain have used since the 1990s, but not for a second did the Brussels-bashing politicians in Warsaw or Budapest suggest the answer was to leave the EU, its customs union or single market, the European Parliament or the overarching authority of the ECJ.

Professor Zielonka predicted in 2014: 'If Syriza wins the next Greek parliamentary election there might also be a referendum in Greece on the issue of membership of the Eurozone.' There was indeed a referendum in Greece in 2015, but it was based on rejecting any idea of leaving the eurozone or the EU. Greece under its nominally leftist government between 2015 and 2019, when Syrzia was replaced by a centre-right New Democracy government, has in fact been the most cooperative member of the EU as the nation confronted what Grexit would mean and decided staying in the EU was a better guarantee of the future, even if the immediate medicine was bitter indeed.

In 2014, Jean-Claude Juncker said that enlargement would be on hold for the five-year period, 2014–19, of the European Parliament and Commission. Yet in 2018 he announced support for the adherence to the EU of the West Balkan European states which emerged from the destruction of the former Yugoslavia during the decade of Slobodan Milosevic's quasi-fascist rule, which ended when the Serbs left Kosovo after a year of wanton savagery that left most of the Kosovo population fleeing their country rather than risk being victims like the Bosniaks at the Srebrenica massacres of 8,000 unarmed, defenceless women, teenagers and men put to death in 1995 in the last genocide in twentieth-century European history.

The eighteen million Europeans squeezed between the Aegean and the Adriatic do not want to join a post-EU Europe as they are already living in the non-EU Europe. They believe their future is best guaranteed and supported if they can become full EU member states.

Another version of EU disappointment comes in Jean Quatremer's *Les Salauds de l'Europe* (The bastards/shits of Europe). Quatremer is a legend in Brussels as the long-serving EU correspondent of *Libération*, the French left daily paper. He regularly exposes the stupidity and corruptions of Eurocrats and MEPs while still maintaining a decades-long faith that European integration as an ideal is worth supporting. Now his dream is dead: 'Europe promises much but achieves little. It has been reduced to a straitjacket that suffocates democracy and an ordo-liberal straitjacket that suffocates national economies.' Of course, for other writers in this year of Europessimism chronicled in these books, Europe is not ordo-liberal enough.

According to Philipp Ther in his contemporary history narrative *Europe Since 1989*, the last near three decades of European development have been about the imposition of 'neo-liberalism' on the suffering Europeans. Yet between 1990 and 2016, the share of GDP taken in tax has increased in all the major eurozone economies save the Netherlands. It is a funny definition of neo-liberalism that sees the state costing more and becoming bigger, not smaller. Britain along with other EU member states had to nationalize banks as a result of the Alan Greenspan crash. The east European economies that protest the most about Brussels, such as Hungary and Poland, have used the state to take shares in major industries. President Macron nationalized France's main shipbuilding firm, refusing a perfectly good offer from an Italian company in order to assert the French state's right to own industry. If this is neo-liberalism, then the word has become very elastic.

As with populism, which is a catch-all term much in vogue, the predictions of journalists and writers such as Jan Werner Muller that an unstoppable tidal wave of right-wing populism would sweep all before it has turned out not to be true in 2017. Left nationalist populists like Syriza had to modify their populism and cooperate with the EU in Greece and right-wing nationalist populists have been beaten back in Albania and Macedonia. Italians voted for populism but gave as many votes to the idiosyncratic left populism of the Five Star Movement as the anti-immigrant populist racists of the Lega. And very quickly, the new Italian coalition government, whose political leaders in opposition had been loud in denouncing the euro single currency, made clear there was no question of leaving it to return to the lira.

So it seems neither neo-liberalism nor populism is sufficient explanation of what is going in European politics. Lega's Matteo Salvini when he entered the Italian government appeared on platforms with Viktor Orban to proclaim unity between Rome and Budapest. He also was seen beaming with Austria's rightist chancellor, Sebastian Kurz, who announced that henceforth there was a 'new axis' between Italy and Austria – not perhaps the best-chosen metaphor. But when Salvini asked his new right-wing Brussels-bashing friends to help by taking in some refugees from Italy, suddenly his new political chums seemed to go instantly deaf.

By 2019, the erratic Salvini had ditched Orban and Kurz and now boasted of an alliance with the far-right AfD in Germany and similar racist rightists in Denmark. In short, there are as many divisions on the European populist right as there are common policies. Salvini and Orban, for example, are keen on getting close to President Putin, but in Warsaw the illiberal PiS government and its party leader, Jarosław Kaczynski, is the sworn enemy of the Kremlin and keeps urging the EU to stop energy pipeline projects to deliver Russian energy to European consumers. This zig-zagging by Europe's hard right nationalists was rejected in the European Parliament elections of May 2019 when the predicted surge of the Salvini–Le Pen–AfD parties failed to materialize. In the choice of women and men to lead the EU between 2019 and 2024 and the choice of committee chairs in the European Parliament, the nationalist xenophobe MEPs flopped miserably. Nigel Farage's band of Brexit MEPs staged a stunt at the opening session of the European Parliament in July 2019 when they turned their backs to the chair and stuck their bottoms into the microphones. Most of Britain just laughed at the undignified posture they adopted.

Olivier Lacoste's *La fin de l'Europe?* (The end of Europe?) is a more levelheaded book written in response to Brexit. It offers the kind of practical suggestions that the Centre for European Reform or the Bruegel Group in

Brussels might come up with. These books tend to fall into the category of Jean-Claude Juncker's lapidary statement: 'Every political leader in Europe knows what needs to be done to make the EU work but no one knows how to get re-elected afterwards.'

EUROPEAN INTELLECTUALS AND THE EU'S APOCALYPSE

There is an appetite in France for apocalyptic books with titles like *Euro: Par ici la sortie?* (This way out for the Euro?) by Patrick Artus and Marie-Paul Virard or *L'Europe a-t-elle un avenir?* (Does Europe have a future?) by Patrick Martin-Genier. But when you examine previous books by the same authors with titles like 'Is it too late to save America?' (2009), 'Globalization: The worst is to come' (2008) or 'Zero growth: How to avoid chaos' (all by Artus and Virard), it seems obligatory to produce a book written by the modern equivalent of Corporal Fraser in *Dad's Army* as he proclaimed: 'We're all doomed! Doomed!' Many of these books, such as Francis Fukuyama's *The End of History?*, Thomas Friedman's *The World is Flat* or Samuel Huntingdon's *The Clash of Civilizations*, are seemingly destined to be quickly forgotten.

Much depends on the starting point of the authors. Pascal Lamy, the former head of the WTO and Jacques Delors's chief aide in the last strong Commission presidency (1985–95), has co-authored with Nicole Gnesotto *Où va le monde?* ('Where is the world heading?'), which is a dialogue rather than a single text but full of useful insights such as the concept of 'polylateralism' – an idea of international relations based on interactions between non-state actors.

Lamy and Gnesotto cannot escape their Frenchness and sense of power plays between commanding nations. They find fault with the EU's handling of Ukraine, which they see through the prism of Moscow's argument that the EU was seeking to integrate Ukraine into the West and remove it from Russia's sphere of influence. This is a constant argument of British anti-European commentators like Liam Halligan and Peter Hitchens who, in debates on Brexit, berated Brussels for stirring up trouble in Ukraine. In fact, most European governments and the EU chiefs in Brussels needed a crisis in Ukraine like a hole in the head. It was the people of Ukraine who filled Kiev with their demand that a corrupt president obedient to Moscow should go. As with the

Solidarity movement in 1980, or the peoples of East Germany, Czechoslovakia or Hungary mobilizing for democracy in 1989, the desire of the peoples of Europe to live under democracy and rule of law remains a constant.

British anti-Europeans join with Vladimir Putin in saying that every expression of European democracy has been artificially created and sustained by dark forces in Brussels seeking to lessen Russian control over its former satellites. On the contrary, Brussels, like EU capitals and Washington, is usually taken by surprise at popular risings demanding that a nation should live by European norms of a free press, human rights, and government by accountable and non-corrupt elected representatives.

Philipp Ther in *Europe Since 1989* takes a different starting point, namely 2005, the year when Ukraine's Orange Revolution took place and there was endless temporization over how to support the clear desire of the Ukrainian people to move away from the Putin mix of authoritarian oligarch state capitalism and cronyism towards a more European model. Perhaps because Ther is based in Vienna – where Austrians recall how the Red Army occupied and then bequeathed a stifling post-1945 settlement that only really ended when Austria joined the EU in 1995 – he is more sensitive to the rights of people to live free from Putin's control. The tragedy of Ukraine is not that the EU meddled or interfered, but that it was far too weak to support civil society and the right of Ukrainians to be free. Putin sought to freeze the conflict with the invasion and Anschluss of Crimea and poured arms and soldiers into a sovereign member state of the United Nations.

Over centuries Russia has invaded, occupied and colonized more European nations and peoples than any other European power. Putin had the choice of turning Russia to Europe and to modernize Russia, but he has opted for a vertical power state based on raw materials and energy exports.

Russia was suspended from the Parliamentary Assembly of the Council of Europe, which is a major humiliation for Putin, even if not much reported in the western media. There are tough EU sanctions in place and the US Congress has voted for new sanctions, even if Putin's man in the White House is not keen on them. The Russians were eventually readmitted to the Council of Europe but, at the G20, announced the era of liberal democracy was over. This was on the eve of the appointment of the most liberal leadership of Europe in recent years following a defeat for Putin's supporters in European Parliament elections.

Philipp Ther takes a diametrically opposed view on the EU and Ukraine to Pascal Lamy and Nicole Gnesotto. Despite the forebodings of intellectuals and academics, Europe is still being forcibly debated by Europeans. In Britain, little of this debate can be seen. The quality of writing in Britain on Europe has become very flat this century. Academics working in university European departments produce their monographs, but little of this influences public debate. Indeed, the triumph of the Brexit referendum was perhaps a reflection of the deep ignorance the British political-media class, let alone the wider British public, have about Europe.

This ignorance was as prevalent as we entered the third year of post-referendum Britain. The BBC's respected political editor, Laura Kuenssberg, told BBC morning listeners during the political party conference season in 2018 that those calling for a new consultation on Brexit were just up to old tricks. She said: 'The EU has form on this. If the leaders' club doesn't like the result, you get the public to vote again until they do.' Ms Kuenssberg is wrong, though her cliché is widely believed to be true, so often has it been repeated by London journalists. When France and the Netherlands said no in 2005 to the EU constitutional treaty, that was accepted; when Switzerland said no in 1992 to joining the European Economic Area, that was accepted, as was Norway's referendum which decided not to join the EU in 1994. So too were referendums in Sweden against the euro in 2003 and the Dutch No vote against the EU Ukraine treaty in 2016. The Swiss held a referendum in 2014 which voted to ban immigration by EU citizens into Switzerland. When the result came through, it was Swiss businesses who rely on European immigrant workers who pushed Swiss MPs to come up with a new plan to help Swiss employees without banning migrants. Denmark and Ireland voted in referendums in 1992 and 2008 to repudiate the Maastricht and Lisbon treaties. But it was national politicians, business leaders, civil society, trade unions and professionals who united within Denmark and Ireland to say that new referendums should take place once the facts about the dangers of amputating Denmark and Ireland from Europe became known. It was not Brussels or any 'leaders' club' that forced the Danes and the Irish to have a second look.

Since the Brexit vote, while there has been unceasing journalism on the future of Britain and Europe, there is no convincing book that has caught the public imagination. The Battle of Brexit is far from over, even if the first round was lost in June 2016. British politics and economics will remain defined by our relationship to Europe for the rest of the century. The sooner good quality writing on Europe is encouraged the better.

But this will be difficult – so pervasive in London writers' salons is a deep, enduring dislike of European integration. There was a sense of personal loss when I ended the latest thriller by Philip Kerr based on his world-weary, sardonic, cynical Berlin detective, Bernie Gunther. The unlucky thirteenth in a wonderful series of novels – nominally crime thrillers – but as rich in character, narrative and exploring the human soul as any Booker Prize entry.

Kerr invented Gunther and sent him on a series of chases across Nazi Germany from the 1930s, through all the occupied countries of the Second World War to the post-war remnants of Nazism. He brought in Göbbels, Heydrich, Himmler and sundry generals and war criminals. The lives of ordinary Berliners surviving the war and non-Nazi Germans just keeping their heads down as great crimes were carried out around them were brought vividly to life.

Sadly Kerr died, aged 62, of cancer earlier in 2018 and so his book *Greeks Bearing Gifts* is the penultimate Bernie Gunther (the fourteenth book in the series was published posthumously). There is plenty of politics in it as it is set in the mid-1950s in Munich and Athens and, as well as being a terrific page-turner, features real live politicians from Greece and Germany of that era.

I knew Kerr slightly, enjoyed his wit and never attached him to strong politics. But the political thesis of his thirteenth Bernie Gunther thriller is part of the most under-reported aspect of the rise of anti-European and Brexit passions in Britain – namely the London salons of Euroscepticism.

In London salons in recent years it has been impossible to discuss Europe without hearing the late Nicholas Ridley's jibe that it was all a 'German racket'. Philip Kerr returned to the charge, claiming that the European Economic Community, the Common Market, was set up in 1957 to allow Germany to accomplish by economic means what it had failed to achieve through the Nazis' military conquests. As Gunther muses:

> Bureaucracy and trade were to be my country's new method of conquering Europe, and lawyers and civil servants were to be its foot soldiers. But if Konrad Adenauer was anything to go by, it was really a coup d'état by a group of politicians who did not believe in democracy, and

we were being guided towards a Soviet system of Europe without
anyone understanding what was planned. Hitler could certainly have
taken a lesson from the Old Man [Adenauer].

In truth, it was the French, Belgians, Dutch and Italians who shaped first
the ECSC in 1950 and then the EEC in 1957 to remove from Germany once
and for all the means to make war. But in London salons, the EEC, then EU,
now the EU has always been a German plot. In his biography of Winston
Churchill, Boris Johnson wrote of a 'Gestapo-controlled Nazi EU' and at the
outset of the 2106 Brexit campaign declared that the EU was following in the
path of Hitler in setting up a superstate. In 1995, the historian Andrew
Roberts wrote a novel, *The Aachen Memorandum*, describing a Britain in
2045 which was just a region of the 'Euro-tyranny' where the monarchy had
been abolished, the Union Jack was banned, and fish and chips could no
longer be sold. Roberts is a popular historian, enjoyable to read but, like
other London salon Eurosceptics, he cannot control his hostility to
Europe.

It is too easy to blame Brexit on the excessive anti-immigrant rhetoric of
Nigel Farage and the tabloids. It was a deep cultural belief in masses of
middle-class living rooms that Europe was bad and rotten from the beginning. In her 1972 novel, *Rule Britannia*, Daphne du Maurier describes
Britain leaving the European Community after a referendum and, as the
economy collapses, deciding to merge with the United States to form a new
nation, USUK, with the Stars and Stripes combined with the Union flag and
the American president and British queen being joint heads of state. It all
goes badly wrong when American troops occupy England to ensure control
of the new USUK and the British rise up against a foreign occupier. It is an
enjoyable satire, but even then Ms du Maurier had to present Europe as a
cause of British problems – a theme that has been a constant for decades,
with few novelists and other opinion shapers making a pro-European case.

At the end of *Greeks Bearing Gifts*, Gunther is involved in a discussion on
the Treaty of Rome and its two German signatories in 1957, Konrad Adenauer
and the German foreign minister, Walter Hallstein, who became the first
European Commission president from 1958 to 1967. One of Kerr's characters states: 'Hallstein was a member of several Nazi organisations.' This is
untrue. Unusually for a career university professor, Hallstein never joined the

Nazi party and was an American prisoner of war when captured as a conscripted low-rank army officer in 1944.

Kerr goes on to write that in exchange for Greece not pursuing Nazi war crimes, 'Adenauer and Hallstein will not only approve the Greek application for membership in the EEC but they will also approve a two-hundred-million-dollar loan to Greece'. Again this is dodgy history. Greece didn't join the European Community until 1981 and today Athens still protests that Germany has never paid war reparations for the damage Germany did to Greece in the Second World War. Indeed, in June 2019, Athens submitted a major claim for reparations to Berlin, contrary to Kerr's assertion that it was all sorted out seventy years ago.

Let me be clear. These historical howlers do not detract from Kerr's storytelling; the Bernie Gunther thrillers are excellent and a great read. But *Greeks Bearing Gifts* tells us more about the mindset in London that produced Brexit than it does about modern Greece and Europe.

The approach of England outside London to Brexit is captured in part in the third volume of Jonathan Coe's roman-fleuve about a group of people who met at the fictionalized King Edward's School in Birmingham in the early 1970s and live out their lives in England in the years and decades that followed. His novel, *Middle England*, set between 2010 and 2017, as Coe's protagonists enter their fifties, politely explores the racism that fuelled Brexit, the differences between the university-educated anti-Brexit characters who work in journalism, in publishing or the media and the non-graduate West Midlanders who vote Leave.

There is the sad nostalgia of the father and grandfather of some of the main characters, a former Birmingham car worker, who has seen his industry disappear and the giant production lines of Longbridge replaced by shopping malls. He harks back to the Second World War when Birmingham metalworkers produced the tanks and guns for the British Army. This nostalgia for an England where there were few foreigners, most citizens were white and understood their place in the regimented ranks of English class divisions, was reflected in endless vox-pop interviews for television and has been heard incessantly on radio phone-ins since the Brexit vote.

Coe is gentle and non-judgemental, as the novel's two EU workers, Lithuanians employed in catering, who are kind to an old English woman who admires Enoch Powell, admit they do not want to stay any longer in a

West Midlands that after June 2016 made unpleasant 'Go home' remarks to anyone with a European accent. He has the grandfather dropping dead just after posting his Brexit ballot paper with its vote to leave Europe.

The man's son and daughter move to France at the end of the novel and the anti-Brexit university teacher of art divorces her West Midlands driving instructor husband who voted Leave. Coe's characters deserve one more novel to round off this long life story of middle England and middling Englishness since the 1970s. As they end their working life sometime around 2030, we may find out how Brexit – the event, not the plebiscite vote – has changed their country and their lives.

Another novel, a political thriller, *The Friends of Harry Perkins* by the former Labour MP Chris Mullin, is set in Brexit Britain in the 2020s. Brexit is the backdrop to Mullin's sequel to his 1980s political novel, *A Very British Coup*, about a charismatic left-wing Sheffield steelworker, Harry Perkins, who becomes prime minister and moves Britain sharply to the left. The novel and a TV serialization grabbed the hearts of all in Labour in the long years of Margaret Thatcher's reign. At the time Chris Mullin was close to Tony Benn. He is of the same generation as Jeremy Corbyn and held the same views on Europe until the big turn of Labour away from anti-European socialism-in-one-country thinking that happened by 1990. The sequel is full of political melodrama and twists and Brexit Britain is a nation in a 'long slow decline into insularity and irrelevance'.

Mullin describes:

an economy going from bad to worse. The symptoms were unmistakeable. A ballooning trade deficit. A drying up of inward investment. A succession of announcements by British business that they would be relocating to the Continent. Regular crises on the border between Northern Ireland and the Republic when the new technology that was supposed to have resolved the customs problem failed to work.

Mullin's thriller was published in the spring of 2019. Novels by Mick Herron and Linda Grant wove Brexit themes into the narrative, mainly on the rise of hate attacks against Europeans and the growing verbal and other aggressions against Europeans unleashed by the language of Boris Johnson, Nigel Farage and the tabloid press. But, in truth, the world of arts – films, TV series, books, theatre, literary festivals, other creative cultural output – did little to change public opinion in the period after 23 June 2016. To a man and woman and trans, the stars and Stakhanovites of Britain's creative and cultural world were opposed to Brexit. But as with so many, they did not know how to turn that opposition into a different route map for political travel. The artists and actors and academics were not as supine as the lemmings of the business world who refused to challenge Tory leaders like Boris Johnson or Theresa May, just as trade union leaders refused to say that Jeremy Corbyn's unwillingness to critique Brexit was damaging to jobs and investment. But they produced few words, few images that caught public imagination and changed the way Britain saw its amputation from Europe.

A film dramatization of the Leave campaign focused on the character of Dominic Cummings, the anti-European political adviser to Michael Gove, who insisted that immigration should be at the heart of the campaign and dreamt up the slogan 'Take Back Control'. Cummings, played by Benedict Cumberbatch, overwhelmed the programme to the point that a broad-based campaign funded by anti-European forces in Britain and America from the 1990s onwards was subsumed into the story of just one of the functionaries used by the anti-EU elites to win Brexit. A top-flight drama or novel on Brexit has yet to be written.

12

HOW BREXIT COST THE BBC ITS REPUTATION FOR IMPARTIAL FACTUAL NEWS COVERAGE

The propaganda for Brexit continued unabated in much of the press and on the BBC. The BBC, notably its main morning Radio 4 current affairs programme, *Today*, continued to allow Brexit propagandists to appear without challenge. Soon after I returned from a visit to Geneva where I witnessed and photographed at a small border crossing between Switzerland and France the queues of cars being checked in case they brought more than a kilo of beef or four chickens into Switzerland – the limit under Switzerland's tough trade regime – I heard the anti-European Tory MEP Daniel Hannam, and then the pro-hard Brexit MP Sir Bernard Jenkin, proclaim on *Newsnight* and then on the *Today* programme that there was 'frictionless trade' and no customs control borders between Switzerland and its neighbours. Having lived for some years 100 metres from exactly one of those EU–Swiss border controls, I waited for *Newsnight's* Evan Davis or *Today's* Nick Robinson to correct these palpable untruths. But they were silent.

In January 2019, the anti-European Tory Dominic Raab appeared on the *Today* programme. He told Nick Robinson that Switzerland offered a model for a frontier in Northern Ireland that 'wouldn't require infrastructure at the border'. The former Brexit secretary who, along with Mrs May and the two other Brexit secretaries in her government, had signed off on the so-called backstop solution in Ireland was now, like the prime minister, reneging on what the government had solemnly agreed to. On the BBC he said there was no need for a guarantee in the withdrawal agreement that no hard border should return to Ireland. He argued that 'practice around the world including on the Swiss border shows it can be done'. Robinson did not correct this blatant untruth and later the same day on LBC, the former BBC presenter Eddie Mair allowed a caller to announce that 'there are no borders in Switzerland'. Mair, who is normally very fast to jump down the throat of any MP he felt was fabulating, allowed this blatant propaganda to be broadcast as truth.

Ignorance? Poor briefing by researchers? Robert Peston, an experienced economics and business correspondent for the *Financial Times* and BBC, now political editor of ITV, explained that during the Brexit campaign the BBC 'put people on with diametrically opposed views and didn't give their viewers and listeners any help in assessing which one was the loony and which one was the genius'. This idea of balance being simply a matter of allowing the advocate of Brexit to proclaim demonstrable untruths and then later in the programme have someone tell the truth has continued in BBC coverage after Brexit. As Peston noted: 'Impartial journalism is not giving equal airtime to two people one of whom says the world is flat and the other one says the world is round. That is not balanced, impartial journalism.'

As Roger Mosey, a senior BBC journalist, now master of a Cambridge college, wrote: 'programmes such as *Question Time* disdain experts and therefore fail to challenge politicians who say whatever's in their head, irrespective of reality.' One expects the offshore-owned newspapers to maintain their relentless propaganda campaign against Europe, but many assumed the BBC would uphold its near century-long tradition of balance, impartiality and fact-checked news. The BBC mattered far more than other broadcasters. Why did the BBC get Brexit wrong?

I started as a graduate news trainee in the BBC, tasked with writing and producing TV news and current affairs programmes in Broadcasting and Bush House and writing news bulletins, and remain devoted to the BBC's public service ethos. But in its twenty-first-century coverage of the EU, the turn against Europe in the Conservative Party and the rise of UKIP and the BNP as vectors for anti-EU ideology, I think the BBC badly lost its way. The problem with looking at BBC coverage of Brexit is the start date. Brexit did not come out of the blue or begin in 2016. It was a culmination of a change of political culture, the rise of identity politics, the open embrace of Europhobe themes mainstreamed into political discourse this century, especially on the issue of Europeans working and living here.

One of the Brexit clichés is that metropolitan BBC elites were all Europhile. On the contrary, BBC elites, like other London elites, took their cues from their favourite newspapers. They disliked the EU's regulatory culture and adopted a condescending, almost sneering contempt for the EU which could be heard at most London salons from the late 1990s onwards. It wasn't just the *Telegraph, Sun* or *Spectator*; the *Guardian* had its star anti-EU columnists including Sir Simon Jenkins and Giles Fraser, or the anti-Euro political and economic editors Michael White and Larry Elliot. This culminated in the *Guardian's* star young left columnist, Owen Jones, calling for Lexit, left-wing Brexit, before the referendum. David Cameron, George Osborne and William Hague may have supported Remain in the summer of 2016, but between 2000 and 2015 they could never find a good word for Europe. The many BBC journalists who were close to the Tory party reflected this anti-EU London elite culture.

Nearly all the reporters and presenters on programmes such as *Question Time, Newsnight* or the Sunday morning political news shows on Brexit were Westminster specialists. They turned the issue into endless mini-Punch and Judy shows between different populist MPs. The rest of Britain was ignored. With the election of mayors for major cities, parliaments in Scotland, the Welsh and Northern Irish assemblies, Britain now has a wider elected political class than just Commons MPs. The BBC over-focused on Westminster with marginal MPs given huge prominence.

The BBC made no effort to find any voices to balance the minority, extreme protestant DUP party. The DUP got 26 per cent of the vote in 2015. There are other elected Northern Irish politicians, unionist protestant as well as nationalist Catholic, who could have put a different point of view since the 2017 election catapulted the DUP to high prominence. The BBC rarely gave Northern Irish elected representative leaders of business or trade unions a chance to air their criticisms of Brexit. The main peers used were unionists with age-old Europhobe axes to grind.

Between January 2013 and February 2018, the BBC's flagship political mass audience television programme, *Question Time*, had thirty-three appearances by UKIP MEPs, usually Nigel Farage, but not a single Labour, Lib Dem or Green MEP. There were only two appearances by a Conservative MEP, Daniel Hannam, who was usually even more extreme in his anti-Europeanism than any UKIP or BNP MEP. Nigel Farage and other UKIP or later Brexit Party candidates failed the critical test of democratic credibility of winning a seat in the Commons. On the single issue of Europe, and under a flawed electoral system, Farage was elected as an MEP, as were BNP candidates. But the BBC elevated Farage far above more knowledgeable and harder-working MEPs of other parties as part of its tabloid approach to reporting Europe this century.

Factual errors were repeatedly made about Europe that would be unthinkable about UK political coverage or even US political coverage. Roger Mosey describes 'the fact-checks somewhere in the output: online or in a genteel programme on Radio 4. This is often true, but there is a gulf between the headlines on the daily mass-audience bulletins and the correctives on the website.' When I worked at BBC World Service in Bush House, it was forbidden to draft any news story without at least three sources. This was time-consuming and painstaking, but it gave World Service news its unchallengeable reputation. On Brexit, anyone, for example, could state as a fact 'The EU is driving towards a federal superstate' – the height of absurdity, when 99 per cent of all UK public spending is determined inside Britain by the government and MPs. Such statements passed without challenge.

That British elites – government, business, media, Whitehall – are not conversant in European languages is notorious. Michel Barnier and Donald Tusk each learnt passable English ahead of their role in Brexit. But as Brexit became a live issue from the moment David Cameron announced his referendum in January 2013, some effort might have been made to pull back into the BBC's UK editorial, commenting, analytical and presenting roles qualified BBC journalists who had worked in European capitals and were at home with EU facts, EU laws and positions adopted in EU27 capitals. The excellent Katya Adler and other BBC Brussels reporters were given limited airtime as exotic specialists but never put into interviewing jobs where they would have exposed the sheer level of untruths about the EU which the monolingual BBC London presenters were not knowledgeable enough to challenge.

The Brexit years (2013–19) deserved a decent journalist view from BBC correspondents and reporters in different EU capitals on what they were seeing happening in the EU: the good, bad, negative and positive. Compared to the wide and deep reporting of any aspect of American political life and the myriad US political players and personalities, the BBC barely reports what is happening in other European countries, not just EU member states but all forty-seven Council of Europe nations. Ask most London-based BBC journalists covering Brexit to name more than two or three EU prime ministers or top EU officials or foreign ministers and they will struggle. Might the BBC have returned to its former practice of educating the public, in addition to its overall handling of Brexit with antagonists battling it out in sterile studio exchanges in London, as a kind of Euro sports contest in which plucky John or perhaps Jane Bull was engaged in combat with the wily, untrustworthy Europeans?

It surely ought to be a cause for concern that the BBC with its 2,000 journalists failed to uncover – as did the much fewer number of Channel 4 News journalists – the details of dubious financial practices by those who financed the Leave campaign. One single reporter, the *Observer*'s Carole Cadwalladr, did more to expose the deep and almost certainly corrupt financing by external sources that helped win the Brexit vote. Why did no BBC journalists investigate and highlight the fact of this outside financing to buy the Brexit vote now being investigated as a potential crime?

Writing of British football reporters and sports columnists, it was once said: 'They are fans with typewriters.' The same might be said of the reporting of Brexit since 2016, notably in the pro-Brexit press such as the *Daily Telegraph*, the *Daily Mail*, the *Sun*, the *Daily Express*, the *Daily Star, City A.M.* and the influential political weekly the *Spectator*. Every article was slanted to paint the EU in as dark a hue as possible. There were attacks on Michel Barnier, but most coverage was about internal British and especially Conservative Party differences on how to handle Brexit. Few bothered to seek to explore the politics of the EU27 nations or explain to readers what the pros and cons of different variations of Brexit might be.

In the first four months after the vote the *Daily Express* published no fewer than seventy-four front pages attacking Europe or making claims about the threat of immigrants. When Theresa May announced the start of Article 50 Brexit negotiations the *Daily Mail* ran fourteen comment articles attacking those who were unsure about Brexit. 'OUT OF TOUCH ELITE WILL DO ANYTHING TO KEEP US IN THE EU' was typical of the *Mail* headlines.

The *Sun*'s former political editor, Trevor Kavanagh, who had been denouncing Europe since the 1990s, attacked the chancellor, Philip Hammond for pointing out that Brexit meant turbulence and volatility. For Kavanagh these were 'scary warnings' and 'Mr Hammond is now at war with his own party'.

One exuberant pro-Brexit Conservative MP, Chris Rycroft-Davis, used a column in the *Daily Express* to attack MPs – as much in his own as in other parties – who suggested that the House of Commons might be allowed to debate and vote on Brexit. This 'rabble of MPs demanding a Commons vote' were guilty of 'snake-like treachery that cannot go unpunished', he proclaimed and added: 'Clap them in the Tower of London. They want to imprison us against our will in the EU so we should give them 28 days against their will to reflect on the true meaning of democracy.'

This feverish tone was caught by Allister Heath, who was one of the most effective journalist crusaders for Brexit as editor of the important London morning free paper *City A.M.* before becoming deputy editor of the *Daily Telegraph* and editor of the *Sunday Telegraph*. Just four months after his camp's victory he felt obliged to write a column in October 2016 under the headline 'WHY IT'S TIME FOR A NEW CAMPAIGN FOR BREXIT'. He urged his fellow anti-European journalists and editors to keep up the struggle and not assume the vote on 23 June 2016 was the end of the story. 'There is no such thing as permanent victory in politics. History never ends: triumphs are fleeting; majorities can turn into minorities; and orthodoxies are inevitably built on foundations of sand', he wrote. This manic right-wing Trotskyist call for a permanent Brexit revolution was reflected in both the daily and Sunday editions of the *Telegraph*. Occasionally tucked away in the business pages there might be a questioning column from an economics or business writer asking if Brexit would be good for the economy and the paper's Europe editor, Peter Foster was allowed to reflect what he was told in Brussels. But no negative economic warnings were allowed onto the front pages and the paper lost its good name for solid news reporting, as writers and page editors obeyed their chief's instruction to fight day and night against Europe and promote Brexit isolationism. This mindset that Brexit could not be challenged was pervasive. I used to write the occasional comment piece for *City A.M.*, which carries a lot of business news. Then a new comment page editor sent me this chilling email: 'I think we as a paper are past the stage where we can question whether or not Brexit should happen.' I have been writing comment pieces on politics for all sorts of papers over many years and have never been concerned if an article was turned down or not published, but never before had I been told I could not mount an argument that represented where at least half the country was known to be.

Other papers were more objective and the *Financial Times, The Times*, the *Guardian, Independent, Sunday Times* and *New Statesman* ran news and comment pieces for and against aspects of Brexit. Columnists like Sir Simon Jenkins, a star of the *Guardian* comment pages, who had been a relentless critic of all things EU and European in his columns this century, suddenly discovered that leaving the EU was not a good idea and began fulminating against a Brexit rupture. If only he had used his writing skills to make these points before June 2016. The *Observer* published a remarkable series of investigative reports which exposed the influence of the Kremlin and illegal accounting by the Brexit campaigns that helped win the referendum. But other papers were sniffy at these well-researched exposés and the issue, while out in the public domain, did not resonate as much as it should have.

And all the time the newspapers that were not rooting-tooting for Brexit and ran plenty of critical news and comment reports did not really have an idea of what should happen. The *Independent* under its editor, Christian Broughton, came out for a second referendum and launched an online petition for its readers, which got the support of more than 750,000 by September 2018 for a new vote. But other Brexit-critical papers were more cautious and as a result had no real line to take, other than a general wringing of hands.

The press, like the business and think-tank community or the Labour Party, were willing to complain but not campaign, to moan but not mount a coherent attack on Brexit with an alternative policy to mobilize public opinion. Three years after the June 2016 plebiscite Britain was rudderless with neither economic deciders, the main opposition party, the opinion-forming intelligentsia nor the press prepared to say *en clair* that Brexit was bad for the country and should be reversed, as had happened in Denmark and Ireland when referendums had secured initial majorities against the EU.

13

BRITISH POLITICIANS JOIN LONG LIST OF ENEMIES OF EUROPE

Matteo Salvini, the Eurosceptic populist nationalist who together with the Five Star Movement had won power in Italy in 2018, spoke for many in England's Brexit camp when he stated after a tumultuous six months loudly bad-mouthing almost every aspect of European Union policy. "The enemies of Europe are those sealed in the bunker of Brussels. It's Juncker and Moscovici who have brought fear and job insecurity to Europe.'

Blaming the EU Commission president and the EU finance commissioner for the state of the Italian economy or the flight of investors from Italian markets as they listened to the extremist policies being proposed by the populists who had formed a government is nothing new. Italy had enjoyed leadership of other corrupt populists, such as the socialist Bettino Craxi in the 1980s or, more notoriously, the right-wing pro-business populist Silvio Berlusconi who was four times prime minister in the 1990s and early 2000s. But neither they nor the more technocratic prime ministers who also served for short periods as head of one of the 61 Italian governments formed since 1945 have been willing or able to bring about reforms that would make Italy into a modern state in line with those north of the Alps.

Instead of setting about reforming and modernizing the Italian state, the first reaction of Salvini, like his friend Marine Le Pen or Viktor Orban, was to adopt the language of British anti-Europeans and start ranting about the European Commission. It is as if Brussels and the European Commission did not exist they would have to be invented as the enemy Salvini, Boris Johnson and Marine Le Pen crave to advance their politics.

This headline approach to Brexit and European politics ignores the deep historical currents of post-1945 Europe and especially the United Kingdom. But if we step back from our noses pressed against the Brexit looking glass, we can see that any form of European partnership or common purpose or sharing of some national sovereignty to a lesser or greater degree has always provoked relentless opposition. The next era of Brexiternity cannot be understood without a sense of the painful post-1945 history of Britain's relationship with Europe.

Here, for example, in 1971 is Britain's future prime minister, Jim Callaghan, telling an audience that to enter Europe was to exchange America and the Commonwealth for 'an aroma of continental claustrophobia' which meant 'a complete rupture of our identity'. The reason was that on the continent people spoke foreign languages, especially the French who spoke French. 'The language of Chaucer, Milton and Shakespeare' would be challenged: 'If we have to prove our Europeanism by accepting that French is the dominant language in the Community, then my answer is quite clear, and I will say it in French in order to prevent misunderstanding: *"Non, merci beaucoup!".*'

Jokey Jim. Comical Callaghan. But this saloon bar pre-UKIP language was more than typical of the British left's approach to Europe between 1945 and 1990. It is too easy to see Brexit and current anti-EU populist narratives as a right-wing or xenophobic response. Throughout the twentieth and so far in the twenty-first century the left and self-proclaimed progressive forces have often found an easy target in the idea of a Europe that was more than just a geographical location for a collection of nation states.

In the case of England, the English do not like Europe because they have been told for decades that they should not like Europe. Margaret Thatcher's favourite minister, Sir Nicholas Ridley always described the European Community as a 'German racket'. At the beginning of the nineteenth century, Britain's foreign secretary, George Canning wrote that the French 'have but two rules of action; to thwart us whenever they know our object, and when they know it not, to imagine one for us, and set about thwarting that'. For centuries England believed the Vatican and Catholic European powers were determined to weaken or destroy English power. For half a millennium the

English have been told that across the Channel lies menace, danger and a threat to the island way of life.

Brexit is a wholly owned Conservative Party product. To be sure, from Enoch Powell to Boris Johnson, many Conservatives have railed against Europe. But it was a Tory prime minister, David Cameron, who gave the nation the Brexit referendum and his successor, Theresa May, who made a political mess of Brexit after June 2016 with her refusal to reach out to Remain voters and her opportunistic 2017 election which delivered her with hands tied to the DUP. Yet the first and biggest refusal of European integration came under the Labour government elected in 1945. On Europe the Labour government led by Clement Attlee from 1945 to 1951 was blind, deaf and without a policy that might have allowed Britain to lead in the construction of a new Europe after 1945. Labour's approach to Europe after 1945 ranged from fear, to indifference, to hostility, with a minority of Labour MPs sharing the positive approach to Europe of their comrades across the Channel.

All of Europe's post-war parties have had moments of doubt about or opposition to aspects of European integration. And within broadly pro-European parties there have been individual politicians who have said no to a particular moment of European construction. Jacques Chirac attacked Europe in 1978 as part of his political manoeuvres against his hated rival Valéry Giscard d'Estaing. In 1976, Chirac said France 'must not dissolve into an Atlanticist colony called Europe'. In 1978, using identical language to English Brexiters forty years later, Chirac said:

> [France must say NON to] becoming a vassal state. A federal Europe cannot fail to be dominated by the Americans. Voting by majority means France is paralyzed and this cannot serve the interests of France or of Europe. The European community is just a big free trade area which favours powerful foreign interests. That is why we say NON to supranational policy, NON to economic slavery, NON to the loss of international influence of France.

In Britain since 1950 one of the two main parties, Conservative or Labour, has usually adopted as its declared policy a critique of or outright opposition to European construction. For long periods either one or the other of the two dominant political formations has preached against Europe. This has been a potent factor in forming public opinion. It is one thing to reject the anti-Europeanism of hard right or left politicians or single-issue anti-EU formations like UKIP and other Nigel Farage one-man parties, but when an entire party capable of forming a government and with thousands of locally elected men and women as well as MPs finds nothing good to say on Europe and every day denounces Europe in negative terms of contempt and opposition, then it is much harder to create a climate of sympathy for the idea of Europe as part of national political discourse.

After Labour won power in 1945, one of the main architects of Labour's rejection of Europe was a young politician called Denis Healey. Healey was a brilliant scholar who had been in the Communist Party at Oxford before 1939. In 1945 he addressed the Labour Party conference wearing his uniform as a war hero. He became the Labour Party's international secretary. He provided the words in notes, articles, speeches and pamphlets that shaped the Labour party response to events and ideas that dominated European politics and decisions between 1945 and 1951.

Later Healey became minister of defence in the Labour government of 1964–70 and chancellor of the exchequer, 1974–79. In the 1970s and 1980s he was Labour's most respected politician, admired as much for his sense of culture and command of German and Italian as for his incisive speeches in the Commons and effective appearances on television attacking Mrs Thatcher. But Healey remained true to his anti-European beliefs. Aged 80, he launched a movement 'Labour Against the Euro'. During more than half a century Healey consistently opposed most aspects of European integration. At the age of 95, Lord Healey said he would vote in favour of Britain leaving the European Union in Mr Cameron's proposed referendum.

In a key Labour Party policy pamphlet, *European Unity*, published in June 1950, on the eve of the Schuman plan's formal adoption by France, Germany, Italy and the Benelux nations to set up the ECSC, the forerunner of today's EU, Healey denounced in Labour's name all moves to set up a European structure which might reduce the power of the British government:

'No Socialist Party with the prospect of forming a government could accept a system by which important fields of national policy were surrendered to a supranational European representative authority, since such an authority would have a permanent anti-Socialist majority and would arouse the suspicions of European workers.'

With these few words Healey set down more than six decades ago the classic sovereignist left case against Europe. By 1950, only a loyal Labour Party apparatchik could believe the Britain of monarchy, of aristocrats sitting as legislators without election, of private schools, of car firms like Ford and General Motors firmly in foreign private ownership and the nation's defence policy subordinate to Washington's control in NATO, and of growing worker discontent against wage restrictions was just around the corner from socialism. Indeed, a few months after Healey said Britain should say no to Europe, Britain said no to Labour in 1951 and voted in a Conservative government that stayed in office until 1964.

LABOUR'S WEATHER VANE APPROACH TO EUROPE

All politicians are entitled to change their minds and positions. But the history of British politics from 1945 until today is full of men and women who have moved from A to Z on the spectrum of Europe. For the British people who, like citizens of other countries, expect a degree of consistency from their leading politicians on the important issues that face a nation, this constant zig-zagging and change of mind and language on Europe is deeply confusing. Some begin as anti-Europeans and become converted to a pro-European position. One such example was Robin Cook, appointed foreign secretary by Tony Blair in 1997, who later became a pro-EU zealot and president of the Party of European Socialists. For many, the journey is in the opposite direction: an early enthusiasm for Europe curdles into hostility flattered and encouraged by the anti-European press. In 1982, David Owen, the Labour MP who had been Britain's youngest-ever foreign secretary between 1977 and 1979, left the Labour Party with other pro-European Labour MPs including Roy Jenkins and Shirley Williams and formed the Social Democratic Party. In 1982, Owen was pro-European. By 2012, still with a voice in British politics and a seat in the House of Lords, Lord Owen was calling for a referendum to take Britain out of Europe. Labour's only consistency has been its inconsistency.

In the 1980s, Jack Straw, later Britain's foreign minister under Tony Blair, was anti-European. As a new leadership took control of the Labour Party in the 1990s, Straw became nominally pro-European. He wrote an essay in the *Economist* in October 2002 calling for a constitution for Europe. His enthusiasm did not last six months, as I noted in my diary:

Monday 29 March 2003

Jack is in a very grumpy mood. Blair has come back from Brussels full of breezy gung-ho optimism on the constitution. Jack wishes it simply wasn't on the agenda at all. 'This constitution won't fly at all,' he says. He really doesn't like the European Union and that is the top and bottom of it.

Of course, in moving from being anti-Europe to being pro-Europe, Straw would never admit inconsistency – no politician ever does. But Labour's shifting one way and then the other on Europe is part of the reason why Britain does not like Europe.

Opposition to European partnership and supranational integration has deep roots. Lenin denounced any idea of a 'United States of Europe as a capitalist entente to divide up colonies'. Pan-Europeanism was also opposed by the Nazis. Hitler's chief ideologue, Alfred Rosenberg said the ideas of European nations working together which emerged in the 1920s were the product of 'the stock market and Jewish journalists'. Hitler denounced the mistake of 'democratic Europeanism' based on unifying racially unequal people which 'is why Jews in particular support this concept'. H. G. Wells wrote against European unity non-stop in the 1920s and 1930s.

I once asked the constitutional political historian, Vernon Bogdanor, who was tutor to David Cameron in Oxford, how one might persuade the English to look more favourably on Europe. He smiled and said quickly: 'Just ensure we had been invaded, conquered and occupied in the 1940s.' The idea that it is the English who are sceptical about Europe and the United Kingdom is alone in criticizing Brussels as the symbol of European integration does not bear a moment's scrutiny. Nor does the conventional wisdom cliché that it is continental Europe's experience of the German conquests 1939–45 and then the Russian takeover of east Europe 1945–90 that makes the continental European nations much more pro-European and fans of Brussels. A moment's examination of the attacks by the current ruling politicians in Hungary,

Poland, Italy, the Czech Republic or Bulgaria on the European Commission or decisions emanating from Brussels shows that Euroscepticism is not an English malady.

It little matters whether it is left- or right-wing Europe. In 1929, R. H. (Richard) Tawney, the Oxford professor of economic history and one of the most prominent ethical socialists with great influence on the British Labour Party between the two big twentieth-century wars, wrote: 'An integration of Europe, whatever its precise form, has reason on its side; but the natural human egotisms of interests and emotions; of locality, class and occupation; of regional loyalties and national pride, will rally to resist it.'

Tawney was right then and is right now. His points, however, can be seen all over Europe today, the day before and in every decade since 1950. Europe has always been a work-in-progress, a never-finished political-economic building site that has required energy, purpose and confidence, new architects and builders or craft workers to begin the next stage of construction. Here is the great French liberal intellectual, Raymond Aron, in 1956, proclaiming: 'The European idea is empty with neither the appeal of messianic ideologies' (i.e. Soviet communism or 1930s fascism) 'out to change humanity nor that of blood-soaked nations' (i.e. France or Britain in two world wars). This dichotomy, so typical of French writing about anything, misses the point about the very nature of European integration: its modesty. Bringing Europe together can only ever work on a step-by-step basis. Occasionally there are big breakthroughs, such as Margaret Thatcher's Single European Act or the euro, but for the most part European partnership construction is slow, evolutionary politics.

All the time there is opposition. Today English and French extreme anti-Europeanism of both right and left denounces the EU as a German-controlled entity imposing Berlin's will on poorer, weaker countries. Go back to the 1950s and it is the German left opposing European integration as it meant the domination of Germany by European powers.

In 1952, the German Social Democratic Party (SPD) voted with German communists in the Bundestag against the ECSC. German social democrats saw the ECSC as benefiting mainly France and even made comparisons with Versailles Treaty reparations. The SPD leader, Kurt Schumacher had spent thirteen years in Buchenwald concentration camp. He complained that the leaders of the six founding members of the ECSC were 'Conservative, clericalist, capitalist and cartellist' and said the SPD rejected the ECSC 'both as convinced internationalists and as German patriots and as Europeans'. The SPD spent the 1950s in the political doldrums thanks to Schumacher's political nationalism. The 1959 Bad Godesberg congress, which modernized the SPD and saw the emergence of a new generation of leaders like Willy Brandt and Helmut Schmidt, saw the main German left party accept that it made sense for Germany to play a full part in Europe, a position Britain's Labour Party did not reach until three decades later.

BOTH LEFT AND RIGHT IN FRANCE ANTI-EUROPE

French anti-Europeanism of both left and right continued unabated. François Mitterrand proclaimed himself pro-European; he had attended the Hague Congress in 1948 presided over by Winston Churchill which gave birth to the European Movement with its national chapters. Yet in 1972, Mitterrand refused to support the French government headed by President Pompidou in the referendum held on Britain joining the European Economic Community. Many key figures in the Parti socialiste after its launch in 1970 adopted French left nationalist sovereignist arguments similar to those of Schumacher. Their leader was Jean-Pierre Chevènement. French left national sovereignists attacked the idea of direct elections to the European Parliament beginning in 1979, which would not change the 'essence of capitalist Europe'. At a meeting in Brussels in the 1980s, Tony Benn asked me to introduce him to Chevènement, which I did, leaving them to have their discussion. It seemed very intense, with Benn waving his pipe about but the Frenchman appearing to do the talking. Afterwards Benn came over to me and said: 'Thank you very much, Denis. That was marvellous. Of course I couldn't understand a word he said but it's clear he is a very principled socialist.'

Mitterrand sent his finance minister, Jacques Delors, to be European Commission president in 1985 to power through the Single European Act with the support of Margaret Thatcher and Helmut Kohl. It was based on abolishing national vetoes. Mrs Thatcher, in 1984, also called for a European Common Foreign and Security policy – a major extension of European competences into an area previously jealously guarded as a national prerogative. Mitterrand told Delors, who was closely linked to the reformist CFDT trade union confederation in France, to develop an effective social policy for Europe. 'Social Europe', a sequence of broad-brush measures aimed at guaranteeing core workplace rights, came into being.

This caused apoplexy in the British Conservative Party, which had governed since 1979 on the basis of anti-union measures that saw the number of trade union members halved and employees losing many of the rights they had taken for granted since 1945. In truth, 'Social Europe' directives were moderate and modest, but they served their purpose of persuading most trade unions and centre-left parties in Europe, notably in Britain, that European construction had a commitment to protecting and supporting workers and their unions.

French anti-Europeanism remained endemic. In the 1992 French referendum on the Maastricht Treaty, Mitterrand insisted that the EU existed 'to protect workers'. The French ratified Maastricht by 51 per cent, thus staying in the EU by a smaller majority than the Brexit majority to leave Europe. France's main centre-right party headed by Jacques Chirac supported a No vote. This produced a backlash from pro-Europeans, much as today pro-European MPs in both the Conservative and Labour parties feel let down by the obsessive defence of Brexit by their party hierarchies.

One young French politician, Michel Barnier, a left-leaning social Gaullist, defied Chirac and voted for the Maastricht Treaty in the National Assembly. 'Chirac was furious', Barnier told me, 'and came up to me after the vote and jabbed his finger in my chest saying "Your career is over, dead, finished". *Eh bien*, I've managed to be France's Foreign and Agricultural Minister, and twice an EU Commissioner, so maybe my decision to stick to my pro-European beliefs and not indulge in political opportunism did not serve me too badly.'

One of the oddest aspects of the Europe-haters in politics is that they are never consistent. In France, the National Front (now rebadged the National Rally) has been led by Jean-Marie Le Pen and subsequently his daughter Marine. In June 1989, Le Pen Snr said Europe should have 'an army, a currency, a diplomatic service, and a European police service to fight illegal frontier crossing, international crime, drug trafficking and counterfeit money'. So just thirty years ago Jean-Marie Le Pen was going well beyond the demands of the most ardent federalist. One wonders where Nigel Farage, Boris Johnson or Jacob Rees-Mogg might end up?

It is almost as if anti-Europeanism is an essential component of modern politics in Europe transcending right and left. As the French Communist Party by the end of the twentieth century finally weaned itself off primitive xenophobic anti-European lines, the extreme right National Front party picks up all the old communist themes and packages them into a populist anti-immigrant appeal that propels Jean-Marie Le Pen into the second round of the French presidential election in 2002 and his daughter into the run-off against Emmanuel Macron to be president of France in 2017. The Conservative Party was the European party from 1950 to 1995 and Labour was hostile to European integration for most of those years. Then the points switch and William Hague, Iain Duncan Smith, Michael Howard and David Cameron decide to make a populist appeal about bossy Brussels and Europeans working in Britain against two Labour prime ministers who accepted EU membership.

THREE COUNTRIES SHARE REFUGEE BURDEN

It is always about political choice. Three EU countries have shared the main burden of receiving the hundreds of thousands of refugees fleeing the West-supported attacks on state structures in Iraq, Libya and Syria. In two of them, Greece and Spain, most politicians of the left and right have not sought to use the refugee issue to whip up political hatred or to attack Brussels and the EU. In Italy, by contrast, ministers who took over in 2018 won power by attacking the EU as if Brussels had ordered the military action in the Middle East or Libya. It is 2,500 km from the refugee camps on Greek, Italian or Spanish territory to Warsaw, Copenhagen or Berlin, but populist politicians used anti-European rhetoric or open xenophobic or anti-Muslim demagogy in order to win votes or stay in power.

Political leaders chose to enter the eurozone as a symbol of modernization and progress. But then they refused to update or reform national economic, fiscal or banking regulatory systems to make their countries able to meet the huge responsibility that came with sharing a currency with other better-managed, less corrupt or clientalist economies. Then they turned angrily on Brussels when the sunny days of low-interest euros pouring in to be used to buy votes or line the pockets of national elites were replaced by the cold winds of the crash or the recessions inevitable under the existing system of deregulated liberal economic management that prevailed from the 1980s onwards. From Yanis Varoufakis on the populist left to Matteo Salvini on the populist right, transferring the blame to Brussels was second nature and would be easily understood by any Freudian psychoanalyst.

The post-communist politicians in central and east Europe were experts at this demagogy. Beginning with Vaclav Klaus in Prague and today with Viktor Orban in Budapest and Jarosław Kaczynski in Warsaw, it seemed at times as if the EU had replaced the Soviet Union as the enemy of the people and nations of central and east Europe. The term EUSSR was used and when the former Czech president Klaus referred to the EU as a new Soviet Empire, he was deadly serious.

The old tunes were the best ones. The French communist historian, Annie Lacroix-Riz insisted in 2016 that Europe was just one of 'the spheres of influence of the United States'. She did not go as far as her fellow anti-European intellectual, Antonin Cohen, whose 2012 book *De Vichy à la Communauté européenne* (From Vichy to the European Community) contained in its title the standard anti-European line that European construction since 1950 has been a corporatist rightist conspiracy.

In fact, anti-European thinking has a whole army of intellectuals and journalists on its side. Here is the venerable founding figure of the *New Left Review* in London, Perry Anderson, much quoted by left populists like Pablo Iglesias, leader of the Podemos party in Spain, explaining how people 'now saw the EU for what it is: an oligarchy, riddled with the gangrene of corruption, built on the denial of popular sovereignty, imposing an economic regime with its privileges for some and constraints for all the rest'. For the post-class-war sociological Marxists like Ernesto Laclau and Chantal Mouffe, the EU stands in the way, not of nations, as anti-EU sovereignists argue, but prevents 'the construction of the people' and their popular sovereignty against the liberal elites. Laclau and Mouffe are followers of the German philosopher Carl Schmitt, who rejected liberal parliamentary democracy and insisted that any attempt to produce harmony or cooperation in politics led inevitably to the reinforcement of those who already wielded power or possessed wealth. Thus the EU, which by its very nature is based on compromise, consensus and liberal rule of law norms, is seen by many left populists as standing in the way of the 'people' obtaining what they should have. Much of this is influenced by Latin American populism and the idea of the people as opposed to the state or an economic system dear to populists from Juan Peron to Hugo Chavez.

Jürgen Habermas, generally seen as a European federalist, writes that EU leaders 'insist on pursuing their elitist project and taking away the rights of the European people'. He deplored the Brexit vote result, but went on to tell *Die Zeit* that the fault lay with the European Union and, in an echo of much of the pro-Brexit arguments in Britain, blamed his own country:

> Germany is a reluctant but insensitive and incapable hegemon that both uses and ignores the disturbed European balance of power at the same time. This provokes resentments, especially in other Eurozone countries. How must a Spaniard, Portuguese or Greek feel if he has lost his job as a result of the policy of spending cuts decided by the European Council? He cannot arraign the German cabinet ministers who got their way with this policy in Brussels: he cannot vote them in or out of office. Instead of which, he could read during the Greek crisis that these very politicians angrily denied any responsibility for the socially disastrous consequences that they had casually taken on board with such programmes of cuts. As long as this undemocratic and faulty structure is not got rid of you can hardly be surprised at anti-European smear campaigns. The only way to get democracy in Europe is through a deepening of European co-operation.

If there was a Nobel prize for political-sociological writing Habermas would surely have won it. His view that the answer to the Brexit result and the so-called democratic deficit 'is through a deepening of European cooperation' will not ring convincingly in the meetings across Europe, where the very idea of the European Union is coming under increasing challenge.

The problem Habermas and most pro-European left intellectuals face is that they posit the idea of Europe in opposition to the failure of nation-state politics to deliver their desired political outcome of a better life for all. This is asking Europe or the EU to carry too much responsibility. Europe can only be built with, not against, its constituent nations. Britain opting out by whatever final means the Brexiternity of negotiations in the 2020s produces is irrelevant. We can no more opt out of Europe than the farmer or fisherman can opt out of the weather. The twenty-first century will see stops and starts, many wrong turnings in European integration – assuming, that is, there is no collapse of democracy and Europe does not become a minor extension of the rising powers and populations in Asia – but the European nations are condemned to live with each other and in each other. The European Union is imperfect, as so many of its political and intellectual critics from all points of the political compass point out. But it is the best effort made in two millennia of European history to allow such different peoples to live relatively harmoniously together.

14

HOW EUROPE SURVIVES BREXIT

So, as Britain settles into a decade of Brexiternity, what happens to the European Union? The next period of European governance 2019–24 with new presidents of the European Commission, European Council and European Central Bank, new MEPs, a new High Representative – the EU foreign policy chief – will determine both what happens in Europe and what happens in the next chapters in the history of Brexit.

A heavy responsibility lies on the shoulders of a young man and an older woman – Emmanuel Macron and Angela Merkel. Macron bucked the trend towards nationalist, closed-society politics when he won election as president of France in 2017, after the triumphs for the nationalist politics of Brexit and President Trump in 2016. Mrs Merkel has steadily upheld core freedoms and insisted on the centrality of European values in Germany based in part on her own experience of living in the unfree Germany up to the demolition of the Berlin Wall.

Both Macron and Merkel ended 2018 on a downbeat note. Angela Merkel stood down as leader of the German Christian Democratic Union Party after eighteen years in leadership. She said she would remain German chancellor to 2021. Some predicted or hoped she might move to Brussels to take over an EU leadership role for the period 2019–24. She was replaced as CDU party leader by her protégé, Annegret Kramp-Karrenbauer. This moderate can-do politician was born in 1962 in the western region of the Saarland. She speaks fluent French. Macron was buffeted by the *Gilets jaunes* (Yellow Vests) protest movements. He failed to find support elsewhere in Europe for many of his

EU reform ideas put forward in the early months of his presidency. The European Parliament voted down his idea of having a transnational list of candidates to stand for the seventy-three seats vacated by British MEPs. The leader of the Socialist and Democrats centre-left grouping of MEPs, the German Social Democrat MEP Udo Bullman, strongly attacked Macron as promoting right-wing policies at the conference of the Party of European Socialists in Lisbon in December 2018 and there is considerable bitterness among French reformist pro-European socialists that Macron refused any alliance or cooperation with them, preferring to rule as a 'Jupiter', to use his own metaphor.

In his 2019 New Year address to the French, Macron said: 'We can't work less, earn more, cut taxes and increase spending and not change any of our habits and still breathe clean air.' There was a time when such obvious banalities of truth would have been on the lips of European reformist social democrats when they used to win elections and govern countries. He added that the era of 'ultra-liberal capitalism is coming to an end'. It is now widely accepted that the thirty-year-long cycle of 'enrichissez-vous' (get rich) capitalism that began with the great deregulation and deindustrialization policies of the 1980s, and which accelerated with the end of European communism and the rise of China as a new source of low-wage production where all workers were denied trade union rights and all citizens denied basic freedom of expression right, is not sustainable.

The way in which Europe restores a sense of social solidarity while maintaining the maximum flexibility and encouraging investment in start-ups and new job-creating enterprises that add value is a key question. Macron at least is trying to ask it. He faces nationalist populists in many countries whose response is to put up economic barriers, especially in the labour market. Matteo Salvini, the right-wing Italian populist leader, calls the euro 'a crime against humanity' and urged a new 'axis' with Vienna and Berlin against the EU's efforts to deal with arrivals from war and conflict zones of the Middle East and Africa.

To anyone with a shred of sensitivity about twentieth-century European history, invoking an 'axis' is disturbing. Salvini's bombast about the euro is not shared by Marine Le Pen, who has dropped her demand that France exits the eurozone. In fact, the rise of the populist right has been matched by the rise of other populists like the Greens, left populists like Podemos in

Spain, Syriza in Greece, *La France Insoumise* in France, or *Die Linke* in Germany. The post-1945 twentieth-century political formations – roughly the conservative, Christian democrat right, the socialist, labour and social democratic left, and the liberals floating in the middle – have all lost ground in Europe. At the start of 2019, half the governments in Europe were minority administrations. Voters are not prepared to entrust total power to just one political grouping. Countries such as Sweden, the Netherlands, Belgium, even Germany can take months to form a governing coalition. European politics begins to resemble those in Switzerland where no party ever wins a majority and where the seven-strong Federal Council – the ruling cabinet in Switzerland – always has three or four parties represented on it.

At least Macron has been putting forward proposals to make Europe work better, unlike most of the rightist populist nationalists who complain about EU obligations while demanding as much money from Brussels as possible. Macron's flagship proposal for a eurozone budget has not been accepted despite warm words from Angela Merkel. His more ambitious plans for a eurozone finance minister or an EU version of the IMF have been pushed aside by the upholder of orthodox financial and economic management, who are as strongly represented among social democratic finance ministers as among conservative ones.

Mrs Merkel has refused to spend any political capital on an alliance with Macron on eurozone reform. A key proposal early in the 2014–19 European Commission and Council was for a banking union. Disagreement over the creation of a Europe-wide deposit insurance scheme has put on hold this long-needed reform which would help complete the single market.

Macron has been prepared to make the case for reforming Europe to avoid the disaster of the austerity years and the EU's poor handling of the debt crisis after the crash of 2008/9. Nearly all of Macron's ideas imply a stronger Europe in line with the great advances of the Delors–Thatcher–Kohl–Mitterrand years before the Maastricht Treaty of 1992. These happened precisely because there was a troika of determined national leaders in Germany, France and Britain and a determined, hard-working, austere social-liberal president of the Commission. Macron has no such partners and EU Commission presidents this century have been less than stellar.

The new populist parties – of the left, the greens, as much as the anti-EU, xenophobic nationalist right – were eating away at the big classic political formations of Europe in the second half of the twentieth century. It is impossible in democratic politics to satisfy all of the people all of the time. The art lies in knowing how to satisfy at least a majority of the people most or some of the time – the necessary requirement for government stability. Without such government stability at home, leaders had little or no room for manoeuvre in agreeing necessary new policy at the EU level.

At the same time as Macron was trying and failing to persuade Berlin to engage as a partner in a renewed push for EU reform, Germany's neighbours to its east and south and north were returning to an early nationalist European politics, though elections at parliamentary, regional and local level may change the current grip of national identity politicians. While much focus has been placed on the growth of support for xenophobic parties such as the Swedish Democrats and Germany's AfD, there have also been surges of support for green and progressive parties outside the framework of classic twentieth-century centre-right and centre-left parties. Nationalist identity politics does not automatically equate with reactionary or rightist politics, as the Scottish National Party shows. New forms of media communication which are post-truth and ignorant of facts, as well as despising the give-and-take arguments of representative parliamentarianism, make partnership politics more challenging.

It would be a foolish head of government who submitted a new EU Treaty to a plebiscite, but the clamour for referendums on EU questions grows daily.

If Europe is to move forward – or move anywhere – new rules are needed. The EU is a legal construction shaped by international treaty law. Strip away the visionary oratory starting with Churchill's 'United States of Europe' appeal in September 1946 and what we have is the practical creation that has allowed European peoples to come together in a manner never known before in their history. Statesmen and one stateswoman – Margaret Thatcher – created the EU as a system of rules and regulations enshrined in international law.

THERE CAN BE NO EUEXIT. EUROPE CANNOT LEAVE EUROPE

There can be no Euexit. Europe cannot leave Europe. But equally it cannot be business as usual for the national heads of government or the EU institutions like the Commission, the Parliament, the European Court of Justice or the

Central Bank who decide Europe's policy and how to interpret or enforce or turn a blind eye to the EU's existing rules. Brexit will change Britain, but will also change Europe.

The Luxembourg politician, Jean-Claude Juncker, president of the European Commission, 2014–19, put it well:

> There is an existential crisis in Europe. We must stop talking about the United States of Europe. The people of Europe don't want it. They like their land, their diversity. If they think Europe is on the way to becoming a state they reject it. Europe cannot be built against the will of nations. Nations will last. Europe must be a complement to nations.

Juncker was fond of the 'last-chance saloon' metaphor for the European Union. As he told a seminar in Paris in October 2016, 'It's the last chance we have to get Europe going again. We need to modernize the economy and make it a digital economy. We need a Europe with a real energy policy. Public finances have to return to health.'

Back in Brussels, officials in the EU Commission's Finance and Regional Directorates circulated a paper which stated: 'More and more citizens are losing faith in the Union's project – as it fails to provide them with confidence and hope for a better future.'

Who can disagree with that? But before we get to a workable solution for the European malaise of which Brexit is the most dramatic symptom, we have to ask more basic questions.

A leading Eurosceptic over the years in Britain is the former governor of the Bank of England, Mervyn King. He had to keep his view under wraps when he was the UK's central banker, but no one who saw him at seminars or had private talks with him could doubt his hostility. Like many in the monolingual London establishment, there was never any sense that King understood how other countries in Europe worked and saw themselves. He incarnates the 1980s Thatcher generation that lives in the world of the London wealthy and believes in the innate superiority of anything England does. Six months after Brexit he insisted that 'being out of what is a pretty unsuccessful European Union gives us opportunities'.

Yet are countries such as Germany, Austria, the Netherlands, large regions in France or northern Italy, or the Nordic nations really so unsuccessful? If

Lord King visited many regions of Britain, he would see levels of poverty, unsuccessful firms, poor public services and many, many smaller businesses only able to survive because of taxpayer-subsidized employment using low-paid European citizens. It is all too easy to set up the straw man of the European Union which has undertaken and is still undertaking the herculean task of bringing backward, impoverished, ex-dictatorship nations of Europe up to the level of modern economics all would wish to achieve.

EU AND UK SHARE COMMON CHALLENGES

In a *Daily Telegraph* column in May 2013, Boris Johnson wrote: 'If we left the EU . . . we would have to recognise that most of our problems are not caused by Brussels but by chronic British short-termism, inadequate management, sloth, low skills, a culture of easy gratification and under-investment in both human and physical capital and infrastructure.' The UK is a nation state and is responsible for its failings. Europe or the EU is not a nation, still less a state, and it is foolish to blame failures by nation states within the EU on the EU's existence, as Boris Johnson and other anti-Europeans in Britain like to do relentlessly.

No one has any clear idea of where Europe and the EU should now go. Almost every week there is a learned or perhaps a polemical book published by an academic, a politician, an intellectual or a journalist seeking to describe the EU's malaise and then suggest ways of reinvigorating the tired, sagging corpus. In a sense Brexit is almost a welcome experiment by which we shall see if a country that decides to leave the European Union can not only survive, but flourish.

The Brexit vote was part of the unfolding process of the failure of global-ized capitalism to win new generations of political support. The governments of EU member states have been unable to deliver or bring into alignment shared economic prosperity, social investment and progress, and a stable programme of development for poorer countries, including those which have joined the EU in the twenty-first century.

Post-national capitalism wants workers to be available at a moment's notice, especially to generate wealth in the new people-intensive industries of cafés, bars, cleaning, caring and transport. Modern capitalism long ago gave up on any sense of a national social contract to train young men and women to given them skills in the non-university graduate labour market.

Will Brexit be the catalyst for European renewal? Or will it further expose the fault lines in the EU, as British anti-Europeans devoutly hope? They dream that following Brexit, the EU slowly sinks under the weight of its contradictions and begins to disintegrate. Those who resist this return to nationalism and protectionism need to embrace more strongly the cause of reforming the EU.

REFORMING THE EUROPEAN UNION – SIX MODEST PROPOSALS

There are so many areas of what happens within Europe's nation states that need reform. Following Brexit, there were calls for a new structure for Europe: a concentric circle Europe, a multi-speed Europe, or a Europe with an inner core of northern eurozone member states and a looser relationship with countries that have difficulty accepting financial and economic discipline. None of this is new. University library shelves are full of books setting out proposals for a different Europe. Every year think tanks or clusters of self-appointed 'wise men' (for some reason, writing on what the EU needs to do seems a male preserve) produce reports and road maps saying what Europe should do or how the EU should be reformatted. Many of them are written by national politicians now out of office. What they were unable to do in office they can proclaim should be done in retirement. Here are six possible reforms.

1. Reform European Universities

Universities are bastions of protection, as many across Europe insist that the diplomas and degrees awarded in other countries have no validity when it comes to offering full tenured posts to foreigners. Indeed, if there is one area of Europe crying out for reform, it is the university sector. Take out British universities, which are full of foreign professors, lecturers and above all students, and there is not a single EU university in the world's top twenty-five universities. Dutch universities now do their undergraduate teaching in English, as the clever Dutch realize they have to adapt to the world's lingua franca if Dutch higher education is to flourish and serve the national interests of the Netherlands. By contrast, British universities will be crippled if the Brexit ministers get their way and slow down the arrival of foreign students and teachers on the grounds of curbing immigration. Universities in North America and Asia have helped source important breakthroughs in new economic added-value activities. Continental European university protectionism has been one of the biggest areas of failure in EU integration or in developing Europe's universities into world-beating excellence, teaching students from all over the world and attracting the best minds to work and help grow the EU.

The example of second-class universities shows that the national traditions and the historical culture and emphasis on the nation state continue to permeate the EU.

2. Treat the Commission as Ally, not Enemy

Sandro Gozi was Italy's Europe minister until the populists won power in Italy. He is one of the most thoughtful and forceful of the next generation of European politicians. He complains that in the second five-year term of the European Commission president José Manuel Barroso between 2009 and 2014, 'the European Commission gave up its role and became a secretariat for national heads of government ever anxious not to oppose them. Berlaymont [the home of the European Commission] was reduced to pointless buildings full of offices.'

Yet whenever the European Commission pleaded with the Italian government of Matteo Renzi, in which Sandro Gozi served, to obey core EU rules on debt and deficit and to reform the economy, especially its banks, along lines agreed at EU level, the Commission was told to go away and stop telling sovereign Italy what to do. The new populist government in Italy is also telling Brussels to drop dead and not insist on Rome meeting its obligation as a state sharing its currency with countries that obey common eurozone rules. The idea of a unified Europe based on the eurozone is easy to declare as an ambition. Yet unless national governments of Europe post-Brexit are as willing to share sovereignty as the generation of, say, Kohl, Thatcher and Mitterrand in the 1980s, the stubborn reality of national priorities and preferences will come to replace the integrated cooperation and acceptance of a common rulebook that is essential to make the EU function.

Europe also needs a new journalism. I cannot think of a single book about Europe that I have seen produced in more than at best two languages. This remains one of the fundamental problems of European discussion. There is no common European history, or philosophy, or intellectual opinion shapers, journalists and media that fully transcend borders.

Worthy efforts are made, but most founder on the problem of language. Occasionally a pan-European historian like the late Tony Judt or political commentators like Timothy Garton Ash or Josef Joffé will get a book or commentaries published in newspapers outside England or Germany. At an elite level, papers like the *Financial Times* or *Economist* have a pan-European readership, but only to English-reading very important people.

Democratic politics depends on public opinion which is influenced by history, today's political leaders and the media. But how can the EU fashion a democratic politics and shape public opinion when it has no history in the sense of war, conquest, culture or sense of meaning, it has no common media, and many elected politicians in EU states find it easier to condemn and blame the EU rather than support it?

3. Reform the European Parliament

The French socialist minister, EU commissioner and dedicated pro-European Pierre Moscovici insists:

> We need to strengthen the European Parliament. How can we do that? By proceeding with the 'Europeanization' of European elections. This implies continuing to elect the *Spitzenkandidaten* – the lead candidates chosen by the different political families to run for the presidency of the Commission. It also implies creating transnational lists and strengthening its role of supervisor and democratic monitor, including when it comes to economic governance of the euro area.

Has this got the process the wrong way round? It is not the European Parliament that needs strengthening, but the role of national parliaments representing the populations of Europe in the democratic supervision of EU decisions. There was much cheer in 2019 when 50 per cent of European voters cast a vote in the European Parliament elections, yet that still leaves one in two voters indifferent to the idea that the European Parliament represents the beating heart of democracy in the EU.

Indeed, there may be a case for arguing that if a nation cannot mobilize more than a quarter or a third of its electorate to vote for representation in the Strasbourg Parliament, it should simply not be permitted to have MEPs and instead nominate national MPs, as is the case in the parliamentary assembly of the Council of Europe. This may be harsh, but would oblige some political education in Europe about the importance of democratic control and surveillance of EU decisions.

As it is, too many political parties use the European Parliament as a rest home for former ministers or party officials who need an income. In Britain, the European Parliament was used in the past as a kind of holding pen for ambitious young politicians like the former Liberal Democrat leader, Nick Clegg, until they won seats in the Commons. It therefore does not have a continuity or permanent esprit de corps. Over the years there have been numerous scandals over pay and expenses. Nigel Farage boasted in the 2009 election that he had claimed £2 million in expenses and allowances from the European Parliament, which puts in the shade the moneys MPs helped themselves to in the House of Commons expenses scandal. Thanks to the pay, staffing and allowances for offices back in national constituencies, the European Parliament has been an important financial source for the promotion of anti-European populist and identity politics of both the right and left.

Few MEPs are held accountable by the national or local media for what they do in Strasbourg and Brussels and, as long as they turn up for a few moments and sign an attendance register, can be very well remunerated. And some from nationalist-populist identitarian parties like the Brexit Party and UKIP or the now rebadged *Front National* in France use the European Parliament mainly as a propaganda platform to attack the EU and obtain funds for anti-EU propaganda back home. On both the hard left and right there are parties that make populist appeals that win seats in the low-turnout elections to the European Parliament and then make no constructive parliamentary contribution to the often detailed and boring oversight work of committees.

It would be useful to associate national parliaments with the work of the European Parliament. One mechanism would be to create a second chamber – a kind of European Senate – consisting of national parliamentarians.

Another modest reform would be to build joint committees covering all the main directorates of the European Commission so that national MPs were directly involved in overseeing the work of the Commission.

A third would be for more joint committees of inquiry to produce special reports relating to EU-wide policy. Much more oversight over EU policy can already be undertaken by national parliaments, including the House of Commons, on their own initiative. One of the first acts of David Cameron when he became prime minister in 2010 was to abolish the regular House of Commons debate that preceded each EU Council meeting and which obliged ministers to come to the floor of the Commons to explain the UK government's approach to EU decisions. This was part of Cameron's disdain and dislike of the EU as an institution. The losers were the British people, who have no idea of how little interest their MPs take in European policy and directives.

The Danish Parliament has set up a committee that requires all Danish government decisions on Europe or proposals for changes in EU policy to be first debated and agreed before ministers are allowed to speak or vote in Brussels. Something similar could be set up in all national parliaments, including the House of Commons, so that elected national representatives would have oversight of EU politics and policy.

Unfortunately the House of Commons, which sees itself as a very superior body, especially in relation to the European Parliament, refuses to alter its practices to allow MPs to become involved in EU affairs. MPs who take a serious interest in EU policy are mocked as Europhiles and getting reimbursement for any travel in Europe to link with other parliamentarians or MEPs is difficult, with accusations of 'junketeering' thrown at any MPs who think finding out on the spot what is going on in Europe is part of their job.

There could also be term limits on MEPs so that no one who had lost a national seat or job as a minister could be instantly parachuted into Strasbourg, with a maximum of two or three five-year terms so that MEPs are regularly renewed and the European Parliament rejuvenated. Most elected politicians in Europe feel left out of the business of the EU. The European Parliament costs 2 billion euros a year to run. Each MEP costs the European taxpayer 2.5 million euros in pay, poorly audited expenses, and levels of staff and assistants unknown in any national parliament in Europe. A major priority post-Brexit should be to downscale the grandiose buildings and declarations in Brussels and Strasbourg and reconnect the EU to democratic politics at the level of the nation state, sub-nation and region.

4. More Work for Europeans Citizens

In 2017 the EU celebrated its sixtieth birthday since the founding Treaty of Rome in 1957. Compared to the age profile of many European states, the EU is a toddler, barely out of nappies. While the EU is young, Europe is getting older, with a declining birth rate. Thanks to its open borders to immigration from Asia, Britain is one of the few EU nations with a growing population. But even in Britain the share of the active employed population has fallen below the inactive population (those without work, the young, retired people and others) and the UK needs more healthy, young, tax paying workers if it is to survive, let alone thrive. Elsewhere Europe is ceasing to reproduce itself and one reason for maintaining free movement of workers is to have enough younger low-paid workers to look after ageing Europeans who are too young to die but too old to wash, clean and feed themselves.

The figures are alarming. In Italy more than 50 per cent of voters are aged over 50. There are only six professors out of 13,000 in Italy under 40. In Britain, an estimated 12.5 million jobs will be opened up in the years to 2025 through people leaving the workforce and an additional two million new jobs will be created, yet only seven million new younger people will be available to enter the workforce to fill these jobs. For the first time in British history we have fewer people at work than the rest of the population. Is it really so dreadful to have a few hundred thousand Poles or Italians coming to live and work in Britain, and gradually integrating into our population the way my father and grandfather did? Europeans have stopped making love – or at least stopped making love in a way that makes babies.

Europeans retire far too early to eke out a third of their life on a pension and become increasingly dependent on supplementary social assistance paid for by taxpayers. The pension age of 65 was dreamt up by Bismarck when the nineteenth-century German leader introduced Europe's first national pension system. Average male life expectancy in Germany in the 1870s was 49, so many more paid into the pension insurance scheme than were paid from it. Today there should be every encouragement for older people to work. The Nordic countries have shown how to keep over-60-year-olds in work, whereas half of citizens in other EU countries have stopped working by age 55.

The current EU population of just over half a billion is expected to reduce to 450 million by 2050. Nor is Europe overcrowded. You can drive for miles in most European nations and see mainly open land. In the 1930s those campaigning against Jews coming to Britain from Nazi Germany said the island was 'overcrowded'. Then the population of the UK was 30 million, half of what it is today. Only 7 per cent of the UK is built-up urban dwelling, office and factory space.

France has roughly the same size population as Britain but twice the amount of territory within its borders. Is it unthinkable for neighbouring European countries to create co-dominium regions of communities and housing in which people from one country feel at home in terms of services provided as if they were living in their own nation? European Union citizenship has given rise to communities in southern Spain, Portugal and areas of France or Greece where citizens of colder northern Europe live for all or part of the year. It is analogous to the movement of Americans from the cold northern United States to have holiday or retirement homes in Florida or warmer zones of the American south. Where the market is leading, can an imaginative state follow so that Europe shares out its space more intelligently among its inhabitants?

In 1958, John F. Kennedy wrote a book entitled *A Nation of Immigrants*. As US president he abolished early twentieth-century laws trying to stop Asians arriving to work and live in the United States and other unworkable quotas on immigration. As a result of this arrival of new energy in the form of hardworking immigrants, America enjoyed some of its best year-on-year growth rates since the First World War. Unlike the older EU member states that tried initially to block all immigration from the new EU member states in the twenty-first century, the UK – up to the Brexit era – welcomed hard-working, tax-paying Europeans. In consequence the UK growth rate outpointed the eurozone member states in most years after 2000 until the anti-immigrant Brexit vote took place.

To be sure, immigration and arrivals need management and controls. This can be done without leaving the EU, as explained earlier. If Europe is to get moving again, then a more welcome and positive approach to people movement into and across its frontiers is required.

5. Europe Must Take More Responsibility for its Own Defence

Winston Churchill, speaking in August 1950 at the Council of Europe, urged the 'immediate creation of a unified European army'. Europe is still waiting. The Czech Republic spends just 1 per cent of GDP on defence and Italy spends 1.3 per cent – both well below the 2 per cent of GDP which is the standard NATO expects of its members. In both countries defence expenditure has gone down despite the threat of Russian aggressive posturing, the continuing neighbourhood crises that Europe faces, and the constant urging from the United States that Europe accept more responsibility for defence. The eastern and southern Mediterranean is a mixture of conflict zone and a region where people-smuggling and trafficking, the transportation of illegal immigrants, occasionally Islamist jihadis into Europe, is rife.

This is Europe's most important external frontier, but it is without defence, regular patrols, or aggressive naval action against criminals. Instead of allocating more of their national budgets to control Europe's external borders and send messages about readiness to defend European interests, Prague and Rome want someone else to do the job. In fact, the EU minus Britain, post-Brexit will lose a major defence capability. EU nations produce thirty-seven different types of tank or armoured vehicle, eighteen different types of warplane and seven different types of naval frigate. The duplication and refusal to copy Airbus and have a single or just a few military products reveal how backward and protectionist EU nations are.

Europe spends nearly four times as much on defence as Russia and just four countries – Britain, France, Germany and Italy – spend US$188.6 billion on defence compared to Russia's $65 billion defence budget. Russia gets more bang for its buck in the sense it can use its military to intervene in Georgia and Ukraine and menace Baltic states with overflight and cyber-interference or send intelligence operatives to England to try to kill a former Russian spy who had defected. But the West also used its military to invade Iraq, overturn the state in Libya, and channelled its funds to support efforts to topple Assad in Syria.

Europe must wake up to the rising power of a China that has nothing but contempt for core European values: political democracy, freedom of expression, self-organization. China is using money power to buy influence in Europe and military power to establish bases in the seas off Asian nations or on the coast of Pakistan. Capitalism has fused with communism in China to create a new force field for the world's most populous nation. At a minimum, the EU should shape a common approach and should step up dialogue with Japan, Korea, Malaysia, India and other democracies closer to China to be ready if at any moment China's advance as a world power threatens European interests.

Europe has to be crystal clear about the menace of Islamist ideology and crystal clear that Muslim citizens of Europe or Muslims living along the Mediterranean shoreline nations are present and future friends. The defence of Europe must start within Europe. It is not the case that poverty or lack of democracy is the main driver of European terrorism, as the attacks in rich countries like France, Germany and Britain suggest. Islamist terrorism is driven by an ideological project rooted in rejection of democracy, women's rights and above all hatred of Jews and the existence of Israel. Tackling this is a long-term project, but one the European Union should engage in if it wants to defend it values.

The Mediterranean needs a strong presence of European naval, coastguard and police vessels able to intercept illegal people-trafficking boats and return them to the African coastline. A simple arms build-up against Russia is not the priority; investing in defeating cyberattacks on democracy coming from Russia is. Indeed as with the Cold War-era broadcasts from the democratic world by the BBC World Service, Deutsche Welle, Radio France Internationale and Radio Free Europe, among others, which sent accurate news and messages of hope to the peoples of east Europe under Soviet occupation, the EU should invest in modern media messaging to give the Russians, Iranians and Arab world accurate information and the chance to discuss issues that are not possible without conditions of freedom of expression.

The key question, however, is:

6. How Can Europe Start Growing Again?

Jean Monnet is said to have said: 'If I was starting all over again, I would begin with culture.' Historians cannot find an actual source for this widely attributed remark, which those in the culture and creative sectors love to cite for obvious reasons. In fact, Monnet and all the serious builders of Europe, including Margaret Thatcher, have understood in a deep Gramscian sense that the material base of Europe – the economic relations between European citizens – is by far the most important source of legitimacy for European integration. A Europe that cannot be shown to be adding value to people's lives via the common currency, or the open border trading system, or the movement of workers, or the adoption of enforced directives on CO_2 emissions will start losing the support of a majority of its citizens, or the elected politicians of its member states.

The British economic historian, Harold James shows in his book written with Markus Brunnermeier and Jean-Pierre Landau, *The Euro and the Battle of Ideas* (2016) that there are no fixed immutabilities about how nations approach economic decision making. There have been times when France was excessively liberal and Germany keen on state intervention and deficit spending, even if more recently the opposite economic theories and practice appear more in evidence. Germany began from *Stunde Nul* (zero hour) in 1945 and invented its own social market economy. The 1947 programme of Germany's Christian Democratic Party began by stating 'The capitalist era is over'. In contrast to Britain or France, Germany after 1945 was built on the basis of a weak, almost non-existent central state, the presence of trade union representatives on the boards of all companies, a devotion to rule of law (*Rechtsstaat*) and a belief in compromise, conciliation and consensus in a manner almost Swiss in its obsession with avoiding dominant leadership by the state or its political leadership. Every German government since the war has been a coalition, just as Europe's richest country, Switzerland, has been run since 1959 by a seven-strong federal cabinet which has equal balance between liberal, socialists, conservatives and national populists. Perhaps coalition rather than single party government is one way forward for better government in Europe?

Germany has been the first major state to adopt green ideas as state policy, culminating in Angela Merkel's decision to pull out of nuclear power. In 1990, Germany took on the burden of financing the incorporation of the bankrupt, almost third-world state of East Germany and bringing it up to West German standards. West Germans were heavily taxed to pay for this remarkable achievement. It was a far bigger transfer in financial terms than the support the United States provided via the Marshall Plan. German workers accepted a pay freeze in order to recapitalize German industry at the end of the 1990s and Germany has provided capital and market access as well as open frontiers to workers from its east European neighbours in a giant project of stabilizing the ex-communist world after the collapse of the Soviet Russian imperium. By any standards, the solidarity the German people, as defined by responsible political parties and labour unions offered first to the Germans from East Germany and then more broadly to the impoverished new democracies trying to find their feet after communism, was quite remarkable.

No one has ever gone from London or Brussels or Paris and publicly thanked the Germans for not retreating into nationalism after 1990 but instead paying extra taxes and foregoing increases in income to turn the peaceful liberation of Europe from Soviet tyranny into a win–win moment of history. By the time the financial crash imported from 'Sir' Alan Greenspan's America hit Europe, Germans were suffering from what they call 'solidarity fatigue'.

The appeals from Greek, Italian or Iberian politicians for extra help to make good their own failures to deal with endemic corruption and remediable inefficiencies did not find much echo in the German public or political class. In his 2017 book on the European Union crisis, *Adults in the Room*, Yanis Varoufakis casts Germany as No. 1 villain. Narcissus at least had the grace to look at his own face.

The twenty-first century opened with the EU gearing up for the absorption of eight new member states from bankrupt ex-communist Europe and embarking on a forlorn search for a constitution to produce what Joschka Fischer called a European *Finalität*. This desire for a final definition of Europe is understandable but not realistic or realizable. The idea that Europe was marble architecture, not a messy garden in need of constant weeding and replanting, was wishful thinking.

Despite claims by anti-Europeans that the EU is a superstate interfering to destroy national economies, the long history of the political crisis that followed the US-led global financial crisis of 2008/9 has shown up the lack of power and authority in the European Commission, or the European Parliament. The two presidents of the European Council, Herman van Rompuy and Donald Tusk, were bystanders in the crisis, as all decisions reverted to national states.

Politics must return to Europe. The Polish political scientist, Leszek Kolakowski, exiled from communist Poland to All Souls, Oxford, once defined social democratic politics as 'an obstinate will to erode by inches the conditions which produce avoidable suffering, oppression, hunger, wars, racial and national hatred, insatiable greed and vindictive envy'. Social democratic or centre-left politics somehow have lost sight of those aims as they seek to locate political action in culture, gender and ecological issues. It was common-place to describe 2016 and the Brexit–Trump voted as uniquely connected to populism, as if politicians had never sought to be popular or use easy-to-grasp slogans.

The Swiss Liberal politician, Christa Markwalder, former speaker of the Swiss Parliament, says: 'It is time for democratically accountable and elected politicians to take back control from the populists.' As Hans Kundnani has written, 'the European Union itself often takes a rather technocratic approach that seeks to insulate economic policy-making from politics'. Until Europe's political parties devote serious resources to forging an effective set of policies that can bring together competing national visions, priories and cultures, or at least decide on a set of key priorities. the crisis will continue and Brexit will be the first sign of the Balkanization of Europe.

No one can magic up a new twenty-first-century social democracy, but the imbalance of power with nearly all key decisions taken by centre-right politicians in today's Europe leaves the European Union like a stork balancing on one political leg. A further problem is the failure of trade unions to modernize themselves. In the 1930s trade unions in Sweden and Switzerland looked at the twin threat to democracy posed by fascism and communism. In 1938 they concluded historic compromise agreements with employers. In broad terms, the unions left the political struggle to politicians and in exchange for recognition as social partners by the bosses and owners of capital, they agreed to push back the strike weapon to one of the ultimate last resort. The unions agreed that the constant renewal and investment in national firms and support for free trade, including inward and outward investment, was essential to national success and the ambitions of trade union members to get more pay, more leisure and investment in the social state of pensions, affordable housing, healthcare and education.

After 1945, unions in Germany, Austria, the Netherlands and the Nordic nations followed within their own national traditions the Swedish–Swiss model developed in the 1930s. Strikes were rare. There was full support for firms investing overseas and opening markets to competition. Contrast this to Britain, where a leading trade union general secretary, Ken Gill, denounced the arrival of Japanese automobile companies in north England in the 1980s as it would lead to the arrival of 'alien practices'. Unemployed workers in north-east England liked such alien practices as jobs and decent pay. In France in 2016, militant trade unions all but destroyed the French socialist government with a series of militant, sometimes violent strikes and protests in opposition to minor labour market reforms that had been accepted by trade unions across the Rhine or further north decades before. The *Gilets jaunes* (Yellow Vests) protests in France at the end of 2018 and the winter of 2019 were a spontaneous expression of anger by many of the left-behinds in France. Despite France having one of the most generous welfare states in the world, too many French citizens were without jobs; or if they did have work, it was poorly paid and they were only just managing. A small increase in the price of fuel for cars and small reductions in pensions paid to state retirees was enough to trigger a protest of blocking roundabouts and taking the anguish of rural and small-town France onto the Champs Elysées. Violent extremists of both the right and left, egged on by populist politicians from the harder end of the French political spectrum, naturally sought to use the protest to prove their points.

The real problem in France was there were no intermediary bodies to represent this anger and discontent. C. Wright Mills, the American sociologist, famously described labour unions as 'managers of discontent'. Dues-paying membership of French trade unions is the lowest in the Organisation for Economic Co-operation and Development (OECD). French unions are only kept alive in the sense of employing staff and organizing events and conferences because they are subsidized by the state or firms allow employees to work as full-time union officials while still being on the company payroll.

The EU institutions cannot oblige workers to join and bring trade unions or some kind of representative bodies back to twenty-first-century life. The only way workers can organize is if they organize themselves. Once again, we hit the problem that the EU – in the sense of the Brussels bodies such as the Commission – has very little power to change Europe's direction of travel unless member states or organizations or movements within member states emerge and prepare for an aggiornamento.

In Italy, Spain, France or Portugal, trade unions were offshoots of political parties or the Catholic Church and obeyed the line of the communist parties or cardinals. Trade union membership slumped as deindustrialization in the

1980s and 1990s eliminated the majority of jobs in the metal industries, where classic working-class trade union organization was strongest. Women and immigrant workers were more difficult to organize and had different priorities from the classic twentieth-century white male proletariat. Unions gave up the difficult task of organizing the new post-industrial proletariat and instead focused on public sector workers: teachers, civil servants, hospital workers, public transport workers, employees of state agencies. These workers needed trade unions, but if ever they took strike or other action, the victims were members of the public who could not leave their children at school or use strike-hit public transport to get to work. In order to get a fairer share of the wealth their labour created, trade unions were no longer confronting capital, but the wider public, who resented having to pay ever higher taxes for the pay and other entitlements public sector employers felt were their due.

As economies and societies reformatted themselves and with so-called AI (artificial intelligence) threatening to replace the human workforce with computers, trade unions were still imprisoned in their early or mid-twentieth-century structures and rhetoric. If the nations of Europe were in the driving seat of EU policy in the twenty-first century especially under weak European Commission presidents, the trade unions of Europe were even more marked by their national heritage and provenance.

Like scales falling from the eyes, more and more of the evangelists of the deregulated, society-destroying, 'greed is good', survival-of-the-fittest economic model, which sunk its roots after the end of post-1945 welfare capitalism, are now running around telling us there are real problems with unequal distribution, poverty and the revolt of voters who have lost confidence in traditional parties of government. But to move to a new paradigm needs new forms of political and labour movement organization.

Referring to the period after the financial crisis of 2008, the economics writer, Anatole Kaletsky argues:

Once the failure of free trade, deregulation, and monetarism came to be seen as leading to a 'new normal' of permanent austerity and diminished expectations, rather than just to a temporary banking crisis, the inequalities, job losses, and cultural dislocations of the pre-crisis period could no longer be legitimized – just as the extortionate taxes of the 1950s and 1960s lost their legitimacy in the stagflation of the 1970s.

Kaletsky believes that:

> governments can redistribute the benefits of growth by supporting
> employment and incomes with regional and industrial subsidies and
> minimum-wage laws. Among the most effective interventions of this
> type, demonstrated in Germany and Scandinavia, is to spend money
> on high-quality vocational education and re-training for workers and
> students outside universities, creating non-academic routes to a middle-
> class standard of living.

Europe needs to shift taxation away from labour and onto capital gains
and wealth, as Ånders Aslund and Simeon Djankov argue in *Europe's Growth
Challenge* (2017). VAT as a tax provides a solid base for national government
income as well as EU revenue. But it is regressive – that is, those on lower
incomes pay a higher share of their income in VAT taxes than those who are
better off. High rates of tax on lower-paid jobs discourage young workers
from entering the labour market if unemployment and other benefits plus
bits and pieces of work in the unofficial labour market or help from parents
allows a lifestyle that is not based on work. Schooling must be more rigorous.
Entry to high-level state functionary posts should require a working knowledge of two European languages and one in two posts should be for those
who have university-level mathematics, computer science or hard sciences
diplomas.

There are other proposals on the table to get Europe moving again, including a banking union and a green European investment bank based on the
successful European Bank for Reconstruction and Development (EBRD),
which lent money for infrastructure projects after 1990. The United States
and Japan are members of the EBRD and as we enter the Brexiternity era,
Britain should seek to be generous and maximize investment and participation in European projects supporting a new economic settlement.

For years I was asked on TV or conference panels in continental cities
what Europe could do to make the Brits less hostile to partnership and
cooperation in the EU. My answer was always the same:

> The British will fall in love again with a Europe that grows. Give me
> 2.5 per cent growth a year, every year, and watch an economy double

in size in fewer than three decades. We Brits are not visionaries, but we understand compound interest and if the EU member states can all regularly increase growth then Britain will fall in love with Europe.

It was crude – and the myriad ways to energize growth by allowing companies to flourish and ensure all citizens have a stake and some benefit from a growing economy call for major political challenges.

Brexiternity will impact Europe as much as it does Britain. Brexiternity is lose–lose for the EU and the UK. Finding a solution will require leadership of a higher order than that on offer in the first two decades of the twenty-first century.

CONCLUSION

Europe is what Europeans want it to be. My father was born in a different Europe. He was a newly commissioned officer in the Polish Army in 1939 and took a Nazi bullet in the shoulder in September of that year as German far right xenophobic politics unleashed war. He came via Romania and France to Scotland to continue the fight against European extreme nationalism. He died when I was 10 from an illness that arose from those wartime privations. My uncle died as his ship bringing vital oil to wartime Britain was torpedoed by a U-boat in the Atlantic. Both my father and uncle were brave men. But if a cowardly tyrant, Stalin, had not been such a close ally of Hitler who did Hitler's dirty work by invading Poland from the east and annexing the Baltic states, perhaps fewer would have been killed in the Second World War. Another uncle long dead was a runner for the Irish patriots who fought for the nation's right to be free against English colonial rulers after 1918.

Although I am as English as can be – a Benedictine school, Oxford, the BBC, the House of Commons, a minister – I cannot ever lose these shadows in my mind of the Europe my forebears grew up in. I have been infinitely luckier. Now a band of swaggering nationalists like Boris Johnson and Matteo Salvini, with endless money from Europe-hating billionaires in America and the Kremlin, want to see Europe return to competing, rival, closed-frontier nation states.

Brexit was their great victory in 2016. I hope a new generation will work to create a Europe for all, including new incomers who can only make us stronger. I look at communist China, corrupt authoritarian Russia, religious supremacist India, the current US president . . . and my Europe, for all its faults and failings, seems to be trying to do its best. It has taken in very poor nations, nations under tyranny, nations that had invaded each other in the decades before the Treaty of Rome was signed in 1957. The European Union has allowed these nations to grow together, strengthening national culture, while sharing an open economy.

Perhaps the greatest lesson of British democracy is the concept of opposition. It is right and necessary to oppose what you believe to be wrong. But the purpose of democratic opposition is not to destroy but to change, modify, reform – in whatever direction you and fellow activists believe is best.

Brexit, alas, may have begun as a reasonable and even necessary critique of how the European Union works and how Britain fits into the EU. But during the course of the twenty-first century it turned into a sour, destructive set of prejudices and passions that allowed liars to win a vote.

Edmund Burke's most famous quote – 'The only thing necessary for the triumph of evil is that good men should do nothing' – has been challenged by scholars who doubt he ever said this, but a century later John Stuart Mill picked up the theme when he said: 'Let not any one pacify his conscience by the delusion that he can do no harm if he takes no part, and forms no opinion. Bad men need nothing more to compass their ends, than that good men should look on and do nothing.'

I do not believe for a second that the 37 per cent of the total electorate (the percentage is even smaller of the total voting age population) who voted for Brexit are bad, evil, or any of the nasty adjectives by which they are sometimes described. That forgiveness does not extend, however, to the demagogic, xenophobic, English nationalist politicians and propagandists in the twin professions of politics and journalism who have told so many deliberate and dishonest untruths in order to win their end.

In January 2015 I wrote a book explaining that Brexit would happen unless 'good men should look on and do nothing'. I hope this latest book will serve to alert my fellow citizens that we must not give up and the cause of defeating, now or in the future, the isolationists who would remove rights from millions of young British citizens and fundamentally weaken our country is as vital now as ever it has been.

I finished writing this book on 6 June 2019, the 75th anniversary of British, American, French, Canadian and Polish soldiers landing on Normandy beaches to liberate Europe from the foulest expression of nationalist extremism ever to gain power. My life has been lived under the peace, democracy, social market economics and ever-growing personal and cultural and citizenship rights shared by all people of my country and the rest of Europe during my lifetime. I would hope my four children can enjoy decades of similar added-value existence. But if the demagogues and ideologues of Brexit and similar nationalist politics hoping to bust apart Europe win out, this will not happen.

AFTERWORD

It would be impossible to list all the many friends and colleagues in politics, government, diplomats, journalism, the academic and think-tank world, and people in business with whom I have discussed Brexit both at home in Britain and in many European capitals since first I used the word in 2012 but there are some I would like to thank by name.

These include Michel Barnier, Alex Barker, Richard Corbett, Hugo Dixon, Flavia Lambert, Jacques Lafitte, Charles Grant, David Hannay, Tom Hayes, Andrew Hilton, William Keegan, John Kerr, Pascal Lamy, John Lloyd, Gerald Lyons, Calum Macdonald, Colin Maccabe, David Mathieson, Margarita Mathiopolous, Edmund Matyjaszek, Martin McShane, Pierre Mosocovici, François Nordmann, George Papandreou, Polly Toynbee, and, Vicky Pryce who sharpens all intellectual tools on Brexit and the European economy.

As ever an incomparable editor, Jo Godfrey, was both essential and a pleasure to work with as were all her colleagues at I.B. Tauris and Bloomsbury.

The book is dedicated to the memory of Isabel McShane and Jan Matyjaszek, both born in 1916 and who luckily were not around to see the folly of English xenophobic nationalism triumph in a corrupt plebiscite a century later. It is also for my four children, Sarah, Laura, Emilie and Benjamin who had the good sense to have a mother who is a French citizen and thus they have the blessing of a passport that will allow them to live, work, love, travel anywhere in Europe. I am sorry my generation was unable to let Britain make its peace with England's demons about the nations and peoples in the region of the world we share with many other proud nation-states co-existing with each other in the European Union. The torch is now passed to twenty-first-century Britons to decide if our country is open or closed to modernity and Enlightenment values.

FURTHER READING

It is reasonably easy to navigate EU institutional websites and those of the British Parliament. It would be helpful if someone put together all the debates and speeches in the Commons and Lords on the question of Europe since 1945. It would be a major but worthwhile task, as nearly every key fact or argument about Britain's relations with the rest of the Europe are on the record somewhere in Hansard. Publishing these statements, exchanges, debates, speeches and questions would at least give the lie to the oft-repeated myth that every MP and peer merely signed up for an economic, free trade arrangement. The European Commission and European Parliament have accessible websites with a great deal of core information. The European Council of Ministers (not the same as the European Council – the quarterly meeting of EU heads of government) also has a good website. The books listed below – many with their own extensive bibliographies – have been helpful in the evolution of my thinking on Europe and the preparation of this book.

Anderson, Perry. *The New Old World* (London: Verso, 2011)
Artus, Patrick and Virard, Marie-Paule. *Euro: Par ici la sortie?* (Paris: Fayard, 2017)
Attali, Jacques. *Europe(s)* (Paris: Fayard, 1994)
Bache, Ian and George, Stephen. *Politics in the European Union* (Oxford: Oxford University Press, 2006)
Balibar, Etienne. *Europe, crise et fin?* (Paris: Le bord de l'eau, 2016)
Beck, Ulrich. *German Europe* (Cambridge: Polity, 2013)
Bergounioux, Alain and Grunberg, Gérard. *L'utopie à l'épreuve: Le socialism européen au XXe siècle* (Paris: Editions de Fallois, 1996)

Blair, Tony. *A Journey* (London: Hutchinson, 2010)

Bogdanor, Vernon. *Beyond Brexit: Towards a British Constitution* (London: I.B. Tauris, 2019)

Bootle, Roger. *The Trouble with Europe: Why the EU isn't Working, How It Could be Reformed, What Could Take its Place* (London: Nicholas Brealey, 2014)

Boris, Pascal and Vaissié, Arnaud. *La France et le Royaume-Uni face à la crise (2008–2014)* (London: Cercle d'outre-manche, 2014)

Brady, Hugh. *Twelve Things Everyone Should Know About the European Court of Justice* (London: Centre for European Reform, 2014)

Bullock, Alan. *Ernest Bevin. Foreign Secretary, 1945–1951* (Oxford: Oxford University Press, 1985)

Butler, Nick, Dodd, Philip, Flanders, Stephanie, Garton Ash, Tim, Grant, Charles and Hughes, Kirsty. *Reshaping Europe: Visions for the Future* (London: Centre for European Reform, 1996)

Calame, Mattieu. *La France contre l'Europe* (Paris: Les Petits matins, 2019)

Campbell, John. *Edward Heath, A Biography* (London: Jonathan Cape, 1993)

Charlton, Michael. *The Price of Victory* (London: BBC, 1983)

Charter, David. *Au Revoir Europe: What if Britain left the EU?* (London: Biteback, 2012)

Charter, David. *Europe: In or Out?* (London: Biteback, 2014)

Clarisse, Yves and Quatremer, Jean. *Les maîtres de l'Europe* (Paris: Grasset, 2005)

Coe, Jonathan. *Middle England* (London: Viking, 2018)

Connolly, Tony. *Brexit and Ireland* (London: Penguin, 2018)

Corner, Mark. *The European Union: An Introduction* (London: I.B. Tauris, 2014)

Crosland, Susan. *Tony Crosland* (London: Jonathan Cape, 1982)

Dahrendorf, Ralf. *Why Europe Matters* (London: Centre for European Reform, 1996)

D'Ancona, Matthew. *In it Together: The Inside Story of the Coalition Government* (London: Penguin, 2014)

Debray, Régis. *Civilisation* (Paris: Folio, 2018)

Dell, Edmund. *The Schuman Plan and the Abdication of Leadership in Europe* (Oxford: Clarendon Press, 1995)

Delors, Jacques. *Mémoires* (Paris: Plon, 2004)

Dixon, Hugo. *The In–Out Question* (London: Amazon Books, 2014)

Dorling, Danny and Tomlinson, Sally. *Rule Britannia: Brexit and the End of Empire* (London: Biteback, 2019)

Dunt, Ian. *Brexit: What the Hell Happens Now?* (Kingston: Canbury Press, 2017)

Eatwell, Roger and Goodwin, Matthew. *National Populism: The Revolt Against Liberal Democracy* (London: Pelican, 2018)

Esler, Gavin. *Brexit Without the Bullshit* (Kingston, Canbury Press, 2019)

Evans, Geoffrey and Menon, Amand. *Brexit and British Politics* (Cambridge: Polity, 2017)

Ferenczi, Thomas. *Pourquoi l'Europe?* (Paris: André Versaille, 2008)

Firsoff, V. A. *The Unity of Europe* (London: Lindsay Drummond, 1947)

Franchesi, Patrice. *Combattre: Comment les États-Unis de l'Europe peuvent sauver la France* (Paris: Éditions de La Martinière, 2017)

Fredet, Jean-Gabriel. *Fabius, les brûlures d'une ambition* (Paris: Hachette, 2002)

Garton Ash, Timothy. *In Europe's Name: Germany and the Divided Continent* (London: Random House, 1993)

Geisbourg, François. *La fin du rêve euro* (Paris: Stock, 2013)

Giddens, Anthony. *Turbulent and Mighty Continent: What Future for Europe?* (Cambridge: Polity, 2014)

Gigou, Jean-Louis. *Le nouveau monde méditerranéen* (Paris: Éditions Descartes, 2012)

Gillingham, John. *The EU: An Obituary* (London: Verso, 2016)

Gimson, Andrew. *Boris: The Rise of Boris Johnson* (London: Simon and Schuster 2012)

Giscard d'Estaing, Valéry. *Europa – la dernière chance de l'Europe* (Paris: XO Éditions, 2014)

Godley, Wynne. 'The Hole in the Treaty', in Gowan, Peter and Anderson, Perry, *The Question of Europe* (London: Verso, 1997)

Goulard, Sylvie. *Europe: Amour ou chambre à part?* (Paris: Flammarion, 2013)

Gowan, Peter and Anderson, Perry. *The Question of Europe* (London: Verso, 1997)

Grant, Charles. *Delors: Inside the House that Jacques Built* (London: Nicholas Brealey, 1994). Subsequently translated into French, Japanese and Russian.

Grant, Charles. *How to Build a Modern European Union* (London: Centre for European Reform, 2013).

Grant, Linda. *A Stranger City* (London: Virago, 2019)

Habermas, Jürgen. *Ach, Europa* (Frankfurt: Suhrkamp, 2008)

Habermas, Jürgen. *La constitution de l'Europe* (Paris: Gallimard, 2013)

Haffner, Sebastien. *Churchill* (London: Haus Publishing, 2013)

Halligan, Liam and Lyons, Gerard. *Clean Brexit: Why Leaving the EU Still Makes Sense* (London: Biteback, 2018)

Hamilton, Daniel S. *Europe 2020: Competitive or Complacent?* (Washington, DC: Johns Hopkins University Press, 2011)

Hayek, F. A. *The Road to Serfdom* (London: Routledge, 1944)

Hazeley, Jack and Morris, Joel. *The Story of Brexit (Ladybirds for Grown-ups)* (London: Penguin, 2018)

Heathcoat Amory, David. *Confessions of a Eurosceptic* (Barnsley: Pen and Sword, 2012)

House of Commons. 'How much legislation comes from Europe?' Research Paper 10/62 (London: House of Commons, 13 October 2010)

Hurd, Douglas. *Memoirs* (London: Little, Brown, 2003)

Johnson, Boris. *The Churchill Factor: How One Man Made History* (London: Hodder and Stoughton, 2014)

Judt, Tony. *Post-war: A History of Europe Since 1945* (London: Viking, 2005)

Julliard, Jacques. *Les gauches françaises 1762–2012* (Paris: Flammarion, 2012)

Juillot, Eric. *La Déconstruction européenne* (Paris: Xenis, 2011)

Kearns, Ian. *Collapse: Europe After the European Union* (London: Biteback, 2018)

Kerr, Philip. *Greeks Bearing Gifts* (London: Random House, 2018)

Kielinger, Thomas. *Grossbritannien* (Munich: C.H. Beck, 2000)

Klos, Felix. *Churchill's Last Stand: The Struggle to Unite Europe* (London: I.B. Tauris, 2018)

Krastev, Ivan. *After Europe* (Philadelphia, PA: University of Pennsylvania Press, 2017)

Lacoste, Olivier. *La fin de l'Europe* (Paris: Éditions Eyrolles, 2016)

Lamy, Pascal and Gnesotto, Nicole. *Où va le monde?* (Paris: Odile Jacob, 2017)

Lapavitsas, Costas. *Crisis in the Eurozone* (London: Verso, 2012)

Laughland, John. *The Tainted Source: The Undemocratic Origins of the European Idea* (London: Little, Brown, 1997)

Leach, Graham. *EU Membership: What's the Bottom Line?* (London: Institute of Directors, 2000)

Leonard, Mark. *Why Europe Will Run the 21st Century* (London: Fourth Estate, 2005)

Leparmentier, Arnaud. *Ces Français, fossoyeurs de l'euro* (Paris: Plon, 2013)

Levy, Jacques and Kahn, Sylvie. *Le pays des Européens* (Paris: Odile Jacob, 2019)

Liddle, Roger. *The Europe Dilemma: Britain and the Drama of EU Integration* (London: I.B. Tauris and Policy Network, 2014)

Lloyd, John and Marconi, Cristina. *Reporting the EU: News, Media and the European Institutions* (London: I.B. Tauris, 2014)

Loew, Peter Oliver (ed.). *Polen denkt Europa* (Frankfurt: Suhrkamp, 2004)

MacShane, Denis. *François Mitterrand: A Political Odyssey* (London: Quartet, 1982)

MacShane, Denis. *International Labour and the Origins of the Cold War* (Oxford: Clarendon Press, 1992)

MacShane, Denis. *Britain's Voice in Europe: Time for Change* (London: Foreign Policy Centre, 2005)

MacShane, Denis. *Heath* (London: Haus Publishing, 2006)

MacShane, Denis. *Brexit: How Britain Will Leave Europe* (London: I.B. Tauris, 2015)

MacShane, Denis. *Brexit – No Exit: Why (in the End) Britain Won't Leave Europe* (London: I.B. Tauris, 2017)

Marsh, David. *The Euro: The Politics of the New Global Currency* (London: Yale University Press, 2009)

Marsh, David. *Beim Geld hört des Spaß auf: Warum die Eurokrise nicht mehr lösbar ist* (Berlin: Europaverlag, 2013)

Martin-Genier, Patrick. *L'Europe a-t-elle un avenir? Une approche critique de la construction européenne* (Paris: Studyrama, 2019)

Maurier, Daphne du. *Rule Britannia* (London: Victor Gollancz, 1972)

McCormick, John. *Europeanism* (Oxford: Oxford University Press, 2010)

McKnight, David. *Murdoch's Politics: How One Man's Thirst for Wealth and Power Shapes Our World* (London: Pluto Press, 2013)

Menon, Anand. *Europe: The State of the Union* (London: Atlantic, 2008)

Mets, Marillis (ed.). *Let's Get Europe Moving Again* (Paris: Centre d'Étude et de Prospective Stratégique – CEPS, 2013)

Middelaar, Luuk Van. *The Passage to Europe: How a Continent Became a Union* (New Haven and London: Yale University Press, 2013)

Middelaar, Luuk Van. *Alarums and Excursions: Improvising Politics on the European Stage* (Newcastle: Agenda, 2019)

Millward, Alan, *The Reconstruction of Western Europe, 1945–1951* (London: Methuen, 1984)

Moscovici, Pierre. *S'il est minuit en Europe* (Paris: Grasset, 2017)

Moïsi, Dominique. *La géopolitique de l'émotion* (Paris: Flammarion, 2008)

Monnet, Jean. *Mémoires* (Paris: Livre de poche, 2007)

Morgan, Kenneth. *Michael Foot, A Life* (London: HarperCollins, 2008)

Müller, Jan-Werner. *What is Populism?* (London: Pelican, 2017)

Mullin, Chris. *The Friends of Harry Perkins* (London: Simon and Schuster, 2019)

Nairn, Tom. *The Left Against Europe* (London: Penguin, 1973)

Offe, Claus. *Europe Entrapped* (Cambridge: Polity, 2014)

Oliver, Craig. *Unleashing Demons: The Inside Story of Brexit* (London: Hodder and Stoughton, 2016)

O'Rourke, Kevin. *A Short History of Brexit* (London: Pelican, 2019)

Ortega, Andrés. *La fuerza de los pocos* (Barcelona: Galaxia Gutenberg, 2007)

Orwell, George. *The Collected Essays, Journalism and Letters of George Orwell in four volumes* (London: Penguin, 1970)

O'Toole, Fintan. *Heroic Failure: Brexit and the Politics of Pain* (London: Head of Zeus, 2019)

Peet, John and La Guardia, Anton. *Unhappy Union: How the Euro crisis – and Europe – Can Be Fixed* (London: Profile Books, 2014)

Peyrefitte, Alain. *C'était de Gaulle* (Paris: Gallimard, 1994)

Pimlott, Ben. *Harold Wilson* (London: HarperCollins, 1992)

Pinder, John and Usherwood, Simon. *The European Union: A Very Short Introduction* (Third edition) (Oxford: Oxford University Press, 2013)

Piris, Jean-Claude. *The Future of Europe* (Cambridge: Cambridge University Press, 2012)

Priestley, Julian and Ford, Glyn (eds). *Our Europe, Not Theirs* (London: Lawrence and Wishart, 2013)

Pryce, Vicky. *Greekonomics: The Euro Crisis and Why Politicians Don't Get It* (London: Biteback, 2013)

Quatremer, Jean. *Les salauds de l'Europe* (Paris: Calmann Levy, 2017)

Quatremer, Jean. *Il faut achever l'euro* (Paris: Calmann Levy, 2019)

Raffy, Serge. *Le Président* (Paris: Fayard/Pluriel, 2013)

Redwood, John. *Our Currency, Our Country: The Dangers of European Monetary Union* (London: Penguin, 1997)

Redwood, John. *The Death of Britain?* (London: Palgrave Macmillan, 1999)

Renterghem, Marion van. *Mon Europe, je t'aime moi non plus* (Paris: Stock, 2019)

Retinger, Joseph and Pomian, John (eds). *Memoirs of an Eminence Grise* (Brighton: Sussex University Press, 1972)

Roberts, Andrew. *The Aachen Memorandum* (London: Weidenfeld and Nicolson, 1995)

Rocard, Michel and Gnesotto Nicole. *Notre Europe* (Paris: Robert Laffont, 2008)

Rogers, Ivan. *9 Lessons in Brexit* (London: Short Publisher, 2019)

Rosen, Greg. *Old Labour to New* (London: Politico's, 2005)

Sarrazin, Thilo. *Deutschland schafft sich ab* (Munich: Deutsche Verlags-Anstalt, 2010)

Sassoon, Donald. *One Hundred Years of Socialism: The West European Left in the Twentieth Century* (London: I.B. Tauris, 2014)

Schaub, Jean-Frédéric. *L'Europe a-t-elle une histoire?* (Paris: Albin Michel, 2008)

Schmidt, Helmut. *Handeln für Deutschland* (Berlin: Rowohlt, 1993)

Schmidt, Helmut. *Mein Europa: Mit einem Gespräch mit Joschka Fischer* (Hamburg: Hoffmann and Campe, 2013)

Schmidt, Helmut and Weizsäcker, Richard von (ed.). *Innenansichten aus Europa* (Munich: C.H. Beck, 2007)

Shipman, Tim. *All-out War: The Full Story of Brexit* (London: HarperCollins, 2017)

Simone, Raffaele. *Come la Democrazia Fallisce* (Milan: Garzanti, 2015)

Sinn, Hans-Werner. *Der Schwarzer Juni* (Freiburg: Herder, 2016)

Solana, Javier. *Reivindicación de la política: Veinte años de relaciones internationales* (Barcelona: Random House Mondadori, 2010)

Springford, John, Tilford, Simon and Whyte, Philip. *The Economic Consequences of Leaving the EU* (London: Centre for European Reform, 2014)

Steiner, George. *The Idea of Europe* (Tilburg: Nexus Institute, 2004)

Thatcher, Margaret. *Statecraft: Strategies for a Changing World* (London: HarperCollins, 2002)

Ther, Philipp. *Europe Since 1989* (Princeton, NJ: Princeton University Press, 2016)

Torreblanca, José Ignacio. *La fragmenatación del poder europeo* (Barcelona: Icaria, 2011)

Varoufakis, Yanis. *Adults in the Room: My Battle with Europe's Deep Establishment* (London: Bodley Head, 2017)

Vedrine, Hubert. *Face au chaos, sauver l'Europe* (Paris: Levi Liana, 2019)

Villepin, Dominique de. *Mémoire de paix pour temps de guerre* (Paris: Grasset, 2016)

Wall, Stephen. *The Official History of Britain and the European Union. Vol. II: From Rejection to Referendum, 1963–1973* (London: Routledge, 2012)

Walter, Norbert. *Europa: Warum unser Kontinent es wert ist, dass wir um ihn kämpfen* (Frankfurt: Campus, 2011)

Young, Hugo. *This Blessed Plot: Britain and Europe from Churchill to Blair* (London: Macmillan, 1998)

Youngs, Richard. *The Uncertain Legacy of Crisis: European Foreign Policy Faces the Future* (Washington, DC: Carnegie Endowment for International Peace, 2014)

Youngs, Richard. *Europe Reset: New Directions for the EU* (London: I.B. Tauris, 2018)

Zielonka, Jan. *Is Europe Doomed?* (Cambridge: Polity, 2014)

INDEX